Almost Worthy

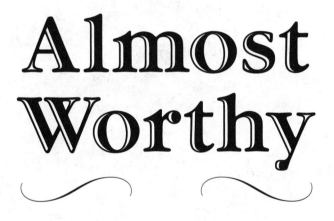

PHILANTHROPIC AND NONPROFIT STUDIES

Dwight F. Burlingame and David C. Hammack, editors

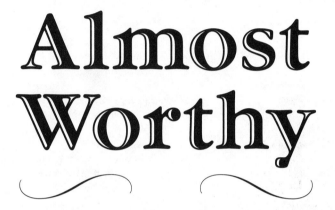

Almost Worthy

THE POOR, PAUPERS, AND THE
SCIENCE OF CHARITY
IN AMERICA, 1877–1917

Brent Ruswick

INDIANA UNIVERSITY PRESS

Bloomington and Indianapolis

This book is a publication of

Indiana University Press
601 North Morton Street
Bloomington, Indiana 47404-3797 USA

iupress.indiana.edu

Telephone orders 800-842-6796
Fax orders 812-855-7931

© 2013 by Brent Ruswick

⊖ The paper used in this publication
meets the minimum requirements of
the American National Standard for
Information Sciences—Permanence
of Paper for Printed Library Materials,
ANSI Z39.48-1992.

Manufactured in the United States
of America

Library of Congress Cataloging-in-
Publication Data

Ruswick, Brent.
Almost worthy : the poor, paupers, and
the science of charity in America, 1877-
1917 / Brent Ruswick.
    p. cm. — (Philanthropic and non-
profit studies)
Includes bibliographical references and
index.
ISBN 978-0-253-00634-9 (clo : alk. paper)
— ISBN 978-0-253-00638-7 (eb)
1. Poor—Services for—United States—
History. 2. Charities—United States—
History. 3. Nature and nurture—United
States—History. 4. Poverty—United
States—History. I. Title.
    HV91.R87 2013
    362.5′57632097309034—dc23
                        2012026049

1 2 3 4 5 17 16 15 14 13

For my students

CONTENTS

ACKNOWLEDGMENTS

The kernel that grew into *Almost Worthy* has been with me since October 2000. As the project grew, it touched every significant element of my life. Too often, I fear, it intruded into space that ought to have been reserved for dear friends, family, and colleagues. It is fitting that they now have the opportunity to encroach upon *Almost Worthy*'s turf.

Victor Hilts, Lynn Nyhart, Joyce Coleman, Christina Matta, Joshua Kundert, Neil Andrews, and Steve Wald have been with me since my arrival in Madison, Wisconsin. As advisors and friends, Vic and Lynn have been unerring in their guidance, unfailing in their support. Along with my closest friend, Joyce, I can see their influence on the entirety of my book and life. Christina, Joshua, Neil, and Steve similarly deserve a special place and recognition for more than twelve years of insight and laughter.

The University of Wisconsin provided a seemingly endless source of critical and sage advisors. Chucho Alvarado, Libbie Freed, Jonathan Seitz, Dan Thurs, Rebecca Kinraide, Erika Milam, Paul Erickson, Rima Apple, Ronald Numbers, Richard Staley, and John Milton Cooper all offered formative insight. John Rensink, Peter Susalla, Bridget Collins, Kristen Hamilton O'Neill, Judy Kaplan, Dana Freiburger, Jocelyn Bosley, Amrys Williams, Jessica Goldberg, Fred Gibbs, Kellen Backer, and Mitch Aso have all been sources of timely help. Dan Hamlin and Katie Reinhart possess an uncanny ability to offer their encouragement and enthusiasm when it is most needed. The John Neu fellowship and University of Wisconsin fellowships provided much needed financial support.

At the University of Central Arkansas, Mike Rosenow's comments on my work have been most helpful and his friendship most appreciated. Kimberly Little, Dave Neilson, and Pat Ramsey deserve special acknowledgment for their humor and support. Chris Craun and Lorien Foote have offered fine insights, and Ken Barnes has generously offered access to departmental funds to assist my work. Most important, I have loved every minute of my work with the students at UCA, and there would be no book were it not for the inspiration I have found in them.

The research for *Almost Worthy* benefited from the kindness and professionalism of many librarians and administrators. At the University of Central Arkansas, Alicia Suitt and Addie Bailey in Periodicals and Microforms and Elizabeth DiPrince and Rosalie Lovelace in Interlibrary Loan and Document Delivery offered unsurpassed support in the friendliest manner. Jane Linzmeyer and Robin Rider patiently helped with all sorts of materials in the Wisconsin libraries. Susan Sutton, Susan Hahn, and Paul Brockman at the Indiana Historical Society aided in securing permissions and hunting down a difficult citation. Mark Vopelak and Brett Abercrombie at the Indiana State Library similarly helped with permissions and working through the McCulloch diaries. Edie Olson and the Family Service of Central Indiana were most accommodating in the use of COS files. Judy Huff, Charlene Bland, and Lila McCauley at UCA and Eileen Ward at UW are first-rate administrators who kept their eyes on every last little thing so that they never became big things.

I am indebted to Indiana University Press for vital support and input from Robert Sloan and David Hammack, who improved *Almost Worthy* in ways too numerous and significant to count. Sarah Wyatt Swanson always was helpful. Elaine Durham Otto served as an excellent and good-natured copyeditor.

Several people who offered critical support do not neatly fit in any larger category. Alan Lessoff sharpened my thinking toward charity applicants. Dawn Bakken improved my understanding of McCulloch's *Open Door Sermons*. Angelo Louisa was my first inspiration to be a historian, and he remains an inspiration to this day. Bre Schrader's friendship has kept me moving forward. Marydale Oppert's singular enthusiasm has helped sustain me.

Finally, I offer a special acknowledgment to my family. Don and Eleanor Gould, my grandparents, are the most remarkable people I know. Their intellectual curiosity and optimism are admirable. My aunt and uncle Rita and Grant Allison never stopped listening. Thank you from the bottom of my heart. My aunt and uncle Nancy and Paul Thornblad and their family, and my stepmother and stepfather, Mari Petersen and Mike Sorensen, are dear and reliable friends. I could not ask for better siblings than Greg and Jannelle Ruswick, whom I love more than I can express. To Jim Ruswick and Carol Sorensen, my parents: thank you for introducing me to and cultivating my interest in reading and learning and supporting me as these interests led me to strange new places. You are the best.

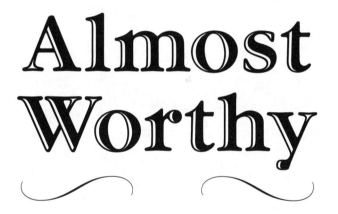

Almost Worthy

1

INTRODUCTION: BIG MOLL
AND THE SCIENCE OF
SCIENTIFIC CHARITY

Big Moll, Pauper

In June 1881 a council of concerned Indiana citizens filed a petition with
the Board of County Commissioners of Marion County, asking that
they investigate the rampant abuse and negligence rumored to be infest-
ing the Marion County Poorhouse. Thomas A. Hendricks, a former Indiana governor, U.S. senator, vice presidential running mate to Samuel
Tilden, and later vice president to Grover Cleveland, headed the petition-
ing council. Their case rested on four contentions: that the poorhouse
overseers did not differentiate between the different types of people re-
siding in their facility, that their negligence and improper training had
resulted in abuse of the inmates, that the poorhouse was part of the local
Republican machine and coerced its residents to vote the party ticket,
and that biology and statistics proved that the poorhouse's system perpetuated pauperism, or willful dependence upon private charity and public welfare.

In spite of concerns voiced to the board by the Reverend Oscar C.
McCulloch, a member of the committee that wrote the petition, that
the inmates feared "they will be thrown in the dungeon" of the poorhouse if they offered critical testimony, several residents chose to share
their experiences.[1] Their remarks brought forth sordid examples of ne-

glect, especially of beatings, solitary imprisonment in the cellar, rancid food and drink, as well as inadequate ventilation, heating, blanketing, medical care, and other injustices. Ed Akins testified that "he had been given the diabetes from drinking a peculiar kind of tea" offered to him by the steward, Dr. Culbertson. With the approval of Peter Wright, a farmer who with his wife and daughter supervised the institution, more a poor farm than poorhouse, Culberson then refused to provide the necessary medicine to Akins.[2] Samuel Churchwell recounted how his two-year-old child had been separated from its mother, left so underclothed during winter that "its legs had been frozen," starved to the point of being unable to recognize its parents upon being returned to them, then caught a cold and died.[3] A newborn died when, allegedly, the professionally inexperienced Dr. Culbertson (whose legal record already included a conviction for assault and battery) waited two days before attending to its illness. Reports suggested that other than to receive beatings or solitary confinement, the insane residents warranted even less attention than the infants.[4]

Hendricks also alerted the commissioners to the consequences of indiscriminately throwing together nearly two hundred people of very different conditions: children, the sick, the insane, the vicious, and the elderly. Oliver Thomas, an "insane idiot" child unable to recognize his own name, reportedly whipped another child, Harry White, two to six times because Harry had screamed after a dog had frightened him. Witnesses reported that Mr. Wright always kept with him a cowhide to beat inmates, and he had also beaten Harry because he "had used careless language and was full of fun." Harry in turn tormented and mistreated other inmates. Hendricks accused Wright of attempting to run the institution without proper discrimination between these classes, an effort "which, in the nature of things, is impossible." To remedy the situation, Hendricks requested that the commissioners remove the children from the poorhouse, build a separate home for the sick, and for those who remained, to separate "the vicious from the virtuous."[5]

In the 1820s and 1830s, local governments across the nation had constructed poorhouses, prisons, and asylums for social outcasts. By creating an institutional system of "indoor relief," Jacksonian era reformers hoped they could discourage the beggars and tramps who searched for towns with better job opportunities or, more likely, more generous levels of "outdoor" public relief. But even as the distrust of the poor amplified calls for their physical isolation, the enthusiasm for poorhouses also reflected a new belief among reformers that poverty was both a moral and a social problem, one that might be solved through concerted effort, especially by building institutions designed either to morally reform or socially isolate the beggar. Almshouses rested "at the center of public policy" toward the poor in the decades before the Civil War.[6]

In practice, however, poorhouse mismanagement was commonplace. The institutions devolved into warehouses that indiscriminately mixed the so-called vicious—paupers, hardened criminals, and the insane— with the virtuous—the elderly, the young, and the "honest" poor—under one poorly repaired roof. The original poorhouse in Indianapolis was "merely a receptacle into which was thrust that inconvenient class in the community who, being unable to help themselves, were put away out of sight and dismissed from public concern. As long as the general public was not informed of the conditions within the asylums few changes were made."[7] Under partisan control, the institutions typically did not answer to any regular form of oversight and often served the interests of the political machine. By the 1870s, a broad range of critics sought to bring charitable and correctional agencies underneath professional, nonpartisan supervision. The Wright family, for instance, had allegedly provided all male inmates over the age of twenty-one with new suits of clothes in October 1880 to encourage their vote in the presidential election, and then only offered the inmates Republican tickets. They confiscated the clothes after the election.[8]

Although the Indianapolis newspapers covered Churchwell and White's tales of abuse with lurid and highly partisan interest, the greatest media sensation was a pair of paupers, Mrs. Pierce and "Big Moll." Newspapers' accounts injected much confusion into the story by using different spellings of the witnesses' names from day to day and paper to paper: Big Moll was Molly, Mollie, or Mary Oliver, and her experiences regularly were juxtaposed with Mrs. Pierce, who sometimes was identified as Miss, and additionally shared her surname and uncertain marital status with a woman at the poorhouse who worked with the insane. When Wright arrived, he placed the pauper Pierce in charge of twenty-five children at the farm. It was not an auspicious choice. Pierce had lived for twelve years at the institution, and according to Hendricks, she was "without education, and as far as Mr. Wright knew, without morality."[9] The Churchwell child who had died from neglect had briefly been one of her charges.[10] Fearing what she might say, Mrs. Wright had given Pierce a new dress and slippers and had promised a second dress and an attempt to secure for her "a set of teeth . . . in consideration of favorable testimony at the trial." Pierce insisted she had not recognized this to be a bribe.[11]

Hendricks warned that leaving a pauper like Mrs. Pierce to raise the children in the poorhouse risked exposing them to a fate worse than death: they would grow up to resemble Big Moll. Could that even be called living? Hendricks presented Moll, who had been raised since infancy in poorhouses, as a monster, a menace to social and moral order, and fundamentally different in nature from both the well-off and the normal poor. The *News* breathlessly reported that the "glimpse of her rude life" so interested the commissioners "that the ordinary rules of evidence were not regarded, and she was more closely questioned as to her own character and career than as to her knowledge of the matters at hand." If not the most accurate description of Molly Oliver, the character constructed by the report indicates the depth of fear and animus that paupers often provoked. Said the *News*:

> She was utterly debased, without a humanizing trait. She was a product of the poor house system. She was reckless and vicious. Her face was without a gleam of virtuous impulse. She was not desperate for she had never hoped. . . . She has only known poor-house care and poverty. She has found nothing in that to awaken the gentler phases of woman's nature. Her moral sense is dull, because it has never been aroused and quickened. She simply exists as she has always existed, friendless, hopeless, and alone, the sport of passions and impulses purely animal, a creature for whom charity regrets the birth. She serves to show, however, wherein our poor farm managements are wrong. She illustrates what is the outcome of such conditions . . . [for] pauper children. She suggests to the humanitarians what should be done. She stands [as] an example and a warning.[12]

Moll was immoral, crude, even unfeeling due to a lifetime spent in poorhouses. She also was "rotten driftwood," an "ill-looking, disgusting woman," and "a great animal."[13]

Life had not been easy for Big Moll. About twenty-eight years old by her own guess, she had either been born or abandoned in a poor farm, spent time in jail, and since shown a "remarkable . . . facility for gaining admission to poor farms." She had four children, each out of wedlock, at least one, scandalously, from a black man, and according to hearsay she had burned one of her children to death by resting it on a steam coil. At the Marion County Poorhouse, Moll seems to have cursed, mistreated, and fought with nearly everyone. She soon ran afoul of Dr. Culbertson, who thought her "a boisterous, high tempered woman." To deal with an alleged outburst, Culbertson needed his male nurse to sit on Moll and bind her with straps, "as she fought us all the way." Once subdued and under the influence of morphine, they bound her wrists, dragged her by her arms along the floor to "a bad-smelling cell" in the basement, where she was kept for three or four days on a straw bed with no pillow, and "with nothing to eat except two pieces of dry bread three times a day. When she was released she was so weak she could scarcely stand." Culbertson dismissed any complaints about her wounds as the product of Moll having syphilis, "which causes her to have pains over the body occasionally."[14]

The intertwined stories of Mrs. Pierce and Big Moll demonstrated several concerns about poorhouses and poverty that had characterized American thinking at least since the early 1800s, but also revealed something much newer: reformers' alarm at the supposedly biological nature of pauperism. In environments such as the poorhouse, individuals already predisposed by their heredity toward pauperism, crime, or insanity might degenerate, hardened into hopelessly irredeemable cases. Hendricks claimed that the poorhouse children already were biologically predisposed toward lives of idleness and that a childhood spent under the tutelage of a pauper like Mrs. Pierce threatened to leave them as hopelessly squalid and degenerate as Big Moll and just as likely to reproduce carelessly. To prove this claim, in the closing arguments he discussed at length the recent findings of Richard Dugdale, whose genealogical study of the Jukes family of upstate New York was widely interpreted by reformers of the period as proof that parents passed the traits of criminality and poverty on to their children the way another family might pass on a prominent chin or nose.[15] In doing so Hendricks hoped to impress upon the commissioners adjudicating the case the magnitude of the threat posed by poorhouse mismanagement. Employing the familiar hereditary imagery of the period, he warned the commissioners that their poorhouse was "raising up plants which would bring forth just such fruit" as Big Moll. Biology and statistics showed that from pauper parentage and supervision arose a new generation of paupers, thieves, and "bad characters."[16]

The defense accepted and even extended upon the hereditarian argument in order to justify Mr. Wright's rough treatment of his inmates. The lead defense attorney, Mr. Norton, argued that the demands placed upon the poorhouse had surpassed the law that had created it; indeed, there should be separate institutions for separate classes of people, staffed with trained physicians instead of farmers. Norton advised the panel to consider the sorts of people with whom Wright and Culbertson dealt. Affirming Dugdale's expertise on the subject, he then reinterpreted Dugdale's research and that of several other recent reports as proof that the inmates were responsible for their pitiful state, thereby justifying Wright and Culbertson's handiwork. Quoting from the findings of an article on the state of the nation's poorhouses that had appeared in the *Atlantic Monthly* in June, he advised the panel, "Probably it is liberal to put down one-tenth of the paupers as people deserving of sympathy. The other nine-tenths are in the Alms House because they have not wit enough or energy enough to get into prison."[17]

Presiding over an investigation of their own institution and employees, the Board of County Commissioners accepted this defense, as they ruled that the food had been adequate and the cells in the basement "reasonably suited to the purposes for which they were intended." With one commissioner dissenting and then resigning, the board also ruled that Wright and Culbertson attended properly to the sick and that they were "not prepared to describe any of the treatments as abusive." Although satisfied that no abuse had occurred, they expressed greater concern for the lack of oversight and proper discrimination between types of dependent persons. The board did recommend that a well-paid physician head the institution, that a farmer serve as steward, that a children's home organized like a kindergarten be established so that the children could be removed from the poorhouse, and that the city and county appoint a board of visitors to supervise the poorhouse continuously.[18] Big Moll disappeared from the public's view as suddenly as she had arrived.

Finding the Worthy among the Unworthy in the Postbellum United States

Big Moll's sorry circumstances aptly illustrate the panic felt by Gilded Age reformers over the seemingly contagious moral and physical disease known as pauperism and the allegedly insufficient or even counterproductive measures then available for addressing it. More drastic reforms of the poor relief system were needed than merely the intermittent patching up of almshouses. Few characters aroused so much fear and condemnation in nineteenth-century America as the pauper. As a general rule, Americans believed that poverty struck those beset by either personal misfortune or moral failings. This understanding of poverty logically demanded that charity be given judiciously. Personal misfortune might strike a man through no fault of his own; in such a case he ought to receive charitable relief. Moral weakness and misconduct, however, were inherent human frailties that would always lead some to value idleness over industriousness if given the chance. Unlike the ordinary worthy poor, who suffered authentic poverty due to some piece of bad fortune like illness or infirmity, the unworthy pauper supposedly chose a life of idleness, living off relief that he won by deceiving charities with fabricated stories of hardship. Conventional wisdom dictated that charity only reinforced the pauper's laziness and willful dependence by creating a disincentive to work. Without needing to labor, his physical and moral vigor would atrophy, and he would descend into a state of permanent dependence, or pauperism, which would furthermore tempt the honest poor to follow his languid ways.

The pauper had lived alongside the worthy poor for centuries, but only with seismic economic, demographic, scientific, and social disruptions in America during the nineteenth century did observers reimagine the pauper as a social problem requiring concentrated and coordinated action. Industrialization and immigration brought a host of new challenges to the towns and cities of antebellum America. Young men migrating from rural settings to the cities and Irish immigrants made the urban poor a new, more foreign, Catholic, and potentially subversive threat congregating in pockets of American cities. The pauper's chronic, willful condition and aggressive pursuit of alms seemingly subverted the classical liberal and Victorian values of independence and thrift, the biblical image of the meek and modest poor, and the transition to a wage-based, modern industrial economy.

While maintaining the traditional moral distinctions between the worthy and unworthy poor, Protestant evangelicals and civic reformers of the Jacksonian generation considered new approaches that might restore community bonds and inspire or coerce the poor toward virtuous lives. In addition to the poorhouse system, Americans established a variety of missions and Sunday school services, charities and community organizations, generally idiosyncratic to their cities of origin.[19] All, however, were designed to bridge the gulf between the poor and the other social classes, relieve the worthy, and "restore a unified moral order in the American city." Given the "Protestant tone" that tended to characterize many of these charities as well and public poor relief, comparable Catholic charities that ministered to Irish immigrants shared in the prolific growth.[20]

After attending to more pressing concerns in the 1850s and 1860s, the swollen northern cities of the 1870s renewed Americans' sense of crisis in poor relief. Massive movements of freed slaves, foreign immigrants, and rural workers and the return of hundreds of thousands of soldiers, many disabled by war, produced poverty and social disorganization on a scale never before seen in the nation. The Civil War created an army of permanently unemployed men estimated at around one million.[21] It also saw the advent of greater mobility for the unemployed and homeless, who now could ride the railroads from town to town as tramps, making them "more visible, and far more assertive . . . than at any other time in American history." Coming into a new town from outside of the community, "of unknown origin and designs," the mobile and supposedly willfully poor threatened cherished American presumptions about opportunity, the moral value of labor and property ownership, and "also threatened another core American value: community control."[22] Adding to this tally of misery were those temporarily unemployed by the depression that began with the banking failures of 1873. The shock of events deeply shook Americans' faith that they were immune from the history of enduring class conflict that plagued Europe. America was, as one historian has described it, "a society without a core" and suffering from "a widespread loss of confidence in the powers of the community."[23]

By the 1870s fears of social disintegration and complaints of disorganized charities liberally giving to the unworthy pauper and the worthy poor alike had confronted the United States' urban centers for two generations. The upheaval of the 1870s, however, created a form of poverty that was more abject, visible, widespread, yet concentrated, and afflicting a more diverse spectrum of people than had been seen in antebellum America. Historical geographer David Ward explained:

> In the antebellum city certain localities were identified with specific social groups, but these discrete sociogeographic patterns were not only very close to each other but collectively described only a small fragment of cities that were not yet highly segregated.... By 1870 the inner sections of large cities were increasingly described as a vast, unknowable "wilderness" housing a "mass" that threatened to engulf the remainder of urban society. [24]

The new mass of poverty challenged charitable institutions designed to identify and relieve just the worthy poor. Unable to attain personalized knowledge of the poor and generally lacking interagency communication, the quiltwork of private and public institutions that made up the social welfare system tended to pass over the deserving poor, argued critics, whereas cunning paupers received relief from a seemingly endless supply of sources. Newspapers fanned readers' fears that they needlessly subsidized the lazy poor by publishing stories of outrageous charity frauds and warning of armies of able-bodied tramps riding the rails from town to town in search of their next handout.

Rivaling pauperism's fecundity, a proliferation of enormous philanthropic trusts and small grassroots organizations arose to complement the existing and already quite heterogeneous system of church-based charity, poorhouses, and public relief. This produced only greater organizational confusion, causing many to argue that the system was ungovernable, economically inefficient, and more susceptible to manipulation and fraud by paupers. Worse still, the pauper seemed poised to swamp the nation not just economically but biologically as well. Scientifically minded critics, applying contemporary understandings of heredity and evolution, considered pauperism to be a hereditary predisposition and a form of biological degeneration. Once activated, it could not be reversed, and this left the pauper's children susceptible to the curse.

The construction of the pauper as someone hopelessly at odds with American values emerged at a moment when ideas of what it meant to be American were themselves in flux. In the Gilded Age, the emergent middle class looked at the poor and the rich and saw each in need of reformation. Given a stronger national government after the Civil War and then a national income tax, issues of who counted as a citizen, what rights citizens were due, and reciprocal obligations between government and citizens gained greater salience. Paupers claiming public relief as a right seemingly threatened the middle class's ambition to regenerate a healthy body politic following the war. Middle-class Americans typically held an individualistic worldview in which society rewarded those who made the most of their opportunities, and opportunities were available to all. They therefore dismissed the idea that America had permanent class divisions and, with it, dismissed as undemocratic any claim that the American government should distinguish between groups or give special prerogatives to one over another.[25] That the pauper now might be biologically distinct, irredeemable by his very nature, and capable of crisscrossing the nation along the railroad lines added unprecedented levels of urgency to these old problems. For charities interested in making sure relief only went to the worthy—those truly in need, of unimpeachable morality, and capable of benefiting from aid—the Gordian knot was trying to identify the worthy when by definition they were the least likely to ask for help or make a show of their want: temptations that the unworthy pauper could not resist. The new pauper menace inspired a cacophony of proposals for reevaluating poor relief and poverty analysis, with the practitioners of a method known as scientific charity, also commonly called charity organization, articulating one of the most influential interpretations.[26]

The most prominent advocates of scientific charity characteristically were college-educated northern professionals, often coming from old Puritan stock, politically and religiously liberal, and invested in a variety of moral and social reform projects. Civic-minded, respected community members, often from influential families, the first and most prominent advocates of scientific charity, served on the supervisory and charitable boards established by city, county, and state governments in the years immediately following the Civil War. Mostly Protestants, they tended to be ecumenical and theologically liberal and well versed in Pauline theology, described by historian James Leiby as the idea "that love is a manifestation of a spirit that links God and His creatures and unites the community of believers." True Christian charity amounted not to material relief but to "a divinely inspired spirit of helpfulness" among a community "held together by sentiments of personal and social responsibility based on the Biblical commandment to love God and thy neighbor."[27] In this spirit and given the desire to coordinate between all charities in order to suppress pauperism, they sought cooperation, on their terms, with religious charities from all faiths.

Indicative of their liberal theology, many of scientific charity's leading thinkers sought to synthesize Christianity with modern science for the purpose of addressing social problems. In late nineteenth-century America, however, science was a concept notable for both its prestige and its ambiguity. As an incomplete but representative sample, science might mean businesslike organization or systematized knowledge of any sort; the compilation of data presented in tabular form; the construction of universal laws inspired by the work of Isaac Newton, whether they concern chemistry, society, or the human mind; precise measurement; the technology then revolutionizing transportation and communication; or the "objective" observation of anything from birds to stars. Increasingly science signified professionalism and was used by groups seeking greater professional recognition. Many occupations increasingly populated in the Gilded Age by the middle class, such as the law, medicine, and engineering, sought greater social authority on the basis of their seeming ability to solve social problems—often ones they themselves had helped to identify and publicize—by command of esoteric knowledge.[28] Ideas of what constituted a science of human society were even more inchoate; the 1870s were "a period of avowed bewilderment" on the exact meaning of social science. No less than the founder of the American Social Science Association, Franklin Sanborn, conceded his inability to define it.[29] Applying science—whatever that might mean—to more ambitious and more diverse projects of social and individual uplift, scientific charity advocates similarly pursued the technocratic dream of saving democratic society by exercising greater control over its institutions and citizens. They initially hoped to bring the new tools of modern science to bear on old goals: suppressing pauperism, rebuilding social bonds, methodically investigating and distinguishing between the worthy and unworthy poor, coordinating poor relief among charities and public officials, cleaning up public relief from the influence of partisan political machines, and thereby drastically curtailing charitable and public welfare expenditures.

Christening their movement scientific signaled more than the hopes of scientific charity organization's founders to benefit from the great cultural authority associated at this time with all things labeled such. It also referenced their actual backgrounds in the social sciences, statistics, and medicine, their enthusiasm for applying biological thought to social problems, and their belief that only by systematic, objective investigation could charity workers see through the pauper's lies to the true causes of his poverty and distinguish him from the worthy poor. The first advocates of charity organization generally conceived of society as an aggregate of moral-free agents responsible for their own destiny; therefore, their initial explications of scientific charity's mission concentrated on using objective investigation to tighten the screws on charitable relief by better identifying the undeserving poor. But scientific charity reformers also believed that they could discover general laws governing the production of pauperism, which suggested the potential for a broader social analysis of poverty and plans for reform.

The Reverend Oscar McCulloch, who played "a leading part" in the poorhouse investigation in Indianapolis and conducted foundational research on the biological nature of pauperism, also gave the earliest and by all accounts most important statement on the principles of scientific charity in America.[30] In a presentation to the National Conference of Charities and Correction, McCulloch asserted that the pauper stole relief intended for the deserving poor and that most poor relief did more harm than good as it subsidized the pauper. Aided by the proliferation of charities and their disorganized state, the pauper with a heart-wrenching (and totally fabricated) story of hardship easily could live off of gullible, overly sentimental givers. McCulloch asserted six propositions about the relationship between pauperism and charity:

1. That pauperism is steadily on the increase in almost every city in the land.

2. That the most truly deserving are those who do not seek and, therefore, very often do not get, relief.

3. That the pauper, the imposter, and the fraud of every description carry off at least half of all charity, public and private; hence there is a constant and deplorable waste in the alms fund of every large city.

4. That, by far, the larger part of all that is given in the name of charity is doing positive harm by teaching the poor to be idle, shiftless, and improvident.

5. That but little effort is made, as a rule, to inculcate provident habits among the poor or to establish provident schemes, based on sound business principles, so as to aid the poor to be self-supporting.

6. That little, if anything, is being done to check the evils arising from overcrowded and unhealthy tenements or to suppress the causes of bastardy, baby-farming, and other evils peculiar to the individual city.[31]

From this departure point McCulloch offered a strongly hereditarian analysis of the origins of pauperism and chronic need that placed the burden of dependence on the pauper's biological and moral weakness, which set him distinctly apart from the ordinary poor. His habit of willful idleness could not be unlearned, because it was a form of degeneration, part of his physical essence. Accordingly, biology taught that the pauper could not be rehabilitated, only suppressed. Belief in the pauper's irredeemableness and the corresponding need to sever all relief to paupers became the bedrock assumptions of several important leaders in scientific charity of the 1870s and 1880s.

McCulloch and other proponents of scientific charity claimed that methodical investigation would reveal scientific laws governing pauperism's origin and its permanent abolition. Scientific charity's founders believed that Moll's debasement and the challenges she posed for public and private charity were more than social questions pertinent to just an individual city; she signified a larger national problem, one open to scientific investigation and treatable by expertly guided corrective measures. It was a problem that, perhaps conveniently, could be solved only by drawing on the specialized expertise of scientific charity reformers.

Investigating Imposters at the Charity Organization Societies

Although countless groups from the Gilded Age could claim with some plausibility to be practicing scientifically guided work in social welfare, those who most vigorously presented their work as the product of scientific methods and theories were the creators of a new charitable agency known as the charity organization society. From the 1870s through the 1910s, scientific charity reformers in nearly two hundred American cities established charity organization societies to reform local relief practices with the intent of better identifying and eliminating pauperism. Again, the Reverend McCulloch offered one of the first and most widely cited explanations of the COS's objectives:

1. The complete severance of charitable relief and other charitable work of the society from all questions of creed, politics and nationality.

2. The social and moral elevation of the poor (1) By bringing the richer and poorer classes into closer relations with each other by means of a thorough system of house-to-house visitation; and (2) By the establishment of provident and humane schemes for the gradual improvement of the condition of the poor.

3. The reduction of vagrancy and pauperism.

4. The prevention of indiscriminate and duplicate giving.

5. The prevention of imposition.

6. The procuring of immediate and adequate relief for the worthy and needy ones in the city.[32]

To accomplish these goals, a COS sought to secure the free exchange of all records from public and private charitable agencies so as to detect paupers trying to collect relief from multiple sources. In each city a COS would send out "friendly visitors" to, at least in theory, befriend the charity applicant and to investigate her moral habits, cleanliness, efforts to secure employment, and general reputation. The visitor or a separate COS investigator then submitted purportedly objective evaluations of the applicant's worthiness and state of need to a committee that made the final determination of what relief would be sent, if any. Although much of the movement's early enthusiasm drew from liberal Protestant theology and American unease with immigrants, McCulloch announced that since pauperism knew no boundaries of religion or race, the COS ought to work for all inhabitants of the city, regardless of race or ethnicity, and without proselytism or religious instruction.[33] Although they often exchanged pointed criticisms with religious charities that held more expansive views of the obligation to minister to all the poor, charity organization advocates thought that pauperism could not be stopped without cooperation among all religious and ethnically oriented charitable projects, and they viewed their work as part of a larger project to ease religious and ethnic rivalries.

Charity organization advocates had no shortage of historical examples of charities dedicated to bringing order to charitable giving through bureaucratic coordination, friendly visiting, and hardheaded investigations of a relief applicant's moral character. For instance, in 1816 New York City reformers created the Society for the Prevention of Pauperism, followed in 1843 by the Association for Improving the Condition of the Poor, which sought to coordinate New York City's disparate private charities, divide the city into districts, and systematically investigate every case of alleged need, categorizing the poor by the causes of their poverty.[34] Such American precedents notwithstanding, the nation's foremost advocates for scientific charity more commonly acknowledge European sources of inspiration for their work. Several cities from the 1600s through the 1800s enacted poor relief reforms that exhibited the principles of coordinated, systematic, and streamlined charity that scientific charity sought to emulate. Among those noted most frequently as a precedent by American reformers was the Prussian city of Elberfeld. An important manufacturing city in the early nineteenth century, Elberfeld's industrial expansion had brought with it a ballooning number of poor residents and public relief expenses. The existing system of relief had been in place for decades, and the first attempt at reforming it led to a 30 percent increase in the cost of poor relief. In response to the failure, the city authorized local banker Daniel von der Heydt to implement citywide reforms in 1852.[35] The "Elberfeld System," as Heydt's reforms came to be known, streamlined relief under a central control board responsible for systematically investigating all cases. His system divided the city into fourteen districts, each managed by an overseer, and further subdivided the city into 364 sections of about three hundred citizens each, with an almoner supervising each section. Almoners were instructed to make thorough investigations of their sections, know the conditions of the poor and the causes of their distress, and provide financial relief where necessary in accordance with a fixed scale designed just to allow for subsistence. They were instructed to encourage self-help among the poor by assisting them in efforts to secure employment. Persons judged to be able-bodied paupers, by contrast, were subject to imprisonment.[36] Examples of rationalized management also could be found closer to home, as Dr. Thomas Chalmers put a similar scheme into effect in his Glasgow parish in 1819. A prominent Scottish theologian, Chalmers similarly advocated dividing his city into districts with a volunteer assigned to visit each one, learn the causes of poverty among its residents, assist them with religious instruction, and provide aid "only when it was desperately needed."[37] Individual American charities began to draw upon his work, especially in Boston, in the 1830s. By the 1880s, Chalmers had become "almost the patron saint" of scientific charity organization.[38]

Scientific charity leaders tended to play down the importance of such precursors in their work, preferring instead to brand it as an entirely new and better approach to pauperism. They therefore often acknowledged only their most immediate institutional relative, the London Charity Organization Society. In elaborating the scientific charity movement's history and how its principles and methods could expose the pauper, McCulloch liberally quoted from the Reverend Stephen Humphreys Gurteen, whom he had met the preceding year. An English émigré to the United States, Gurteen in turn had learned his principles of scientific charity from Octavia Hill and the London Charity Organization Society. Hill and other reformers founded the London COS in 1869 amidst conditions similar to the upheaval faced by Americans a decade later.

Octavia Hill and other London observers noted with alarm the growing geographic separation between rich and poor and the subsequent dissolution of personal relations between the classes. By 1860, London was quickly segregating along class lines.[39] As the trend accelerated, the wealthier west end residents increased their charitable contributions in an attempt to shore up the east end's failing system of local poor relief. Critics of this new, distanced relief labeled it "indiscriminate almsgiving," asserting that the relief could not precisely target the truly needy and deserving, since the giver lacked personal knowledge of the recipient. First in London and then later in America, the literature on charitable reform treated the indiscriminate giver as an equal or even greater menace than the targets of his donations. Indiscriminate giving taught dependence, and dependence only reinforced bad habits, demoralized the poor, weakened their desire to work, and thereby turned them into chronic paupers.[40]

Abhorring the pauper's continued existence and concerned by the effects of impersonal charity, Hill shared the common Victorian assumption that individual flaws in character were the primary causes of poverty. The only way to effect permanent relief of poverty was to change the poor's behavior, but to Hill this could never be achieved through institutions like the poorhouses. It instead required reestablishing social relationships between charitable givers and recipients. This belief motivated her conception of charitable giving as well as Hill's better- known work as a housing reformer in the East London slums.[41]

Hill envisioned her society as a central hub coordinating the investigation of poor persons' claims to relief and subsequent charitable action. While much of this work meant distinguishing the worthy from unworthy poor, Hill also insisted of her charitable volunteers that they get to know the poor, befriend them, and act as exemplars of frugality and responsibility. Not that this was to be a friendship among equals. Hill centered her analysis of poverty on the fear that charitable relief caused moral degeneration in its recipients. In an often-cited 1869 paper to the National Association for the Promotion of Social Science, "The Importance of Aiding the Poor without Almsgiving," she argued that it was more important to restore the poor's spirit than to provide material goods. Charitable gifts, she warned, "foster an ungracious, discontented spirit." Aid "eats out the independence of the poor."[42] In lieu of tangible aid, the poor needed the firm but friendly guidance of the COS. One historian noted that her peers regarded Hill as "among the sternest of COS members" and that "her language of moral earnestness and Victorian spirituality suffocates the modern reader."[43]

The COS pursued seemingly dissonant goals: systematizing relief by methodically and disinterestedly investigating all cases, while personalizing relief with charitable volunteers who would provide the poor with moral uplift. The apparent tension in goals can be understood by considering the reformers' alarm over demoralization and interest in "truly" knowing the poor. Indiscriminately given charity supposedly weakened the resolve of the poor to work their way up from the bottom, allowing them instead to give in to lives of deceit and idleness or demoralization. Such charity at once made the poor their own worst enemies while it also obscured the real incomes and expenditures of the poor, thereby concealing the true sources and nature of dependence. Breaking these moral habits and seeing through to the true nature of pauperism required at once a systematic, rigorous approach and individualized moral supervision. Given that, Hill confidently announced, "I see no limit to the power of raising even the lowest classes if we will know and love them."[44] The London COS articulated this mission most coherently in its fifth annual report. It declared that improving the poor would come through cooperating with both the Poor Law and charitable agencies so as to thoroughly investigate and consider every request for relief. Those judged deserving would receive "judicious and effectual assistance" from one of the cooperating agencies. Investigators would promote "habits of providence and self-reliance . . . social and sanitary principles" among the poor and work to repress "mendacity and imposture" among paupers. This approach promised "to deal with the causes of pauperism rather than its effects, and permanently to elevate the condition of the poor."[45]

Although an English creation, charity organization's greatest success would come in America. The goals of systematic coordination of charitable work, investigation of all relief requests, promotion of moral uplift, repression of pauperism, and investigation of the true causes of pauperism quickly became part of the transatlantic exchange of reformist projects that characterized the period.[46] Oscar McCulloch, for instance, compared Hill to Florence Nightingale and recommended her writings in his highly influential "Associated Charities" paper, in which he spelled out the principles of charity organization at the National Conference of Charities and Correction.[47]

Few nondenominational charity or reform groups rivaled the COS's rate of growth. From Stephen Humphreys Gurteen's founding of the Buffalo COS in 1877, the first COSs clustered around large cities in the mid-Atlantic and Great Lakes regions, but they soon began to appear across the continent and enjoyed great popularity in midsize cities, small towns, and even a few rural counties. Determined to keep abreast of and coordinate these developments, a committee at the National Conference of Charities and Correction worked to keep in correspondence with each COS. In 1885 it collected survey results from a questionnaire sent to 121 charities in towns of 12,000 residents or more that adhered to the principles of charity organization in its "widest meaning." Combined with information culled from elsewhere, the committee announced that it was in correspondence with 170 charities that claimed to be reforming charitable giving in their city along scientific lines.[48] A survey using a stricter definition of scientific charity done in 1887 found thirty-four COSs functioning in cities that contained one-eighth of the U.S. population and one-sixth of its pauperism, about 456,000 paupers.[49] The 1890 committee gave much more grandiose numbers, citing seventy-eight societies covering a population of more than eleven million.[50] Finally, at the 1893 conference of the NCCC in Chicago, Charles Kellogg claimed the COS numbers had enjoyed a growth rate of 228 percent in a decade, from twenty-two societies in 1882 to ninety-two in 1892. By state, the distribution of COSs was as follows:

New York	16	Michigan	2
Massachusetts	14	Illinois	2
New Jersey	8	Kentucky	2
Ohio	5	Nebraska	2
Connecticut	4	Minnesota	2
Maine	3	Missouri	2
Rhode Island	3	South Carolina	1
Pennsylvania	3	Tennessee	1
Colorado	3	Louisiana	1
Indiana	3	Oregon	1
Wisconsin	3	Delaware	1
California	3	Washington	1
Iowa	2		

By region, Kellogg identified twenty-nine societies in mid-Atlantic states, twenty-four in New England, eleven in states north of Ohio, eleven between the Mississippi River and the Rocky Mountains, seven in the old South, five in the Pacific states, and eighteen states without a COS. Only thirteen were known to have folded, generally in smaller communities concentrated around the Great Lakes, mid-Atlantic, and New England states with old systems of charitable relief that were well entrenched. Kellogg concluded that the north Atlantic seaboard and Pacific coast had experienced the most rapid expansion, while mining and manufacturing towns, traditionally home to strong union movements and benevolent societies, adopted charity organization more slowly. Agricultural regions also were slow to adopt the COS method, as they lacked the commercial growth that brought about such needs.[51] If the relative lack of urbanization, migration, and immigration that tended to promote the establishment of charity organization societies were not enough to dissuade southern communities from creating charity organization societies, their association with northern Civil War era philanthropists also must explain the scant presence of COSs in the south. Southern states similarly had little engagement with the most prominent national organization to discuss the principles of scientific charity, the National Conference of Charities and Correction. In the early years of the NCCC, its public face arguably was its secretary, Franklin Sanborn. While northern reformers might have known him for his earlier efforts to found the American Social Science Association and his service as chairman of the Massachusetts State Board of Charities, southerners more likely would have remembered that he was one of the six abolitionists who had funded John Brown.

The National Conference of Charities and Correction

Scientific charity advocates considered biological pauperism a national threat that respected no jurisdiction, but that might be removed by methodically identifying its underlying causes and effective treatments. They therefore sought national forums for the exchange of scientific and charitable theories and methods. Historians have given considerable attention to the creation of a national network of scientifically minded social reformers in the Gilded Age and Progressive Era, with particular emphasis on New York City. The United Charities Building is rightly identified as "the single most important center of reform activity during the Progressive Era," since it housed the New York City COS and eventually "the National Consumers League, the National Child Labor Committee, the Association for Improving Conditions among the

Poor, the editorial offices of the applied social science and reform magazine *Charities* . . . and offices for some of the Russell Sage Foundation's
staff."[52] For those without immediate access to Manhattan, however, the
most important forum for the dissemination and exchange of scientifically motivated social reform projects during the Gilded Age and Progressive Era was the NCCC.

From its inception in 1874 through the 1880s, the NCCC mostly comprised representatives from the state boards of charities, a recent administrative invention designed to supervise and investigate all charitable, correctional, and in some early cases medical institutions within
a state. The boards often were modeled off of the work of the U.S. Sanitary Commission in the Civil War. Faced with shocking numbers of sick
and wounded northern soldiers, the commission worked as a comprehensive voluntary organization possessing the legal authority to coordinate medical relief, make sanitary inspections of army hospitals, provide
nursing, hospital, and ambulance services to augment the army's, and finally, to gather vital statistics. Run by members of the highest rungs of
northern society, commissioners' motives involved more than a noble or
sentimentalized humanitarianism; it advanced what historian George
Frederickson described as a "dollars-and-cents approach" to medical relief and their interest in using their work to impose order and discipline
on the unwashed mass of northern troops.[53]

Governors in several northern states quickly authorized bodies similar
to the Sanitary Commission to oversee public charitable institutions.
Historian and social worker Frank Bruno noted that "as originally conceived, the boards were intended to cover the four fields of health, penology, mental diseases, and dependence; health, however, was usually
separated early from the other fields."[54] Nonpartisan, unsalaried appoin-
tees staffed these state boards of charity, where they applied the administrative and investigative techniques honed from their Civil War experiences. Most boards possessed only the power to investigate state
charitable institutions, although Rhode Island's also enjoyed considerable policy-making authority.[55] Reformers placed great hope in the
boards' potential for identifying and eradicating root causes of dependency. In the early 1870s, reformers generally viewed society as simply
"an aggregate of individual wills."[56] Therefore, one had to scratch only

a small distance below the surface before uncovering the causes of dependence, and reform of society could be achieved by reforming its individual constituents.[57]

The board members' approach to charity informed the development of modern American social science, scientific charity, and social work; the lineage of each extends back directly to the state boards of charity. In 1865, from his position as secretary of the Massachusetts State Board, Franklin Sanborn called a meeting of a select group of state board members, academic and amateur social thinkers, and other reformers from across the nation. He wrote in his invitation to the first meeting that the new organization would pursue social progress through the discovery and application of scientific laws of society. The new organization, the American Social Science Association, soon grew to be the most respected body for the production of social knowledge in America. Almost as quickly it fractured into more specific subgroups addressing particular areas of social science and social reform. Most historical attention has been spent on the splinter groups such as the American Economic Association and the importance of these groups to the advancement of professional social science.[58] Considerably less has gone to the organization that initiated the exodus, the National Conference of Charities and Correction.

The state board members who created the ASSA soon felt that the scholarly direction of the association crowded out their interests in reform and charity and looked to create a group more amenable to their focus. Representatives of the state boards of charity from Massachusetts, Connecticut, New York, and Wisconsin met in New York on 20 May 1874, where they organized the first Conference of Boards of Public Charities within the ASSA. Momentum for an independent forum soon grew within the Conference, leading to the formation of the National Conference of Charities in 1879, adding "and Correction" to the title a few years later.[59]

Designed by the executives of the state boards of charity, it is unsurprising that the state boards exerted great influence on the development of the National Conference. Its first twenty-one presidents were all state board members, including three state governors. Similar to the charity organization societies, the presidents of the NCCC hailed mostly from the north Atlantic and northern Mississippi Valley states. From 1874 through 1946, New York State sent twenty-seven men to the conference as presidents, whereas the entirety of the old South sent one, and western states sent five. New York's overrepresentation is perhaps slightly less dramatic, considering how many national associations for reform had headquarters in New York City. Over the same period, the conference appointed 609 committee chairs. Frank Bruno has identified the geographic distribution of those chairs: New York, 164; Illinois, 72; Ohio, 60; Massachusetts, 56; District of Columbia, 38; Pennsylvania, 33; Minnesota, 32; Indiana, 23; Michigan, 22; New Jersey, 17; Missouri, 15; Maryland, 14; and Wisconsin, 14. Other than the District of Columbia, which gained greater influence due to the emergence of a stronger relationship between social work and charity organizations and the federal government, the distribution of influence between states remained relatively stable. The choice of host cities shows much greater attention to geographic balance, including several southern and western cities and two trips to Canada. Finally, although no woman served as president until Jane Addams in 1910, women did serve as committee chairs, approximately 8 percent of all chairs from 1874 through 1898.[60]

The four most important founders of the conference, as identified by Bruno, were Sanborn, of the Massachusetts State Board of Charity; Frederick Wines, of the Illinois Board; Andrew Elmore, of the Wisconsin Board; and William Letchworth, of the New York Board. Sanborn, the founder of greatest significance, also was the most radical. A Harvard-educated transcendentalist who studied with Emerson, he had helped finance John Brown's raid on Harpers Ferry, an act that necessitated his flight to Canada when summoned by the Senate. Bruno observed, "To the end of his life . . . he was considered a subversive thinker by his conservative contemporaries."[61]

Historians have tended to focus on what the NCCC was not. It was not a professional association until its rechristening as the National Conference of Social Work in 1917. It never functioned as the primary home of an academic discipline, like the American Historical Association, or of a coherent social reform agenda, like the Women's Christian Temperance Union. It held no formal power to shape charitable policy or to affect the practices of its members beyond its power to persuade, publicize, and coordinate. The NCCC began as an exclusive debating society for a subset of northern reformers who shared a very specific background and set of charitable interests. Bruno described the social composition of the first conferences as an "aristocracy" of "tight little oligarchies, directed by a few men identified with state boards who invited and tolerated others from the wider area of the social services, but did not draw them into their councils."[62] Attending the National Conference required more funds than the average charitable volunteer could afford, so it tended to attract professionally employed academics, administrators of charitable and correctional institutions, and individuals like the state boards of charity members who were well off enough as to be able to afford to take unsalaried positions.

These limitations notwithstanding, the conference quickly emerged as a highly influential national platform for religious, academic, and secular communities to exchange theories and research pertaining to a dizzying array of social reform topics. It was the only such association for connecting salaried professionals in charity and reform work for the first fifty years of its existence, and historians describe it in terms like "the principle reform organization" of the Gilded Age and Progressive Era.[63] Although it did not represent a particular scientific or professional community, its membership shared an aspiration to bring data-driven methods and scientific theories to the study of social problems. The founders of the NCCC presented their work as "applied sociology" and believed that human ills could be combated with proper scientific methods. As an organization with personal and institutional ties to the state boards of charities, the American Social Science Association, the nascent university-based social sciences, the charity organization and settlement house movements, the social gospel movement, the Russell Sage Foundation, and the U.S. Census, and as a handmaid to the birth of modern social work, the NCCC influenced and drew from most of the major nodes of American reform and social science from the 1870s through the 1910s. Issues of prison reform were of particular importance to several founding members, especially Frederick Wines and Zebulon Brockway, while crime, juvenile delinquency and the treatment of the mentally ill also received great attention. Frank Bruno's tabulations indicate that the most frequent topics of discussion at the conference were

"Children," "Prisons and Prisoners," "Charity Organization," and "Insanity and Feeblemindedness."[64] The annual publication of the *Proceedings* became an important medium for the expression of scientifically guided social reform, and it quickly became required reading for students of sociology, criminology, and charity from the University of Chicago to men's and women's clubs across America.

Among the many groups that used the National Conference as a meeting place for discussing scientifically guided social reform, the creators of the charity organization societies—or "associated charities," as another name commonly used to indicate the same approach—grew to become the most significant faction within the conference. Historians identify the NCCC as "the national forum" for charity organization.[65] Initially the NCCC's founders from the state boards of charity responded favorably. Sanborn described it as "a matter every way worthy of the attention of all charitable persons."[66] Letchworth explained the charity organizers' prominence in the conference as due to their skill with scientific investigation. He remarked that their statistical work and comparative method constructed "systems of law on true principles of social science" that brought social evils to public attention.[67] Such endorsements notwithstanding, the NCCC's founders proved reluctant to turn so much of their forum over to groups from outside the state boards of charity. Charity organization gained "a position both in numbers and in importance that caused some of the earlier promoters of the Conference to raise the question whether the original idea of the Conference was not being smothered." In an ironic twist, the same individuals who initiated the NCCC's secession from the ASSA contemplated leaving the NCCC to its charity organization interlopers.[68]

The representatives of local charity organization societies who attended the conference, typically an executive officer of that COS, in conjunction with the like-minded academicians and public administrators with whom they sought to collaborate, can be characterized as the leadership of the scientific charity movement. Not that it was an easy movement to lead. The COSs shared a dynamic if sometimes contentious relationship with the NCCC: the two groups claimed different origins and overlapping but not identical missions and constituencies. In contrast to the NCCC, the COSs were diffuse, found in more than one hundred cit-

ies across America. While some of the more prominent societies might
boast one or two nationally known reformers with the time and inclination to travel to a national meeting, for the most part civic-minded
lay volunteers staffed these COSs. Some participants appropriated the
rhetoric of scientific rigor, even taking scientific training courses to in-
form their work. But mostly the common volunteers did not actively
identify with the scientific aspirations or with the increasingly progressive politics of the attendees at the NCCC. The charity organization
committee at the National Conference regularly surveyed the COSs for
their data on poverty and pauperism, sought to standardize their investigative and relief practices, and generally sought to promote the exchange
of practices, theories, and data between the different COSs in pursuit of
standardized investigations that might reveal the causes of pauperism
and means for its elimination. Lacking any authority to compel cooperation, however, the COSs and other local charities were under no obligation to honor the requests coming from the NCCC. The result was a
very fruitful if complex federated relationship between national leaders
in scientific charity reform and local charity organization society volunteers as they pursued greater understanding of what it meant to be a pauper and how to identify and treat one.

From Almost Parasites to Almost Normal and Back: Scientific
Charity's Evolving Approach to Pauperism and Worthiness

Scientific charity does not enjoy a good historical reputation. Historians
of science conclude it was not scientific, and historians of charity conclude it was not charitable. Strong cases can be made for both positions.
In many ways the original mission of the scientific charity reformers
amounted to a deeply conservative defense of the industrial wage society's economic class structure and laissez-faire economics. In the 1880s
the dominant themes in scientific charity reformers' thinking were punitive and suppressive: they direly predicted that the pauper's libertine
ways would biologically and economically swamp America, and therefore they demanded severe restraints on his freedom and opportunity
to receive aid. Scientific charity's theoreticians and the founders of the
COSs initially employed purportedly scientific investigation in a manner designed to keep the onus for chronic dependence on the moral and

biological shortcomings of the pauper. Its most repressive elements have been well chronicled by historians of social welfare. Concentrating on the period from 1877 to 1895, the historical literature has emphasized the middle-class moralizing of the scientific charity leaders' and their belief that only by reconstructing the poor in their own image could they prevent pauperism. Central to this interpretation has been the landmark thesis offered in 1971 by Frances Fox Piven and Richard Cloward, who contended that throughout virtually all of American history, relief policies have been designed not so much to relieve the suffering or deprivation of the poor as to stigmatize charity, thereby preserving a pliant and inexpensive pool of labor. Furthermore, the conditions of relief have been designed to be "so degrading and punitive as to instill in the laboring masses a fear of the fate that awaits them should they relax into beggary and pauperism."[69] A generation of historians sympathetic to social control arguments and writing in the shadow of the Reagan, Bush Sr., Clinton, and W. Bush administrations has found in scientific charity a continuation of the punitive English Poor Laws and a precursor to the contemporary American war against welfare.[70] Adherents to this interpretation typically conclude that the scientific charity movement's approach became obsolete in the face of the depression of the 1890s, but the obstinate reformers refused to believe that any greater forces were at work in explaining poverty than an individual's honesty and work ethic.

Much less has been written about the scientific element of scientific charity. If anything, historians of charity seem more open to the importance of science in shaping scientific charity reformers' practices than historians of science are. When it is included at all, the most prominent texts in the history of science portray it as a group of amateurish cranks lacking intellectual rigor, their claims to scientific authority just a veneer for Victorian moralism. The creation of professional social science in the universities out of amateur organizations like the American Social Science Association has received the preponderance of historical attention.[71] Those histories document professional social scientists casting social reformers, charity workers, and other amateurs out of the scientific pale in the 1890s, as wary professors distanced themselves from the amateurs' various reform agendas and seemingly unsophisticated social analysis. Excellent historical work has chronicled how academic sociology kept outstanding researchers at the periphery of the American university system, especially Jane Addams and W. E. B. Du Bois, and more generally, black and female scholars.[72] Historians have written far less about charity reformers' interest in science and their application of it and virtually nothing to suggest that they might have created scientific knowledge or in any way altered the course of science's development in the United States.

An approach that takes seriously the scientific context of scientific charity, however, reveals a much more complex and historically significant movement. Scientific charity organization was not swept into the dustbins of history in the 1890s as an intellectually moribund ideology, unable or unwilling to accept the trends toward more environmental and causally complex explanations for poverty, the more generous proposals for relieving the poor, and more liberal guidelines constituting worthiness that characterized the decade. Instead, leading figures in scientific charity who gathered at the NCCC not only followed these trends but often led them. Their work is marked by an uneasy and fluid coexistence of several attitudes toward poverty, pauperism, science, and social reform. Biographical studies of scientific charity reformers already have established that they held less monolithic and more flexible understandings of dependence than historians once thought. Joan Waugh's biography of Josephine Shaw Lowell reveals a woman who moved from a rigidly moralistic approach to the poor in her youth to become a friend of the labor movement and who personally struggled to come to terms with a new analysis of the interdependent, social, and economic causes of poverty. It is no coincidence that Waugh also highlights Josephine Shaw Lowell's credentials as an amateur social scientist respected by professional peers, as Lowell's efforts to produce a charity based on the principles of science had much to do with the evolution of her poverty analysis. Elizabeth Agnew observes a similar change in Mary Richmond's understanding of poverty and likewise explores her complicated relationship with university-based social scientists.[73]

Expanding the study of scientific charity to encompass the relationship between friendly visitors, COS executives, statisticians, sociologists, and psychologists further suggests the movement's influence on the study and relief of poverty. For forty years the scientific charity reformers shared research and pedagogical methods with their university-based counterparts. Heirs to the American Social Science Association, they saw themselves—and were seen by academic social scientists—not just as producers of raw data on poverty but as conductors of crucial experimental work and authors of scientific treatises affecting the experience of poverty for countless numbers of people. Scientific charity's luminaries produced theoretical treatises and empirical studies of remarkable scope addressing the causes and treatment of poverty, work that the period's academic community recognized as making important contributions to economics, sociology, heredity and eugenics, psychology, and social work. The proponents of scientific charity helped pioneer the use of statistical surveys in America and worked to reform university curricula in the social sciences to reflect their practical knowledge of social problems. Movement leaders collaborated with leaders in sociology, psychology, and biology, while some of the more prominent charity organization societies offered courses to train their local volunteer members in the elements of properly scientific social investigation. Outside of the universities, the Russell Sage Foundation's board of trustees was "dominated" by "partisans of the COS" and "served as a think tank for the charity organization movement."[74] Its research efforts included support for *Charities and the Commons,* a national journal edited by one of the leading scientific charity advocates and that inspired The Pittsburgh Survey, arguably the most influential sociological work of the early twentieth century.[75] Scientific charity's amateur elite were not delegitimized by professionals or excluded from the scientific community; their end as amateur social scientists came about by their own decision to change approaches and to professionalize their work, transforming it into what is now the field of social work. The zeal with which members initially labored to suppress the pauper, their construction of the pauper as not just a local problem but a national concern, their eventual rejection of the pauper category, the worthy/unworthy dichotomy, the calls for social and economic justice made by the movement's leadership, their success at expanding the movement in the two decades after the 1890s depression, and their eventual abandonment of a progressive poverty analysis cannot be properly understood without considering the scientific context of scientific charity.

Throughout the history of scientific charity, science generally meant quantification and classification. In an era known for its enthusiasm to count and group, scientific charity reformers set the pace for investigating charity applicants, counting incidents of various types of misfortune, distilling those cases into groups, and pronouncing laws of society based on the inductive method. Especially before the late 1890s but carrying into the twentieth century, quantification and classification typically served the search for biological explanations of social phenomena. As chapter 2 demonstrates, COS and NCCC leaders rooted their approach to charitable relief in a biological analysis of pauperism. Throughout the Gilded Age, scientific charity's leaders spoke confidently of a parasite class of paupers whose mendicancy came from a hereditary disposition. They readily linked pauperism with criminality, insanity, intemperance, and feeblemindedness as diseases that shared a common origin in biological degeneration and that parents passed on to their children as a predisposition toward the same weaknesses. Oscar McCulloch conducted an often-cited genealogical investigation that purportedly demonstrated the hereditary nature of pauperism, a study later appropriated by the Eugenics Record Office as proof of the need to sterilize the feebleminded. Some scientific charity reformers recommended programs of negative eugenics, like sequestering these groups in institutions during their childbearing years, while a few speculated about sterilization. Trends in prison and poorhouse reform supported by scientific charity leaders also had a eugenic bent, like the indeterminate sentencing movement which sought to keep potential social menaces institutionalized, regardless of standard sentencing guidelines, for as long as they might create offspring.[76] Efforts to segregate poorhouses by age and by sex grew from the same logic. Entering the final years of the nineteenth century, the scientific charity elite held a basically eugenic outlook toward the Big Molls of the world.

Local COS volunteers remained more committed to diagnosing traditional moral symptoms of unworthiness than to finding scientific signs of biological weakness. COS executives and social scientists often used the NCCC to express concern for the friendly visitors' and investigators' overly sentimentalized approach to charity, their lack of scientific training in the methods of objective investigation, and therefore their inability to identify the pauper from the common poor or contribute toward the endeavor to systematize investigation and relief across the nation. As the visitors of the COSs produced data on poverty to be consumed first by their own society's leadership and then by the NCCC, a hail of complaints came pouring down about the visitor's reliability as a scientific observer. If she were not reliable, how could the movement ever have confidence that it had identified and eliminated root causes of pauperism like bad heredity? From the 1890s to about 1910, a scientific charity also meant one where charity volunteers had adequate training in the use of statistics and application of sociology.

As the movement expanded, members turned their attention from repressing the pauper to relieving the poor and from eliminating pauperism to eliminating poverty. Reformers' efforts to bring a scientific study to worthiness and dependence somewhat unwittingly introduced a more subtle and potentially radical critique of chronic dependence as a problem that remained one of morality, but that also might be open to social engineering by purportedly objective experts. Scientific charity's most prominent proponents began advancing the proposition that poverty and pauperism were not just matters of distinguishing between one person's bad circumstances and another person's bad character. Neither were they discrete social problems unique to the circumstances of individual cities and towns. Instead, pauperism was a common national problem that could be described scientifically in terms of underlying causes and could conceivably be ended by concerted social reform. Chapters 4 and 5 chronicle how several of the movement's most prominent national leaders had by 1900 constructed a new synthesis of scientific and moral perspectives that rejected the very notion of pauperism, of a biological basis to chronic economic dependence, and the worthy/unworthy dichotomy, in favor of a progressive and at times even radical interpretation of the poverty problem.

With their rejection of the pauper category came two other important developments. First, the movement began to uncouple chronic poverty from the forms of social deviance open to eugenic solutions, because chronic poverty alone no longer was sufficient proof of biological degradation or unworthiness. While the poor certainly still could provoke dread and loathing in these respectable middle-class reformers, they held out a promise of redemption and a presumption of moral worthiness that the pauper had never offered. Second, when virtually all of the poor became in some sense worthy in the eyes of the scientific charity leaders, poverty to them ceased being primarily a matter of distinguishing between types of individuals; instead, it became an issue of the very social and economic organization of American life, open to the same diverse assortment of environmental reforms favored by other progressive reformers, ranging from the public health, hygiene, and sanitation efforts to pro-labor legislation and health insurance. Americans had located the cause for at least some poverty in society and the environment since the early 1800s. But propositions that perhaps every last one of the poor was worthy, and could be redeemed through reform, previously belonged to the exclusive domain of utopianists, socialists, and radicals. Now they were given a receptive audience at the NCCC, an organization founded by moderate, upper-class mainline Protestant reformers dedicated to preserving social order. Again these changes are best understood by considering the changing use and meaning of science among scientific charity reformers, as cooperative interpretations of evolution, progressive economic theories, and victories scored over disease by the public health movement all inspired efforts to reform environmental causes of poverty.

Charity workers slowly removed chronic poverty from the types of social dependency they had once ascribed to a common source: biological degeneracy. What factors account for the finer discrimination between types of dependency? Why did mental illness and criminality become eugenic categories when chronic poverty did not? Most of scientific charity and social workers' closest professional cousins, groups including psychologists and intelligence testers, social hygienists and mental institution superintendents, stood at the center of the eugenics movement. Yet historian Daniel Kevles notes that social workers were among the first groups to resist calls for sterilization of the "unfit" at the turn of the twentieth century. His remarks here are most brief, saying only that workers "who confronted face to face the human objects of eugenic attack in charitable agencies, settlement houses, and institutions for the mentally deficient" were more likely to resist the call for sterilization than those with less immediate ties to the afflicted.[77] Since Kevles's observation, historians have extended the eugenic period back into the 1880s while broadening the diverse cast of persons, professions, and reform agendas involved in the movement.[78] However, there still is no thorough examination of the charity and social workers' complex relationship with eugenic thinking and treatment.

The answers lie in charity workers' abandonment of the "pauper" category and their decision to fold most cases of what once had been pauperism into the larger category of "the poor," while explaining the remaining cases of chronic poverty as a problem of psychiatry, a topic relevant to their work yet involving an expertise beyond their ken. Once scientific charity and social workers reoriented their work around the deserving poor and expanded that definition to recognize more and more persons as deserving, dependence no longer necessarily signified social deviance, degeneracy, or otherness as it had in the 1880s. For a group that aspired to professional and scientific recognition and increasingly turned toward psychiatry as the science most relevant to their work, the move away from eugenics was fraught with peril. Indeed, most scientific charity and social workers continued to accept eugenic solutions for other dependent classes, just not for the chronic poor. Exploring the professional and scientific aspirations of charity and social workers provides an interesting new cut into the well-carved topic of American eugenics by examining the motivations behind one of the first groups to revisit at least some of their eugenic assumptions.

The new perspective, however, did not last. By the end of the 1910s the scientific charity movement's leading thinkers had moderated their interpretation, abandoning calls for systematic social reconstruction in order to pursue their own professional ambitions. Chapter 6 illustrates how charity workers and their professional offspring, social workers, withdrew from their search for underlying economic and sociological principles of poverty in favor of a more individualistic analysis that stressed understanding the psychological traits of the poor in explaining their poverty. As historian Alice O'Connor astutely describes it, modern poverty knowledge rests on the state's commitment to using scientific investigation to alleviate poverty in a manner that does not challenge the basis of a liberal capitalist economy. It instead emphasizes individual responsibility and reinforces the assumption "that poverty occurs outside or in spite of core American values and practices."[79] Although O'Connor locates the introduction of this viewpoint in the 1920s and the Chicago School of Sociology, such a description fits just as well for the scientific charity movement's origin in the 1880s and conclusion in the 1910s.

Almost Worthy is the story of the scientific charity movement's transformation of the pauper from the well-known local mendicant or Dickensian character into an object of scientific research. Most of this story seeks to explain why the pauper suddenly provoked such a strong and organized response and the nature of that response, but just as important, to explain why that response, like the pauper, evaporated. America has not since witnessed the sort of mass-movement interest in addressing poverty and chronic dependence that characterized this period. Neither has it seen much of the pauper. Although the distinction between the deserving and undeserving poor extends back in western history at least to the Middle Ages, the pauper, like those who would either eradicate or reform him, has disappeared from the modern American landscape. Where did the pauper go? American poverty discourse today continues to be guided by concerns for individual deservingness. However, we do not imagine today's icons of the "undeserving poor" like supposed "welfare queens" and workmen's compensation frauds to be so numerous, distinct, wretched, threatening, or requiring of new policy initiatives as Gilded Age observers imagined the pauper. What happened to Big Moll?

2

"ARMIES OF VICE": EVOLUTION, HEREDITY, AND THE PAUPER MENACE

The Biological Pauper

In the late 1870s, the pauper became a threat not only to the nation's economic and moral health but to its biological health as well. Americans learned of Darwinian biology and the various social implications that commentators drew from the "struggle for existence" at the same moment that economic depression threw more people deeper into that struggle. Chronic, intergenerational dependence could easily be explained as the consequence of charitable relief obstructing the natural course of evolution by unnaturally protecting humanity's weakest members and allowing them to perpetuate that weakness, instead of strengthening them to better face life's struggles. Proponents of scientific charity soon adopted and expanded this analysis, announcing that they had found proof that some and perhaps most pauperism was hereditary. Children born to pauper parents suffered a hereditary predisposition to pauperism. Without intervention, the filth and depravity of their environment almost certainly would activate that predisposition, from which they could not escape.

Much of the urgency, even the sense of looming disaster found in reformers' condemnations of traditional approaches to charity, drew from the idea of hereditary predisposition. Once activated, no force on earth could resist the pull of degeneration as it dragged the individual further down into depravity. Worse, since popular belief held the pauper to be licentious, his numerous offspring, weakened by hereditary taint, eventually would flood America in a sea of dependents. Pauperism now became a problem transcending individuals, relief agencies, or even cities. At a moment when native-born Caucasian Americans already were sounding the alarm at the perceived dilution of the nation's biological strength due to immigration, interracial couplings, and the dissipation of white moral and biological health, the biological analysis applied to pauperism transformed it into a problem of national concern.

This analysis guided and justified the scientific charity leadership's tough-minded approach to poor relief and its contemptuous dismissal of other approaches to social welfare. They argued for extreme restrictions in outdoor relief coupled with close scrutiny of all relief applicants to cut the pauper off from the source of his sustenance, in part because they held that the biological pauper could not be redeemed. From the late 1870s through the 1890s, scientific charity's cognoscenti reported on the results of their investigations into the local pauper populations at the annual meetings of the National Conference of Charities and Correction. In conversation with criminologists, biologists, sociologists, psychiatrists, and others, they built the scientific arguments from which emerged the eugenics movement for restricting the reproductive rights of "degenerate" groups. It further justified the frequently noted disparity in reformers' interest in preventing pauperism as opposed to relieving poverty.

The belief that a hereditary predisposition required some sort of environmental trigger for its activation suggested other sorts of intervention as well. The scientific charity movement pushed for better investigation and supervision of state and private institutions, particularly poorhouses and reformatories, so that impressionable children did not mix with hardened paupers like Big Moll. Similarly, children possessing hereditary predispositions toward pauperism might be saved if they were removed from the contaminating influence of their environment. The causal relationship between degeneracy and economic dependence worked in both directions: chronic dependence could also cause an otherwise healthy person to slide into a biologically degenerate state.

Environmental reforms therefore could be effective prophylactic measures to keep the honest poor from descending into pauperism. The result was a movement that, in spite of superficially seeming to adhere to a
crude biological determinism, contained the kernels of a more complex,
expansive view of heredity's relationship with the larger environment.

The Reverend Oscar C. McCulloch, who helped define the scientific
charity movement in the early 1880s, also informed its leaders' biological
understanding of pauperism. In addition to authoring a foundational
paper concerning the philosophical basis of the movement and the proper
work of charity organization societies, he produced one of the earliest
and most influential inquiries into the biological basis of pauperism,
known as the Tribe of Ishmael study. The Ishmael study helped construct the biological pauper, thereby justifying the movement's forceful
and dogmatic approach to ending indiscriminately given relief. Eugenicists later used the work to validate the sterilization of the supposed unfit.
More immediately, his research inspired the construction of the Indianapolis COS in 1879, the fifth COS founded on American soil and one
of the most successful and influential in the nation.[1] McCulloch served
on the Charitable Organization in Cities Committee at the NCCC for
eight years, served as a secretary to the conference twice, and was elected
the National Conference's vice president in 1890 and president in 1891.
Papers nationwide noted his death a few months later, and conference
members referred to his influence for years afterwards.[2]

Following McCulloch's travels from Indianapolis to the National
Conference and back also allows for an examination of how the idea of
the biological pauper circulated between the local volunteering community and national bodies for discussions of social reform and how the
NCCC sought to shape the contours of local charitable relief where it
had no practical authority. While observing the Ishmaels, an extended
family of wandering poor known around Indianapolis for their chronic
dependence, McCulloch drew on his reading of prominent social scientists, biologists, anthropologists, and reformers to transform this local
family into a national menace. When the Ishmael study was discussed at
the National Conference, it joined data on local conditions gathered by
reformers from around the country to create the biological pauper, transcending all regional boundaries and demanding new approaches to an

old problem. Conference attendees then returned home to spread the alarm regarding the pauper's hopelessly corrupted moral and physical state, justifying further investigations and restrictions on his charitable relief.

The Appearance of Mass Poverty in Indianapolis

Scientific charity arrived in Indianapolis as reformers attempted to ease the city's transition into a booming city, one increasingly integrated into a nationwide industrial economy. Designed in 1821 to create a state capital as near as possible to the geographic center of Indiana, Indianapolis remained an agrarian town in spite of its growth as a railway hub. As late as 1860 the city possessed just two blocks of paved road. Still an agriculturally oriented town, at that date it ranked forty-eighth nationally in population but only ninetieth in manufacturing.[3] Indianapolis additionally appears to have entered the 1860s lacking strong class divisions, at least relative to those found in other American cities at the time.[4] Historian Frederick Kershner noted that "social amalgamation was more characteristic than social cleavage. Rich and poor still moved in the same world, consciously aware of one another as individuals." Instead, fault lines ran along ethnic and religious lines, including strong anti-German and Irish sentiments and race riots against the African American population. Religious affiliation mattered more than political allegiance, with Methodists and then Baptists and Presbyterians claiming the largest number of practitioners.[5]

Indianapolis exemplified the national trends of urban growth and poverty that prompted the calls to better organize and coordinate charity. A postwar economic boom spanned 1865 through 1874 and created new family fortunes that threatened the privileged social and economic position of the old rich.[6] As it became a major railroad center, the city's population grew from 18,611 to 48,244 during the 1860s: this was a 160 percent growth rate matched only by San Francisco and Chicago. By 1877 the population had leaped to 75,000. Recent emigrants from elsewhere in the United States, mostly rural laborers from southern and border states, especially Ohio and the uplands in Kentucky, accounted for half the population and held even greater claim to the state's cultural development. As the joke went, "Kentucky had taken Indiana without firing a shot."[7]

The boom, however, drew on strong speculation in real estate and the growth of competing railroads that could not be sustained. The collapse of the House of Cooke and other banks that had propped up weak railroads with easily available credit sparked a national panic in September 1873. As the capital of a state with a primarily agricultural economy, Indianapolis weathered the worst of the panic's first months, although Indiana historian Emma Lou Thornbrough notes, "Within a few weeks there were reports of hundreds of unemployed vainly seeking work at the pork-packing establishments in Indianapolis." Wages, which had risen steadily since the war, now plummeted.[8] In early 1875, crop and bank failures and railroad consolidation caught up to the city "with a completeness that was paralyzing."[9] When the nationwide railroad strikes hit in 1877, Indianapolis's status as a railroad town left it especially vulnerable; the mayor, John Caven, responded with stockyard and railroad construction projects that immediately employed hundreds and defused a potentially violent uprising by getting out in front of a march of the unemployed and leading them to the bakeries where he paid for bread from his own pocket.[10]

The mayor's visit to the bakeries illustrates the failure of Indianapolis's private and public relief agencies to fulfill their missions in a changing economic and social landscape. Charitable relief in antebellum Indianapolis was "an extraordinary tangle of confused responsibility."[11] Lacking the periods of mass unemployment that came with a fully industrialized economy, the city had not pursued a coordinated approach to the challenge of identifying deceitful paupers. The city's main charitable organization, the Indianapolis Benevolent Society (IBS), had dispensed private charity in the form of food and clothing to the local poor since 1835. Distribution occurred face-to-face, with persons reportedly of the "highest respectability" delivering to citizens known within the community to be in dire need of help. Typical of many American communities at this time, Indianapolis's charities sought to distinguish not just the worthy from the unworthy poor but also the local needy from strangers outside of the community. According to the IBS, the first tramps—men traveling from town to town looking for work or, from the IBS's view, malingerers in search of the most generous relief accommodation—had arrived in 1851 to a reaction "so immediate and hostile that it led at once to recommendations that assistance either at the door or on the street be refused them."[12] This approach to pauperism seems to have functioned well enough in antebellum Indianapolis, but faltered under the transition to an industrial economy and even greater population mobility introduced by the Civil War. Complicating the situation, Indianapolis's borders sprawled out in all directions as the population continued to swell.[13] Indianapolis residents did not know one another, did not know who was poor or why they were poor, and had no infrastructure for finding out. Calls increased for centralized coordination of the city's charities and public works projects.

The Tribe of Ishmael and Oscar McCulloch's Integrated Laws of Christianity, Nature, and Society

In this confusion Oscar McCulloch rose to become a key national figure in the effort to construct a new charitable infrastructure and new theories for addressing pauperism and poverty. A man possessing myriad interests and tied to several strands of late nineteenth-century American history, McCulloch has been examined by scholars from a range of specialties as diverse as his own eclectic work. Economic historians have examined his work with the COS to evaluate the efficacy of welfare reform. Historians of eugenics see McCulloch's research as inspiration and scientific support for sterilization of the unfit, noting that Indiana became the first state to pass a sterilization law in 1907 and that the Eugenics Record Office picked up on his work almost a quarter-century after his death. Others have sought to understand the history of the actual members of the Tribe of Ishmael and the diverse, often contradictory observations made by their contemporaries and equally schizophrenic historical narratives constructed around them.[14] Missing from this kaleidoscopic view is an examination of what McCulloch actually thought he was doing: synthesizing his understanding of the biological and social sciences with his liberal biblical exegesis in order to address contemporary questions of social welfare.

McCulloch entered into his investigation of pauperism possessing a blend of theological liberalism and scientific enthusiasm. This informed his initial, biologically deterministic and pessimistic analysis of pauperism, but it also prompted his analysis toward a much more biologically plastic, optimistic, even radical perspective (to be discussed in chapter 5). Raised as a Presbyterian in a religiously strict family, McCulloch avowed his dedication to God after experiencing a conversion at age fourteen, a highly prized event among evangelical youth in the 1850s, characterized by the work of revivalist preachers like Dwight Moody.[15] He began his professional career as a traveling salesman in the American West.

Biographer Genevieve Weeks speculates that his encounters with diverse characters in this line of work might have been responsible for his movement toward a more liberal theology than his father's.[16] McCulloch eventually chose to abandon this career in favor of becoming a minister, and he enrolled at the Congregationalist Chicago Theological Seminary in September 1867. Through extensive reading and debating with classmates, McCulloch crystallized his new theology and became one of the first ministers identified with the social gospel movement, or "applied Christianity," whose adherents argued that the lack of church attendance among the poorer classes reflected the indifference of the clergy toward social issues relevant to the poor. McCulloch warned, "Into minds worried by poverty and debased by pauperism the Lord cannot enter."[17] He regularly used writings from the leading social gospel theologian, Washington Gladden, in his sermons and other writings. Opposing biblical literalism, McCulloch and most social gospelers accepted Darwinian biology and believed that evolutionary principles could be harmonized with Christianity in order to shed light on the social problems of the day. Intellect secured more lasting conversions to Christianity, not the emotionally charged tactics employed by Moody and other revivalists that had appealed to McCulloch in his youth.[18] His liberal biblical exegesis saw science and religion as complementary, and he filled his diaries with extensive notes and commentaries on the great books of cultural anthropology, evolutionary biology, sociology, criminology, education, and economics.[19] An admirer of transcendentalism and more progressive theologians like Gladden, Henry Ward Beecher, and Theodore Parker, McCulloch likewise stressed "a loving, forgiving Father instead of Calvin's punishing, revengeful God" and advised that individuals should discover the "liberty of religion" and not just the "law of religion." He did not believe in Hell and expressed no eschatological inter-

ests.[20] Weeks points out that from the start of his first pastorate in Sheboygan, Wisconsin, he gave more sermons on topics of practical interest
and concern than on theological doctrine. Several sermons analyzed
the latest scientific and technological discoveries and their application
to Christian ethics.

McCulloch's theology represented part of a larger challenge to the
complacency that characterized Reconstruction Era Protestantism, once
described as "a massive, almost unbroken front in its defense of the social status quo."[21] Conservative elements in Sheboygan's religious establishment quickly condemned his theology. The *Sheboygan Herald*
accused him of preaching "another gospel," and one of his supporters
had to maneuver to secure McCulloch's reappointment to the church
after he had taken a leave of absence due to illness. As the criticisms
forced McCulloch to consider resigning, members of Plymouth Congregational Church in Indianapolis invited him to come preach at the
end of April 1877 and then extended a formal call to him to head the
church. After initially sending a letter declining the offer, McCulloch
had a change of heart and telegraphed his acceptance to the church before the letter arrived.[22] When he moved on to Indianapolis in 1877 to
lead Plymouth, McCulloch's reputation as an unorthodox theologian
preceded him.

In the months before his arrival in Indianapolis, McCulloch read extensively in the social sciences, including cultural anthropologist E. B. Ty-
lor's *Primitive Cultures,* John Fiske's *Triumph of Darwinism,* and Herbert
Spencer's *Sociology.* He seemed especially interested in anthropology,
reading Oskar Peschel's *Races of Man* and several smaller articles during
the year. He also purchased Spencer's *Psychology* and *Social Statics* that
fall, and he regularly read *Popular Science Monthly* and a variety of literary magazines. The analysis of natural and social laws McCulloch entered into his diary indicate that he anchored his worldview with an un-
shakable belief in the force of inexorable laws of nature, unforgiving yet
basically benevolent to those who observed their lessons. He held faith
in general human progress and the omnipresence of God in all human-
kind, tempered by the knowledge that not all would share in the good
fortune of progress.

Portrait of Oscar C. McCulloch from title page of his book
The Open Door: Sermons and Prayers and the 1891 *Proceedings*
of the National Conference of Charities and Correction.

Excerpts from his 1877 diary shed considerable light on the analysis of science, Christianity, and society that McCulloch brought to Indianapolis and guided his involvement with the scientific charity movement. Thoughtful observers often found lessons on the intersection of human progress and human misery by sifting through the wreckage of railroad accidents, and January saw a particularly wrenching disaster at Ashtabula, Ohio. A train of two locomotives, eleven cars, and nearly two hundred passengers was slogging its way through blizzard conditions when it crossed an iron bridge seventy-five feet above a frozen creek. As the first engine reached the other side, the bridge snapped, sending the cars into the creek below. An estimated fifty-five passengers perished from the fall, the resulting fire, and exposure to the cold and the current of the river. The event stayed at the front of the *New York Times* for a week, which described the combination of perils as "an ideal tragedy."[23]

To McCulloch, the events demonstrated the relationship between natural law and the universe's moral order, which he articulated first as a sermon on the seventh of January, "The Meaning and Moral of Accidents," then expanded upon in his diary. Like so many scientifically minded reformers of his era, McCulloch sought to harmonize human law with natural law. He believed pain and suffering were the unavoidable moral consequences brought about by violating the natural order of things: "Death according to nature ought to be at the end of a full life and as painless as birth. That it is not, is due to the disobedience of natural laws." These laws were simultaneously benevolent yet merciless. They existed "for good" and "to bring about a habitable world," but "do not stop to consider ignorance or weakness. . . . They make no mistakes and forgive none." The conclusion evinced little sympathy for persons in suffering: "The moral is that these are not accidents but that men are in the way" of natural law.[24] He soon came to understand the pauper's suffering as the consequence of a lifestyle and of charitable practices contrary to natural law.

McCulloch's first thoughts on the interplay of heredity and environment appear in May 1877, in the form of an outline for a lecture he delivered to the Northern Wisconsin Sunday School Association, "The Science of Childhood."[25] In his notes McCulloch broke down the factors affecting behavior, growth, and development of children into "Internal

Factors" and "External Factors." In comments closely echoing the analysis he later applied to the children of paupers, McCulloch concluded that "a child is to be looked upon as a *composite* and studied in the light of his ancient history," "inheritance demands individual study," and "progress pledges us to all effort." The lecture was the first of many addresses McCulloch gave to audiences that may not have been particularly receptive to his message. A newspaper clipping McCulloch kept in his diary described the address as "eloquent, thoughtful and much of it philosophical," but also "a singular address to a Sunday school convention because of the speaker's close adherence to the narrow speculations of the materialistic evolutionists."[26] Although not the predominant theme in his early writing, this optimistic interpretation in which the force of heredity might be superseded by early environmental intervention eventually became more significant to McCulloch's thinking than the punitive interpretation of natural law found in his diary entry on the Ashtabula disaster.

The final entry, from 7 June 1877, "The Problem of Life," articulated what the study of nature entailed and what it offered mankind. McCulloch wrote that two oppositional forces comprised the totality of the world: the human will and that of nature. Humanity's struggle against the force of nature came from its sense of the divine, of "a certain ideal which man instinctively puts before himself. An ideal of happiness or an ideal of perfection."[27] Man, thought McCulloch, most advantageously applied the force of his will against that of nature by applying the methods of science. With his belief in the beneficence of natural law and the dangers that befell men ignorant of those laws, McCulloch soon moved to reconstruct charitable giving so as best to resemble his understanding of human, natural, and divine law.

No evidence exists that McCulloch ever dealt with poverty in Sheboygan—a lack due perhaps in part to the dearth of surviving newspaper articles relating to his Wisconsin sermons and in part to the scarcity of the minister's own writings. Yet the first recorded impression of the city of Indianapolis was that its residents "have not had much hand in relieving the poor, I judge."[28] The most recent historian to study McCulloch's work, Nathaniel Deutsch, observes that McCulloch had entered the ranks of "a small but powerful minority" of northerners who "sought to transform Indianapolis from an overgrown frontier town into a modern, industrialized metropolis."[29] His efforts at transformation often focused on the habits of the poor. Six months later, he recorded a meeting with members of a severely impoverished family, which appeared in his 18 January 1878 diary entry under the title "A Case of Poverty." He described:

> A family composed of a man, half-blind, a woman, and two children, the woman's sister and child, the man's mother, blind, all in one room six feet square. One bed, a stove, no other furniture. When found they had no coal, no food. Dirty, filthy because of no fire, no soap, no towels. It was the most abject poverty I ever saw. We carried supplies to them.[30]

The family's condition shocked him, moving McCulloch to investigate the family's history at the office of the Center Township trustee, the office in charge of overseeing relief for the poor and where all records of public poor relief in Indianapolis were kept. There he discovered the astonishing extent and historical depth of the family's dependence on public relief. Generations had grown up depending on charitable or public relief and suffering from the full gamut of social dysfunctions.

McCulloch extended upon his diary remarks two days later in an entry titled "The Ishmaelites." McCulloch mistakenly thought Ishmael was a pejorative nickname presumably intended to reference the story of Ishmael, son of Abraham and Hagar. As told in the book of Genesis 16:12, an angel prophesied that Ishmael "will be a wild donkey of a man; his hand will be against everyone and everyone's hand against him." Deutsch insightfully notes: "By employing the name Ishmaelite, therefore, McCulloch had tapped into a biblical narrative that resonated with many Protestant Americans who saw themselves as the New Israel. To be an Ishmaelite within this context signified kinship with, but ultimately exclusion from, the chosen community."[31]

McCulloch saw a more contemporary parallel for the Ishmael family with Richard Dugdale's study of the Jukes family's generations of malfeasance. He wrote:

> The case alluded to under date of Friday seems to be a case similar to that of the "Jukes." I went to the office of the township trustee this morning and found them under the above name. They are called the "Rest-house mob." Real name is not known but called so from wandering habits. They are a

wandering lot of beings, marrying, intermarrying, co-habiting. They live
mostly out of doors in the river bottoms, in old houses. They are largely illegitimate, subject to fits. There have been in all one hundred and thirteen
who have received aid at different times from the county of this family and
its connections. Two years ago they lived out of doors all winter. Most of
the children died. They are hardly human beings. But still they can be made
something of by changed surroundings. The children ought to be taken from
them and brought up separately.[32]

In suggesting the removal of the children, McCulloch echoed Charles
Brace's work with the New York Children's Aid Society, which removed
children from poor, urban, and often immigrant Catholic families and
placed them with better-off and generally Protestant families. One of
the central reform efforts to originate in the 1850s, the topic remained
a fiercely debated issue in the 1870s and 1880s, locally as well as in national forums like the NCCC. While the plan as originally conceived
and executed by Brace may have originated in denominational rivalries
and suspicions between charities, it gained further saliency among scientific charity advocates of the 1870s and 1880s due to their interest in
the power of heredity and the malleability of children.[33]

His encounter with the Ishmael family sparked a year of social investigation in which McCulloch visited poorhouses and tramps' lodging houses, the county asylum, a women's reformatory, and a women's
prison. The research eventually grew into one of the great nineteenth-
century studies on heredity and pauperism. By 1889 he had traced the familial connections of 1,789 individuals who had lived in the state since
1830. This amounted to just a fraction of his investigations, which he
claimed spanned another 350 families and 6,000 individuals.[34] A 2′5″ by
5′6″ diagram of the Ishmael family tree hung on the office walls of the
Indianapolis Charity Organization Society for many years, illustrating
the supposed hereditary origins of pauperism, and copies sold for fifty
cents. To one twentieth-century observer, it resembled "a cross between
a seismographic reading of the San Francisco earthquake and an electro-
cardiogram of a man who has just sat through a triple feature of X-rated
movies."[35] Closer scrutiny of the research into the Ishmael family has
been conducted by Stephen Ray Hall and Deutsch, who each strongly in-
dict McCulloch for the eugenic implications of his work and cast doubt
on the reliability of his observations. A local journalist and member of

the Board of Children's Guardians of Indianapolis, James Frank Wright, conducted most of the investigations, and his research notes diverged wildly from McCulloch in their assessments of the Ishmael family's racial identity and their drinking, sexual, and religious habits, to name a few. McCulloch and Wright's own assessments of the family are further riddled with clear testaments to their prejudiced observations, seeming contradictions, and possible fabrications.[36]

Such limitations in the quality of its visual presentation and research notwithstanding, McCulloch's study of family histories in pursuit of proof that individuals inherited antisocial behaviors and other personality traits was a prominent part of a widespread phenomenon in the late nineteenth and early twentieth centuries, one inspired by Francis Galton's study of genius in England and Dugdale's study of pauperism and criminality in the Jukes.[37] The genealogical investigations appeared to give irrefutable proof that injudicious charity so demoralized the poor that their dependence perpetuated from one generation to the next—a powerful rhetorical device in welfare debates and one easily visualized through a genealogical tree. Like Dugdale, McCulloch gained national attention for his research, and reformers spoke of the Tribe of Ishmael in the same breath as the Jukes. Eugenicists soon hailed both as scientific arguments for sterilization. Motivated by his research, McCulloch looked for an organization that could harmonize the practice of charitable relief with his scientific discoveries.

A Society for the Suppression of Benevolence?

His Tribe of Ishmael investigations motivated McCulloch to breathe new life into the foundering Indianapolis Benevolent Society. Although the IBS had been the city's most prominent private charity since 1835, by the January 1879 meeting its members were debating motions on its possible dissolution. There future president Benjamin Harrison moved to reorganize the society to fight poverty and pauperism in Indianapolis, and members elected McCulloch as president, a post he held until his death in 1891.[38] A pamphlet he produced within the week announced the revival of the IBS and its new objectives: to thoroughly investigate every case of relief, to disseminate the results to all charitable societies in town, to secure help "for every deserving applicant," to cooperate with public officials, other charities, and churches, and "to exert all its influence for the prevention of begging, the diminution of pauperism, and the encouragement of habits of thrift and self-dependence among the poor."[39]

McCulloch concluded that IBS officials could not manage the tasks of registering and investigating relief applicants while also distributing relief to the worthy poor.[40] In order to relieve the IBS of the burdens of investigation and registration, he took steps to establish a charity organization society that would shoulder those responsibilities and then report the results to the IBS so that it could administer relief knowing it only went to those judged worthy. With the auspicious endorsement of "sixty prominent business and civic leaders," the Indianapolis COS emerged from these meetings and began operations in 1880.[41]

Charity organizers in Indianapolis and across the nation struggled to explain the importance they attached to distinguishing the biologically hopeless and morally lax pauper from the noble and potentially redeemable poor. In their demand that no aid be given to anyone suspected of being a pauper, the movement quickly gained a tightfisted reputation. Popular perception held that charity organization societies were designed to reduce charitable giving. Critics of their methods soon renamed the Indianapolis COS the SSB: the Society for the Suppression of Benevolence.[42] Defending the COS's focus on pauperism in its first public statement, McCulloch sought to explain the unique biological threat the pauper posed, one unsolvable by traditional relief.

> The prevention of pauperism is as important as the relief of poverty. While the poor we will always have with us, it is our fault and our disgrace if we have the pauper. The pauper is one whose Saxon or Teutonic self-help has given place to a parasitic life. He hangs upon the city, sucking thence his sustenance and giving nothing back. He is willing to be fed and clothed at the public expense. He propagates children who are after his kind, recruiting armies of vice. It is folly to dole out charity, year after year, without making an effort to cut off the source of this deep, black river of pauperism. The first thing necessary in the administration of charity is to know who are the poor and who are the paupers.[43]

McCulloch initially believed these "armies of vice" to be beyond any hope for redemption. Charity should instead concentrate on preventing the pauper from receiving relief and from having additional children or raising his existing offspring. McCulloch listed suppressive efforts

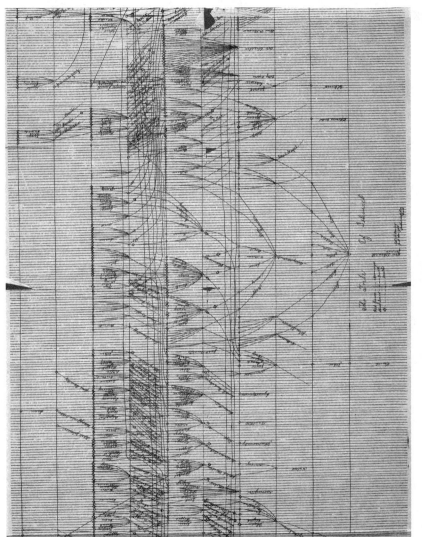

Oscar McCulloch, *The Tribe of Ishmael. Diagram.* Box 5, folder 5, used by permission of the Family Service Association archives located at the Indiana Historical Society.

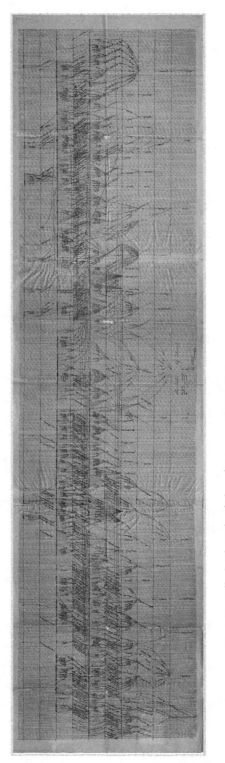

Oscar McCulloch, *The Tribe of Ishmael. Diagram*. IB M13 Cutter, Special Collections, Memorial Library, University of Wisconsin–Madison.

against pauperism as the first, second, and third priorities in a letter he wrote to the editor of the *Indianapolis News*. Collectively, the charity organizers in Indianapolis declared that relief of the honest poor must be predicated first on the prevention and suppression of pauperism.

Prevention meant investigation, and the COS quickly developed arrangements with most of the city's existing charities to scrutinize the moral, social, and economic circumstances of every poor person who requested relief. To determine what help, if any, to give relief applicants, the Indianapolis COS investigated tens of thousands of cases over forty years. In just the first weeks of its operations in December 1879, the COS's agents investigated 362 applications for relief. McCulloch declared, "Their history, habits and characters are known and recorded.... [Therefore] intelligent relief or refusal have been possible."[44] By April 1880, the COS had secured cooperation from the township trustee, Smith King, who provided records of more than 7,000 cases. The COS hailed this trove of cases as a source of information for students of pauperism "unequaled" in the nation, one that would advance the "scientific frontier" of determining the proper line between public and private relief.[45]

In a more detailed report issued to the local newspapers on 1 May 1880, McCulloch declared that the COS's investigations already totaled 1,779 families containing about 8,000 persons. The investigations allowed the COS to "trace family connections and lines of descent through three and four generations." Of those families, 1,193 had been deemed eligible for outdoor relief and 693 for free medical attention. McCulloch also trumpeted anecdotal evidence suggesting that the COS's work already had lessened street begging. More important, he asserted that the statistics gathered from these cases revealed "knots" of related families living in pauperism, a confirmation of its biological nature. The COS had found 165 such knots, he claimed, one of which contained forty-five families. It is unclear whether or not any of these were references to the Ishmael family, and McCulloch's own language suggests some confusion on where the family ended and pauperism in general began, but the terms McCulloch used to describe them was the same: "a mass of parasitic growth" that yielded "armies of pauperism." Lest a reader get the impression that the society indeed concerned itself only with the suppression of parasites, he ended with the reminder that the ultimate goal of investigation was to "point the way to helping" the poor and to avoid "mechanical charity" by treating all the dependent class as individuals who were "the victims of civilization."[46]

Deutsch views this press announcement as evidence that McCulloch perhaps "dramatically inflated numbers when it came to his charity work," since 8,000 would amount to more than a tenth of the population of Indianapolis in 1880, and the surviving COS casebook from 1880 contains only a few hundred entries.[47] The discrepancy between the 8,000 investigated cases claimed by McCulloch and the couple hundred entries in the casebook, however, might alternately be explained as the rounded-up sum of the 7,000 cases shared by the trustee and the fruits of the first few months of the COS's original work. That one-tenth of Indianapolis's 1880 population may have received public relief also seems less than suspicious, especially after appreciating that the files shared by the trustee did not represent the state of relief in Indianapolis for 1880, but were the compilation of several years, perhaps even decades worth of investigations. Hall's claim that McCulloch's work was "fraught with . . . fabrications" similarly rests heavily on the supposition that someone clearly so prejudiced and at times sloppy with his record keeping, as judged by to-day's social and scientific standards, must also have been outright dishonest.[48]

Gurteen's Darwinian Analysis of Pauperism

As part of his efforts to establish the COS, McCulloch invited the founder of the first American COS at Buffalo, the Reverend Stephen Humphreys Gurteen, to address the annual IBS meeting in November 1879 on the topic "Methods of Organization in Charitable Relief." He then met privately with the city's leading businessmen, politicians, and professionals, including Benjamin Harrison and future U.S. attorney general William Henry Harrison Miller, to deliver a more detailed explication of charity organization.[49] Almost singlehandedly, Gurteen introduced the archetypical organizational plan and rationale for reconstructing American charity. He then worked to present it as a scientific enterprise to American reformers like McCulloch by emphasizing the biological nature of pauperism. Many of McCulloch's early statements on charity organization and pauperism point to Gurteen's influence. Gurteen had emigrated

from England to New York City in 1863, entered the Episcopal priest-
hood at the end of 1875, and served as associate rector of St. Paul's Cathedral in Buffalo. His distress at witnessing the New York City draft riots
in 1863 and then the full force of the 1870s depression in Buffalo led him
to inquire into methods for reorganizing charitable relief to better meet
the growing threat of social dissolution. To that end he visited England
in the summer of 1876, worked alongside Octavia Hill and the London
COS, and upon his return established the COS in Buffalo in 1877. A tire-
less promoter and organizer, Gurteen also established Chicago's COS in
1883 and advised several others.[50]

Gurteen explained why pauperism steadily increased and why combating it required a new and coordinated scientific approach in his promotional address to Indianapolis's civic leaders, "What Is Charity Organization?" In it he sought to explain how best to balance kindness with
wisdom in charitable relief, given that the "most truly deserving," those
who would work if they could, shunned assistance and did not seek help.
As a result, Gurteen claimed, "the pauper, the imposter and the fraud . . .
carry off at least one-half of all charity." Worse, whatever sum found its
way to the honest poor did positive harm, he argued, by teaching the
habits of idleness, improvidence, and shiftlessness.[51]

The enormity of the problem required nothing less than mobilizing
and reorganizing all of a city's relief institutions through a charity organization society. He envisioned the COS acting as a "business scheme"
that gave no relief of its own but would investigate "thoroughly and free
of charge" all cases of need brought to its attention. Through investigation, COS agents would distinguish the honest poor from the paupers,
connect the honest poor with the appropriate relief society, and promote thrift and self-help among all the poor. There would be no dupli-
cation of existing benevolent work, no relief given directly by the COS
except in the most urgent cases, and "no sentiment in the matter."[52]
Gurteen argued that there must be no discrimination by religion, creed,
race, or ethnicity, as the only distinction that mattered was that between
the deserving and undeserving poor, and the corrosive effects of pauperism could be found across all these groups. For similar reasons the
COS should also eschew proselytism. Like several COS leaders, Gurteen extended an olive branch to established religious charities with one

hand, while writing pointed criticism of the inefficacious and ignorant approach of many such charities with the other.

Because it rested on scientific laws of nature, Gurteen insisted that his plan for organized charities could not fail. In "The Scientific Basis of Charity Organization," a chapter from his influential 1882 *Handbook of Charity Organization,* he elaborated on this boastful claim in order, ironically, to rebuke allegations that charity organization was too utopian. In an essentially social Darwinist analysis he laid forth "some of the best established facts of science" such as "the fate of the vast majority of human beings to have what is called a 'struggle for existence'" and that those "best fitted to live have the best chance of living, and those who are the least fitted to live are the most likely to die early. This is what is known as the law of 'the survival of the fittest.'"[53] Perhaps disingenuously he insisted that anyone could accept these principles regardless of his or her opinion concerning evolution.

In Gurteen's world, human sociability caused poverty. Man stood out from the biological kingdom as the only "social and sympathetic" animal, one that "has always and everywhere banded together with man to defeat this law of Natural Selection." Social cooperation had allowed persons who would otherwise be defeated by the struggle for existence to survive. Though "a not unwelcome burden upon society," the effort to support these persons was the origin of modern poverty.[54] The weak and sick survived "only from the fact that they form part of a social organism and are aided in the struggle by common consent." But while poverty arose as an unfortunate by-product of man's gregariousness, Gurteen insisted that pauperism did not come inevitably by aiding the weak, so long as they "keep up a good average of labor" relative to the strong. It was when this average was broken and a fair division of labor was not maintained that the poor descended into pauperism.

Typical of those influenced by English sociologist Herbert Spencer's evolutionary views, Gurteen saw society as analogous to a biological organism. To maintain the organism's health, each component part must serve its proper function. By this reasoning, pauperism would be ended by properly fitting each individual within the greater social organism so that everyone kept up an amount of labor appropriate to his unique constitutions and talents.[55] Gurteen illustrated the idea of the social organism and the manner by which its weaker members might share in the labor with a fetching analogy. The title page of *A Handbook of Charity Organization* included an image in which a stout, grizzled blind man, clad only with a pelt around his waist and a staff in his hand, carries a "crippled" boy up a rocky path. The boy holds up a lit lantern and serves as the eyes for the man. Gurteen explained that their relationship was analogous to members of a well-functioning society, which through the division of labor accomplishes collectively what no one person can do on his own.[56] Effective charity must be rooted in natural law, and therefore any society that wished to prevent pauperism must follow the proper division of labor. A longer passage is instructive in appreciating the importance Gurteen attached to the concept.

> [I]f the keen sighted cripple had always been compelled to use his eyesight as a return for being allowed to mount the strong back of his blind brother, he might have performed as truly his proportionate share of labor as the strong and vigorous.
>
> The cripple may not be able to gain his living as a farm hand, but he may be able to keep the books of the produce merchant. The sick may not be able physically to pass an army examination, but he may be able to perform duty in the manufactory which makes army supplies.
>
> In other words, the "division of labor," which is one factor in the great law of the "survival of the unfit," cannot be ignored in any scientific system for the relief of the physically weak, the physically sick, the physically defective. In order to carry out nature's own idea, in thus making possible the survival of the unfit, each member of the community must perform that part which he is best able to perform, so as to keep up the just *average of labor* and not become an unnecessary burden upon the community at large.
>
> This is the underlying principle of the [Charity Organization] Society's method of dealing with Poverty and Pauperism.[57]

Gurteen seemingly venerated the moral and therapeutic power of hard work, tailored to fit the capacities of the individual. By thorough and methodical investigation of all poor, the COS would discover what particular niche each individual "is best adapted to fill as a worker in the great workshop of the world."[58] It was just a matter of conducting proper investigations into the social organism.

Historian and economist Stephen Ziliak observes that Gurteen described poverty in terms of simple dichotomies of "unworthy/worthy,

Image from title page of Gurteen's *Handbook of Charity Organization*.

pauper/rich, idle/industrious, careless/provident, dependent/indepen-
dent."[59] In addition to his distinction between the honest poor and the
pauper, he also distinguished between the poor in general and the rest
of society. Gurteen viewed all the poor, not just paupers, as a sociolog-
ically and perhaps biologically distinct category, all of whom were in
some respect unworthy and unreliable. This fundamental mistrust of
the poor necessitated scientific charity's systematic investigation. His
strongest comments on the subject came from the "Woman's Work" chapter in *Handbook of Charity Organization*, where he discussed the role
of the volunteer investigators. He warned, "It is the experience of all
who have ever had much to do with the poor . . . that their statements,
as a rule, are utterly untrustworthy. . . . [T]he poor will take your gifts
and laugh at your credulity."[60] The statement underscored the ambiva-
lent and contradictory attitudes that reformers in both England and the
United States brought to the charity reform movement. The poor were
at once honest and untrustworthy, unfit yet redeemable. Paupers might
be beyond hope, and yet poverty was ameliorable, an unnecessary consequence of social organization. In his writing, Gurteen exemplified many
of the traits that characterized the first American scientific charity reformers' approach to the poor: an interest in how the force of scientific
theory and method could be brought to bear upon the problem of poverty, blended with many of the value judgments toward the poor common to the middle class, including conflicting feelings of concern, fear,
sympathy, and revulsion.

An Early Eugenics? Degeneracy and Dependence at the NCCC

As cities across America created charity organization societies to identify paupers, end indiscriminate aid, and promote environmental reform
to rescue potential paupers, increasingly the executives of the COSs
would meet at the annual gathering of the National Conference of Charities and Correction. There the charity organization leaders, amateur and
professional social scientists, and other reformers interested in scientific charity pooled the investigatory data they accumulated from their
respective cities and institutions and exchanged theories on the nature
of poverty and pauperism. In the process this eclectic group built an ap-

proach toward pauperism that required the competent managerial skills and cool scientific detachment of trained experts.

Debate over the influence of biological degeneration, heredity, and environment quickly emerged as a central matter in the discussions of pauperism at the National Conference. Since the concepts might be of use in understanding not just pauperism but also criminality, feeblemindedness, and more, and since reformers commonly observed that these forms of social deviance often were found in the same cases, examination of hereditary pauperism took place within a larger tangle of discussions about the administration of the correctional and mental health system that included not only charity organization representatives but also penologists, experts in feeblemindedness, and administrators of poorhouses, reformatories, and asylums.[61] Reflective of broader trends in American attitudes, the discussion evolved from one that evaluated both heredity and environment in a complex interaction, to one steeped in the language of irreparable biological degeneracy. Influential voices at the National Conference in the 1880s spoke of a future in which the state registered all paupers and feebleminded persons, sequestered unfit women in institutions during their reproductive years, and denied marriage licenses to the feebleminded, the paupers, and other supposedly biologically defective groups. In so doing, charity organizers and their fellow travelers in scientific charity at the National Conference articulated the core principles that gave direction to the early twentieth-century eugenics movement.

Richard Dugdale's research inspired McCulloch and several other genealogical investigators. It informed the Big Moll trial and certainly other cases, and generally set the terms for late nineteenth-century American discussions of heredity, environment, and social deviance. Unsurprisingly, Dugdale won the unofficial award for "most noted paper" delivered at the conference on any topic for an 1877 paper he delivered concerning the Jukes. Indicative of the centrality of pauperism as a topic within the conference even before the emergence of the charity organization societies, in this paper Dugdale limited his discussion of the Jukes not to his findings regarding their criminality but to their pauperism.[62] Casual readers of Dugdale's work both then and now have tended to miss his criticism of the "extremists" who would insist on the exclusive importance of heredity using "doubtful" and "unsound analogies."[63] He offered an optimistic assessment of the power of environment to reform criminals and paupers and a latitudinarian understanding of heredity that included "all the influences which shape the personality of the individual," suggesting that he understood heredity to include the inheritance of a parent's environmental circumstances.[64] Regarding the causes of hereditary pauperism, Dugdale pointed to "the nature of the environment, geographical, industrial and social," especially the "inferior natural resources of soil," "low wages" among the poor "because they possess little skill," the seasonal closing of workplaces in winter, "a high rate of local taxation [which] decreases the purchasing power of their income," and "lax and lavish administration of the poor-laws."[65]

Instead, conference attendees remembered Dugdale's work for its description of the progressive degradation of the family line across generations, the data chronicling a downward trajectory as inexorable as the family's profligate reproduction, the importance of the "blood" in the transmission of characteristics, and the deleterious consequences of miscegenation. They similarly shared his premise that whatever the nature of the combination of environment and heredity, it created a class of paupers fundamentally different from the common poor. Listeners concluded furthermore that if pauperism could be identified, it might be eliminated with relative ease. Dr. Diller Luther, the secretary of the Pennsylvania Board of Charities, confidently pronounced a "marked distinction" between the paupers and the common poor. Pauperism was "often hereditary" and sometimes immutable, but in other cases it might be manageable, a biological inheritance transmitted as "a condition or tendency to be developed or diverted during the life, as circumstances may favor or oppose." Some cases might even be due entirely to the environmental conditions found in a person's childhood. Among environmental triggers, indiscriminately given charity was the greatest bane; the only persons who would seek aid "are of rather a low moral and intellectual type." Luther claimed that the Pennsylvania State Board's survey of fifty-eight poorhouses showed that 42.7 percent of inmates were able-bodied poor who could have been working. This statistic suggested to Luther that the cause of pauperism had been identified and now could be removed through universal education and employment, "proper moral training," and repair of the leaky system of charitable relief.[66]

Reformers at the NCCC typically expressed less sanguinity about the prospects for environmental reform. Instead, they suggested that only through the confinement and physical segregation of paupers could they ensure that ill-gotten relief would not give rise to another generation of the willfully idle poor. In her paper to the 1879 conference, "Girls in Reformatories," reformatory matron Louise Rockwood Wardner claimed, "It has been found that a very large proportion of this [pauper] class are the direct descendants of paupers." She warned that a girl tainted with pauperism was "likely to increase her kind three to five fold." Evidently referring to a case in her home state of Illinois, Wardner asserted that the descendants from two pauper sisters totaled one thousand, of which only twenty-two had not become wards of the state. The rest had cost the state $1,823,000 in care.[67]

Again taking a page from Dugdale, reformers used calculations to great dramatic effect in the 1870s and 1880s, illustrating the supposed financial burden that profligate paupers imposed upon the middle class. Both locally at the COS and in pronouncements at the NCCC, the interest in fighting pauperism was informed by and dovetailed into a broader political agenda favoring reductions in taxation and government spending, especially on charitable and correctional institutions.

While Wardner did not follow her thinking to its eugenic implications, the following speaker did. Josephine Shaw Lowell, a pioneer of charity organization, member of the New York State Board of Charities, founder of the New York City COS, and almost an icon for reformers, argued for the segregation of pauper women during their childbearing years. Citing the results of an investigation by the New York State Board of Charities into the rise of crime, pauperism, and insanity, she said that "even a casual perusal" of the statistics quickly proved that one of the greatest causes of their increase was "the unrestrained liberty allowed to vagrant and degraded women." Several examples followed before Lowell concluded that the women began life by "inheriting strong passions and weak wills, born and bred in a poorhouse." Lowell asked her listeners, "What right have we to-day to allow men and women who are diseased and vicious to reproduce their kind, and bring into the world beings whose existence must be one long misery to themselves and others?" Although she targeted women exclusively, claiming they were "visible links in the direful chain of hereditary pauperism," Lowell concluded by noting that the same treatment should be provided to pauper men as well.[68]

The Parasitic Pauper: The Tribe of Ishmael Goes National

Although Dugdale is better remembered today and was more widely known by the public then, Oscar McCulloch's presentation of his preliminary findings on the Ishmael family to the 1880 meeting of the NCCC and follow-up report in 1888 most influenced charity organization societies' thinking about biological degeneration and pauperism. In the "Associated Charities" paper discussed in chapter 1 for its importance in defining the proper methods and goals of charity organization, McCulloch rooted his argument for rigorous investigation and a punitive approach to pauperism in a strongly hereditarian analysis of the Tribe of Ishmael.

McCulloch told about his discovery of the family to his audience at the NCCC, describing that first encounter with poverty mentioned in his diary, in which he visited a blind woman, her daughter and the daughter's child, her son, his wife and their two children, all living in a one-room house with "no chair, table or stool, a little 'monkey stove,' but no fire, no plates, or kettles, or knife, fork or spoon." He recounted his visit to the township trustee's office where he learned that the family was "one knot of a large family known as 'American Gypsies'" that had dotted the records of Indiana's charitable and correctional institutions for generations. McCulloch's records showed that 125 members and three generations of the Ishmael family were receiving public relief, and he argued that public relief was "chargeable in a large degree with the perpetuation of this stock." His initial report in 1880 found that 65 percent of the children were illegitimate, and 57 percent of those children died before reaching the age of five.[69] In his final presentation to the National Conference on the Tribe of Ishmael eight years later, McCulloch also noted a high degree of intermarriage, disease, child mortality, petty theft and begging, licentiousness, and "wandering blood" inherited by a "half-breed mother."

McCulloch regularly described the mostly southern, rural, and white Ishmael family as wanderers and Gypsies, a group that had weakened its

Teutonic heritage through intermarriage. Marking the Ishmael family as a threat to Teutonic ancestry tapped into white American social science enthusiasts' pride in their supposed Teutonic racial legacy, mythologized in the late nineteenth century to represent the pinnacle of freedom-loving culture and subsequent concern for its loss in the face of immigration and miscegenation.[70] Nathanial Deutsch additionally suggests that McCulloch chose to present the Ishmael family as the "Tribe of Ishmael" or "Ishmaelites," suggestive of Islam to late nineteenth-century Americans, or "half-breeds" suggestive of Natives, or as Roma, in order to better give this clan of poor whites distinctive markers that demonstrated the clan "did not live by middle-class norms, were functionally equivalent to outcast groups," and "were even more dangerous to respectable society . . . since the white physical appearance of most Ishmaelites disguised their true perfidy."[71] Their unwillingness to stay settled in one location or work stable jobs that urban reformers recognized as part of the industrial wage economy was "tantamount to rejecting whiteness" in a world where white racial anxiety made such identity a paramount concern.[72] Alexandra Minna Stern documents that when sterilization came to Indiana, "eugenicists demarcated difference by dividing northern from southerner" and "branded destitute white southerners as the state's most serious biological hazard."[73] Dugdale similarly expressed his anxiety and disapproval at intermarriage, pointing to it as one of the many causes of hereditary weakness in paupers.

McCulloch clucked that the Ishmaels were "met by the benevolent public with almost unlimited public and private aid, thus encouraging them in this idle, wandering life." Linking the problem of unlimited public relief to another favorite hobbyhorse of scientific charity reformers, the patronage of city political machines, McCulloch accused the trustee appointment of being a political plum. Its powers to disburse relief went unchecked, functioning as a mechanism for doling out patronage to the poor in exchange for their votes.[74]

But here again McCulloch may have been playing fast and loose with the lessons drawn from the Ishmael family. Deutsch noted that while outdoor relief in Indianapolis nearly doubled from 1874 to 1876, when it reached $55,542, the election of B. F. King as trustee reversed that trend, as he and a team of investigators reduced expenditures from $31,733 in

1877 to $6,743 in 1879. A study of the COS casebooks also is telling in the relative absence of the Ishmael family, contrary to McCulloch's claims. Given their nomadic habits, ability to eke out a life outside the regular economy, and preservation of rowdy, rural, upland southern mannerisms that often clashed with midwestern and northern sensibilities, Deutsch speculates, "It may have been the Ishmaels' social independence rather than their economic dependence that made them seem dangerous and undeserving in the eyes of Oscar McCulloch."[75] An examination of case files from the 1880 record book of the Indianapolis COS further suggests that "impudence" and other expressions of contrarianism or independence on the part of charity applicants often were greater marks against them than their poverty.[76]

McCulloch saw in his research proof that pauperism was a degenerative condition passed from parents to offspring, activated by a poor environment. If a child with a hereditary predisposition to pauperism grew up in a family of paupers, her predisposition would be activated and she would descend into the pauper's lifestyle, producing children in turn with even less hope of escaping the pull of heredity. Hostages to their appetites, paupers would breed armies of mendicants willing to say anything to acquire the charitable relief necessary to avoid working. McCulloch concluded that charitable and public relief must be reformed in order to guarantee that the deceitful paupers were identified and denied relief, and he endorsed the removal of young children from pauper families in order to prevent their predisposition from activating—a proposal that routinely generated controversy at the NCCC, between competing charities within a city, and between cities sending out children and those receiving.

Referring to British phrenologist George Combe's work for support, he argued that unsanitary habits could cause the onset of degeneration in people just as it did in animals. Combe had discovered that "when the rabbit warren was not properly cleaned, the female killed her young and the male became quarrelsome. The organism of the animal was injured and rendered miserable by dirt, and nervous irritability akin to insanity was the result." Likewise, McCulloch argued that the "sufferings and crimes" of pauperism might be caused by filthy physical conditions. To justify his analogy between humans and rabbits, he cited Ray Lancaster, a British biologist popular among leaders of the scientific charity movement, for proof that "the law of degeneration is as active as that of gravitation" and just as universal.[77]

McCulloch spared no rhetorical expense arguing for a hereditary basis to pauperism. In a comparison that became famous within the movement, he announced that the pauper had an analog in the biological kingdom: the sacculina, parasitic barnacles that "fasten themselves to a hermit crab and live on the juices of his body." Before invading the crab, the barnacle began its life as "a highly organized crustacean . . . six-legged and self-supporting." The life of ease won at the expense of its host, however, brought about physical degeneration. "Their legs drop off, they lose their original form," leaving only "a sac-like body, with root appendages and reproductive organs." With a deft skill for avoiding subtlety, McCulloch pronounced:

> No social student will question the existence of such a law of degeneration in society, or has failed to see such degraded forms of life. He sees the social parasite, the pauper in whom the instinct of self-help has disappeared. He sees the children, under the same law, becoming like their parents; and all this he is powerless to help.[78]

His own efforts to help raise the Ishmael family to independence had failed because "they are a decaying stock; they can no longer live self-dependent." Like the parasite, their sense of self-help had disappeared, along with "all the organs and powers that belong to free life." A consideration of how an organism might strengthen or weaken both its physical and moral faculties through use or disuse, which was a linchpin of the Lamarckian theories that then characterized American views on heredity, might also have reminded McCulloch's audience at the National Conference of their concern about the biological fate of future generations of African Americans and poor whites.[79] He claimed to know of only one who had escaped pauperism for good to become "an honorable man." McCulloch reinforced the idea that this class was distinct both socially and biologically from the poor, saying, "These are not tramps, as we know tramps, nor poor, but paupers."[80]

The eugenic implications of the Ishmael study and the parasite analogy circulated from McCulloch's presentation at the NCCC and into academic discourse. Jacob Riis referenced it in his famous study of the poor

in New York City, *How the Other Half Lives*.[81] University of Chicago sociologist, scientific charity enthusiast, and NCCC attendant Charles Henderson repeated the sacculina comparison and its lessons in detail in the
introductory chapter of his 1893 college textbook, *An Introduction to the
Study of the Dependent, Defective, and Delinquent Classes*.[82] Its lessons
were "quoted in the schemes of study in Johns Hopkins University, An-
dover Seminary, and several colleges."[83] David Starr Jordan, the prominent biologist, pacifist, president of Stanford University, and national
advocate for eugenics, became a friend and one of McCulloch's parishioners at Plymouth Church when Jordan was a young professor at Butler College. Jordan had asked McCulloch if he might join without being
baptized, and with McCulloch's assent, he later boasted it was the "only
religious organization I ever formally joined."[84] In 1908 Jordan addressed
one of the first and most important institutional homes dedicated to eugenics research, the American Breeders Association, and insisted the
National Conference of Charities and Correction was the first American organization to consider eugenic solutions to social problems.[85]

McCulloch occasionally drew on his experiences at the NCCC for
sermon material, and his relationship with Jordan similarly proved useful in the pulpit.[86] In one from 1886 he told of how he and Jordan climbed
the Matterhorn along with several of Jordan's friends. All were tied together for the ascent, and when one fell, the strain could be borne by
the rest of the climbers. McCulloch observed that so too in society, "the
stumbling of one might bring all down, or the rise of one bring all up."
Turning his attention from mountain climbing to social dependency,
McCulloch noted that the Jukes family had cost New York State $10 mil-
lion and that in his own county "no fewer than 800 inter-related people of
the pauper and criminal classes have caused us to bear taxes and shame.
We are responsible for it."[87]

While McCulloch's two papers were the most important statements
from a scientific charity associate suggesting the potential of eugenic
solutions for pauperism, several other participants at the annual conference gave even stronger enunciations of the potential for prophylactic social reform to end the menace permanently. One speaker from 1882, C. S.
Watkins, recommended removing susceptible children from their pau-

per parents and placing them "within an environment that shall irresist-
ibly guide . . . [their] growth in a direction away from . . . [their] otherwise inevitable tendency."[88] Similarly, William Letchworth of the New
York State Board of Charities used his presidential address to the 1884
conference to press the absoluteness with which pauperism dominated
its victims, as well as its needlessness in the face of good government
and environmental intervention. Letchworth concluded that pauperism, like criminality and insanity, was inescapable after onset but also
quite preventable. Playing on the popular garden metaphors used to explain degeneration, he described how the pauper immigrant stock from
Europe "takes root, multiplies, and perpetuates itself." Studying hereditary pauperism one quickly learned that "an adult, able-bodied, chronic
pauper is one of the most limpsy, hopelessly inert, and utterly good-for-
nothing objects in the world; and the community that is not continuously active in extirpating this fungous growth will soon find itself in the
condition of the gardener, who, after planting the fruitful seeds, leaves
his garden to the weeds."[89] Fortunately, preventative measures could ex-
terminate the "fungous growth," as the pauper problem was "unquestionably one of the results of misgovernment."[90] Working with children
"while the mind is plastic and character may be shaped," they might develop habits of good citizenship before degradation and degeneration
set in.

Although the National Conference did not possess a mechanism for
giving its imprimatur to any policy approach or philosophical statement,
Letchworth's blend of biological pessimism toward paupers with optimism that it might be abated through early environmental intervention represented something close to an orthodox position among conference members and advocates of scientific charity in the 1880s. Josephine
Shaw Lowell believed the "catastrophe" of hereditary pauperism could
be avoided. "Paupers and paupers' children may be re-educated and re-
developed into self-respecting men and women, full of noble independence, instead of following a course which will surely degrade into the
pauper rank."[91] Conference presidents and other core figures gave similar
reports blending dire warnings of degenerates swamping America with
hopes that social reform might save children from their heredity.[92]

A Local Problem, a National Menace

In the late 1870s and 1880s, reformers made pauperism the paramount issue in charity and poor relief, part of a broader if somewhat inchoate political agenda of governmental reform and the pursuit of interclass harmony through the transmission of more or less scientific, professional,
middle-class Protestant mores. While the moral distinction between
worthy and unworthy poor existed in western charitable relief for centuries, now the pauper also became a biological menace and scapegoat
for the inequities, injustices, and general growing pains of an industrial-
izing and urbanizing economy and an expression of racial anxiety. The
initial pronouncements from McCulloch, Gurteen, Lowell, and others
made the pauper not just a drain on the nation's economy and a source of
temptation upon the honest poor, as he had been since at least the 1820s;
now he also was constitutionally irredeemable and could potentially
contaminate the broader populace with his heredity. The genealogical
and statistical examinations, the rhetoric and policy recommendations
produced in the 1880s by the scientific charity movement's leaders advanced their contention that only they possessed the means for reliably
identifying and ending pauperism. The scientific and moral hubris, biological pessimism, and cold economic calculations of the cost to taxpayers for supporting dependents all anticipated the eugenics movement, as
contemporaries and historians alike have observed.

The creation of the pauper menace holds greater historical importance than discovering another eugenic precursor. Locally, the COS's
evaluation of a relief applicant might mean the difference between being fed or going hungry, and now COS executives were returning from
the National Conference with warnings to the friendly visitors and investigators that a bad habit observed in an applicant might be a sign not
just of poor morality but also of unsolvable biological failings. Meanwhile, although the NCCC lacked any practical authority, it effectively
positioned itself as the central hub of correspondence between charity
organization societies and state boards of charity, a hub that also drew
in many of the nation's leading figures in sociology, social surveying, biology, and eugenics. It drew upon COS investigatory data submitted
from towns and cities across the nation as well as reports from chari-

table, criminal, reformatory, and medical institutions both public and private, and from it created a composite sketch of the biologically degenerate pauper. From the NCCC, these eugenic metaphors and data filtered out into college textbooks, organizations explicitly dedicated to eugenics, government officials, and of course back to the local organizations charged with the task of identifying the unworthy and unredeemable poor and excluding them from charitable relief.

The scientific charity movement's leaders, however, were no crude biological determinists. Entering the 1890s, the scientific charity reformers attending the NCCC held a complex view of how heredity and environment worked as complementary elements upon the pauper. It was a view well tailored toward the mission of scientific charity, as it simultaneously grounded the pauper/poor distinction in biology, thus justifying severe and repressive, proto-eugenic measures against the pauper, while also justifying social reform so that children might be saved from corruption and adults might not be tempted by the debasing influence of alms. But this view also led its adherents in unanticipated new directions. Of great importance in the history of poverty analysis, the reformers' turn toward a biological analysis of pauperism gave them another tool with which they might stigmatize the poor, but also moved pauperism from an atomistic issue of individual behavior and more toward generalized causes beyond the person's control, like poor civic administration and eventually into matters of chronic unemployment and public health reform. Beginning in the late 1890s, scientific charity reformers confronted a nettlesome set of questions: if heredity determined a person's social dependency, and environment determined the activation of heredity, then in what sense could the pauper be held morally responsible for his condition?

3

FRIENDLY VISITORS OR SCIENTIFIC INVESTIGATORS? BEFRIENDING AND MEASURING THE POOR

The Uncertain Authority of the Friendly Visitors

Through daily encounters with the needy in dozens of North American cities from Vancouver to Atlanta, volunteers of the scientific charity movement investigated, registered, classified, and sometimes aided the poor. Far removed from the annual gatherings of leading reformers and academics at the National Conference of Charities and Correction, the efforts of COS investigators and the "friendly visitors" kept the movement running. Visitors were at once to befriend the poor, supervise their moral development with an eye especially toward matters of finances and cleanliness, and evaluate their worthiness for relief so that the local COS could fulfill its mission of aiding only the worthy poor. Contrary to the visitors' historical anonymity today, leading members regarded visiting as the single most important component of the scientific charity movement, since it ideally put the scientific theories of pauperism and principles of scientific investigation espoused by reformers into action, via personal engagements that crossed class lines. As Haverford College professor of sociology and social work and NCCC stalwart Frank Dekker Watson explained, "Where there are the largest number of volunteers coming into firsthand and constant touch with the disadvantaged groups, there you are likely to have a more intelligent interest in the poor and the causes of poverty."[1]

Historians commonly interpret scientific charity members' use of friendly visiting as a form of middle-class meddling justified by the poor's supposed immorality and untrustworthiness. Befriending the poor amounted to serving as exemplars or enforcers of cleanliness, thrift, and sobriety. In their promotional and didactic writings on visiting, scientific charity authors rarely bothered disguising those intentions beneath a veil of humanitarianism. More commonly they argued that in addition to its moralizing effect, visiting also helped the movement maintain a fresh and unprejudiced scientific perspective toward poverty. By keeping field volunteers in close proximity with their objects of charity, they would not be beguiled by the paupers' contrived, emotional pleas, would not fall into fixed patterns of thought, and would better learn the causes behind "honest" poverty. Even as visiting kept the movement appropriately scientific, it also promised to act as a bulwark against an overly mechanized charity. The theoreticians of scientific charity who sought to restore interclass harmony worried that the local COS tended to let their work "crystallize into fixed forms and methods," as Oscar McCulloch put it. If such mechanization were to occur, the movement would become just another charitable group contributing to the glut of sources upon which the pauper preyed. Visiting was to be objective yet also personalized and flexible.[2]

The friendly visitor played several roles: friend, moral instructor, snoop, scientific investigator. She aspired to know the poor in the subjective capacity of a neighbor, restoring the personal bond between giver and recipient that the movement thought characterized an earlier, nobler charity. Yet visitors might also serve as investigators, observing the conditions of the poor objectively, providing raw data to be interpreted by a committee at the local COS and then perhaps at the national level. Given these complex and often contradictory demands, her role, responsibilities, and the meaning of the data she collected became topics of much controversy and even greater pontification. With time, leading members increasingly came to see her preparation as insufficient for the task of investigating pauperism. Much like the pauper, the visitors and investigators required scientific intervention to be reformed and improved if the movement was truly to know the causes of poverty and distinguish the worthy from the unworthy.

Many in the movement thought of friendly visitors' work in terms of medical metaphors. Influenced by their biological analysis of pauperism and their ties first to the Sanitary Commission and then to the public health movement, several leading thinkers in scientific charity claimed that pauperism was a disease with causes that could be discovered by rigorous examination, that had regular symptoms to be diagnosed, and that potentially could be cured. At the 1885 meeting of the National Conference, Alexander Johnson, the general secretary of the Cincinnati COS who later became one of the most prominent members of the conference, a nationally recognized expert in charity as well as feeblemindedness, explained the "general law of social science," that "the defective classes are to be considered, not as objects of punishment, but of treatment; diseased persons to be cured, or persons in danger of disease to be protected, quarantined, or disinfected." Johnson claimed the laws of medicine were "especially applicable to scientific charity" and compared scientific charity's investigators to physicians, since both sought diagnosis of a disease and prescription of a remedy. To staff the local charity organization societies, Johnson insisted on "a committee of clear-headed, warm-hearted men and women—a consultation of physicians carefully to consider and decide on the case." Finally, scientific charity required someone to guide the poor in their pursuit of thrift, "a volunteer visitor,—a trained nurse, to take the case in hand, and carry out the system of treatment as ordered by the physician."[3] In this spirit Johnson often claimed to be an "asthenontologist." Coined by a classics professor at the University of Pennsylvania, the neologism referred to one who studies "the science of weak beings."[4]

The medical analogy also advanced the visitor's pursuit of authority over the visited. By the early 1880s, medicine had identified the causes of leprosy, anthrax, tuberculosis, and gonorrhea, among other scourges. Louis Pasteur announced that man could "rid himself of every parasitic disease." Small wonder that advocates of scientific charity would employ medical rhetoric in their pursuit of the parasitic pauper. Perceived triumphs of the scientific method, notes historian Sheila Rothman, brought greater authority to physicians.[5] Just as the period's physicians expressed their professional ambitions by exercising greater claims of authority over their patients, the scientifically minded visitor also sought to supervise and discipline the poor. At the 1881 convening of the National Conference, a Mrs. James Fields from the Boston COS stressed the importance of a visitor's influence in "the disciplining of our immense poor population" and their power to transform "a mob of paupers and semipaupers, into a body of self-dependent workers." Again, the model for such exertions of authority came from professional medicine. Fields observed: "A physician is sometimes obliged to see a case many times before the nature of the disease is made clear to his mind; but once discovered, he can prescribe the remedy. How many visitors fail in this long undertaking!"[6] Effective treatment of poverty, then, required the visitor to pursue the same diligent, empirical search for the cause behind the condition that the physician pursued in diagnosing illness.

The danger posed by pauperism justified extreme measures to thwart it. A pamphlet issued by the Indianapolis COS cited Octavia Hill's warning that "we must at times do what almost seems like cruelty, if it is for the ultimate good of the poor." Again, the medical analogy could be used in support of radical prophylactic measures against paupers:

> Sentimental charity may do as much evil as if a physician should give stimulant or narcotic, simply because the habit of using these is set up. . . . When a community begins seriously to ask what it can do to prevent poverty and to cure pauperism, its decisions will seem severe, but they are radical and merciful. The physician must not hesitate to cut off a limb, or to give pain, if by so doing he can save life.[7]

Here the pain or metaphorical amputation had a double meaning: the rescinding of charity from some of the poor, and the subsequent extinguishing of pauperism.

Unlike medicine, Americans saw charitable work, especially investigation and friendly visiting, as suitable affairs for Gilded Age women. Historically, Americans have imagined charitable work with the poor as an issue appropriate for women's interest.[8] In addition to Octavia Hill in England, scientific charity's brightest American stars included Josephine Shaw Lowell and Mary Richmond. Although outnumbered by men at the NCCC, women and men alike participated in the highest ranks of charitable work; women led committees and eventually served as conference presidents at the NCCC. Both sexes, however, conceived of friendly visiting as a distinctly feminine project, with one estimate indicating that up to 89 percent of visitors were women.[9] Visiting demanded patience, understanding, empathy, good moral standing, and knowledge of proper parenting and familial relations—skills that scientific charity reformers and the general public associated with femininity. As Louise Wolcott explained, a visitor should induce the mother—and it was almost always the mother that a visitor interviewed and purportedly befriended—to "tell all her little plans and hopes; wherein she has failed and why, and what she still hopes to do."[10] A woman identified only as Mrs. Jacobs of Denver declared in an 1890 discussion session that the foundation of scientific charity "rests upon the women of the world. . . . Men are not good investigators: they are too easily blinded. It takes a woman with a woman's heart to go to a poor and stricken soul, and find out what she needs." When a visitor calls upon a man in need, "he will open his heart to a true-hearted woman, and she can lead him where she will."[11] An interesting synthesis of objectivity and sentiment lay in Jacobs's claim, one used repeatedly by women reformers from the period: due to the unique nature of a "woman's heart," she was simultaneously more objective and more sympathetic than a man. Her sympathetic approach and shared bond of womanhood would, in theory, bring the poor to lower their guard and thereby reveal the true causes of their poverty.

An instructive pamphlet authored by one of the Indianapolis COS's friendly visitors, Harriet Noble, most lucidly illustrated the visitor's role in disciplining the poor while also illustrating the visitor's contested status in the fields of charitable relief and social scientific investigation. The worthy poor suffered due to ignorance of "physiological and moral laws, and their penalties" as well as ignorance of religion. The well-trained visitor, Noble believed, would enlighten the poor to the habits necessary for escaping dependence. While many of these habits amounted to moral regulations like encouraging church attendance, economic advising also figured prominently. Life insurance should be advised against, but weekly deposits in a savings account should be encouraged, no matter how small the amount. Noble boasted that she had taught some of the "infinitesimal economies" to the poor, and she believed that "the best friendly visitor would be one who has lived the life she would inculcate."[12]

Such a demanding and complex task could not be done by just any well-intentioned busybody. The visitor needed to possess vast practical knowledge that she could pass on to the poor without seeming to dictate. As Noble described it, a visitor must "cultivate three attitudes of mind":

> the alertness of a detective, that he may not easily be deceived; the methodicalness of the scientific investigator, that he may apprehend a situation fully; and an ardent humanitarianism that is not easily discouraged at the faults and failures of individuals, but perceives in these the effects of a defective training which calls for charity and patience.[13]

Although Noble referred to her hypothetical visitor as a man, the qualities she described suggest more feminine traits. The visitor had to be modest and sincere to win the confidence of the family she visited. She must be "companionable" and "inspiring" as well as "cheery, chatty, humorous, or witty." Most important of all, the friendly visitor must be unselfish. Noble dismissed as vain any woman who would take up the work for the experience she might get out of it. "Such visiting would be an offense to poor people as much as to rich, and do much harm." The need for complete unselfishness and personal modesty, of course, fit well with the gendered understanding of visiting.[14]

A visitor instilled with a sense of modesty, Noble hoped, would in turn instill modesty and maintain class discipline in those she visited. She must inspire in the visited "a clear apprehension of the place" that the poor family "is fitted to occupy": right where it already stood. Noble charged: "We all of us are more or less victims of a wrong idea of what it is to rise in the world; and we foster that wrong idea in the hearts of those whom we are trying to help." Insisting that the poor must "become sensible of the dignity of work," there could be no doubt that when given the options of either inspiring the poor to rise to a higher station in life or teaching them the value of manual toil, the visitor should advocate the latter.[15]

In spite of these supposed feminine advantages and women's sizable presence at all levels of charity work, the qualities women supposedly brought to charity remained a source of ambivalence within the field of charity reform. Scientific charity leaders associated earlier "sentimentalized" charity with feminine charity and the image of "Lady Bountiful" indiscriminately giving alms. Like the visitors who employed them, the instruments of investigation also became sites of controversy. The members of the scientific charity movement had to construct the tools of their investigation: statistical forms, ledger books, tables, charts, questionnaires, oral interviews, and countless other particulars. Especially at the NCCC, questions abounded concerning how to design an effective questionnaire, how to represent the "true" causes of poverty on forms that would allow for easy use in the field, and how to design instruments that would remove the visitor's or relief committee's biases from the equation. Out of these controversies emerged a consensus that the friendly visitor could not be trusted to fulfill the scientific requirements of her position. She was to be a data gatherer, with conclusions about the true causes of poverty and individuals' worthiness for relief decided upon by others. Stephen Humphreys Gurteen said that women "must take the lead [in charity]; and that by this, we do not mean that they should be asked to work as members of Council or as members of District Committees, for this is especially a man's work." Instead, they could shoulder "that higher and more difficult task of visiting the poor."[16] This division of labor could be found at the Indianapolis COS, where women served both as friendly visitors and as the investigators of charity applications, then reported their findings to the men who staffed the committees that made final decisions on worthiness.[17]

In Search of the Worthy Poor in Indianapolis

Oscar McCulloch conducted many investigations himself in the Indianapolis COS's first year of work, but soon gave those duties over to the forty or so visitors who volunteered for the work each year in the 1880s and 1890s.[18] By 1881 the Indianapolis society had developed for its investigators an elaborate form to be filed for every charity applicant they encountered. The application included names, addresses, reasons for coming to the city, all relatives in the city and elsewhere, former marriages, children, children living elsewhere, married children, those in school and at work, wages, occupations (his and hers), last employers, rent, number of rooms, landlord, reason for removal, and other categories.[19] When a charity applicant arrived at the COS office or was brought to its attention by a neighbor, investigators filed the application, checked the

Center Township trustee's records, and submitted a personal evaluation of the relief applicant to a COS committee on relief that decided which cooperating charity, if any, should give assistance in the form of groceries, wood, coal, clothes, or temporary employment. Of 6,170 cases from 1880 through 1893 for which the COS secured relief, sometimes from multiple sources, 46.7 percent were relieved by the IBS; 35.2 percent by the trustee; 14.1 percent by the Flower Mission; 6.6 percent by the Friendly Inn and Wood-yard, and most of the rest by the city's dispensary and hospital. Relatives and churches relieved surprisingly few cases: 199 and 73, respectively.[20] Although this process represented something close to the ideal to which charity organization societies ought to strive, Indianapolis's COS was somewhat unusual in the extent to which it emphasized the organization in charity organization. Frank Bruno speculates that its isolation from eastern COSs may explain some of the unique position of the Indianapolis COS, which "became the nerve center of all the city's philanthropic activities, public and private, a center of ideas and of planning."[21]

Little information remains about investigators, visitors, and relief committee members, but the qualitative descriptions of the poor they left in their record books show an enthusiasm for explaining to the poor the errors of their ways and thereby strengthening interclass social harmony, at least in theory. In a promotional flier for the COS mailed to 12,000 Indianapolis homes, John Butler claimed that scientific charity could serve as a bulwark against communism and civic unrest by promoting better cross-class relations and relieving "real" poverty. Arguing that charity should not be equated with mere giving, he insisted that an "essential part of true charity" included "friendly counsel, words of sympathy and manifestations of brotherhood." In words indicative of the broader vision held by middle-class reformers of the Gilded Age that, contrary to the growing labor agitation, America was and ought to be a land free of permanent classes and class conflict, Butler claimed that visiting "tends to keep down the spirit of communism by manifesting a friendly spirit and disposition between all classes and conditions of society."[22]

That friendly spirit and disposition could be hard to find when the friendly visitors came knocking on the doors of the poor. Among the record books that document the visitors' assessments, the one from 1880

Above and facing. Charity application record from Indianapolis. Case record no. 14, Charity Organization Casebook, 1880, BV 1198, used by permission of the Family Service Association archives located at the Indiana Historical Society.

RECORD

DECISION.

is flush with comments about charity applicants that perhaps say as much about the intentions and presuppositions of investigators as they do about the state of the investigated. Marinda D.'s home had a general look of "don't care-a-tive-ness."[23] Mary G. was a "lazy careless creature not capable of self-government or support."[24] The records further indicate that the poor were equally unimpressed with the visitors, refusing them entrance or even threatening suicide before following recommendations to enter the poorhouse or county asylum. Mary D., a fifty-year-old widow known to her neighbors as "a half-crazed needy old woman," wrote to the mayor of Indianapolis in June 1881, explaining that she was starving:

> Mayor Grubbs—I have written to you once before, but received no answer. There was a lady called to see me and said or rather asked me if I had written to you. She declined to tell her name, said any one that saw me could see I was not able to work, yet did not do anything for me. I have lived in the city 17 years, worked when I was able. My object in addressing you is to have you come to see me, or send some one that you have confidence in, to see my suffering condition and relieve me. I am unable to work. I have nothing to eat and nothing comfortable. I would prefer to see you, but if you cannot come, please send some responsible person to see me as soon as you receive this. Come to my room No. 8 and oblige Mrs. Mary D.[25]

Mary's husband had abandoned her without further communication for twelve to fifteen years when he suddenly returned and, discovering she had remarried, cut her out of his pension. Mary's second husband died a short time after this, necessitating that from 1873 onward the Marion County and Center Township of Indianapolis relief agencies support her through the winters with fuel and an occasional payment of her rent. Those sources of relief, however, often proved unreliable, reducing her to begging. When Mrs. Kline, a shopkeeper, complained to the trustee that she "cannot 'shake' her" from begging around her store, it prompted one of the Center Township trustee's agents to pay Mary a visit in November 1878. Advised that she would have to go to the poorhouse, Mary threatened to drown herself first.

The COS first sent their own visitor in April 1880 to inspect her circumstances, with the trip yielding a similar conclusion: Mrs. D. ought not to receive charitable relief but go instead to a public institution like the county asylum or the home for the aged. A visitor sent to follow up on Mary D.'s letter to the mayor in 1881 noted the cost of rent and that Mrs. D. reportedly had moved there after she "got into trouble with the janitor" at her previous residence. The visitor was unimpressed by what she saw. The small room was "completely filled by old bedding, trunks, stove, wood," and Mary herself "was barefooted and moving things about without any particular object that could be discovered." Intent on identifying any hint of fraud, the visitor noticed that although Mary claimed to have gone three days without food, she "saw some new biscuit and cold victuals in a trunk, evidently given her," a sin of omission that Mrs. D. then acknowledged. Again she swore that she "won't go to the P. H. and even if it is made decent to live in, will commit suicide first." While she proposed that the COS help her find a room somewhere "on a floor where there is water," they decided that unless Mrs. D. had a change of mind about going to an institution, she did not need further aid.[26] Mrs. Mary D.'s refusal to move to the poorhouse—at the time a sign of her purported insanity or perhaps, as the COS described several other opinionated applicants, "impudence"—might instead have been proof of her lucidity. The COS entry that recorded her threat to kill herself is dated 18 June 1881. Four days earlier, the newspapers had begun printing the first testimonies to the horrific poorhouse conditions taken in the Big Moll trial.

Taken in aggregate, these records compiled by the COS produced social data that they hoped would reveal objective laws governing the causes and relief of poverty. To historians, the data illuminate scientific charity reformers' changing views of worthiness. The 1883–84 annual report of the Indianapolis COS announced that the society had evaluated 1,070 applications for aid concerning 3,579 family members during the year. In every case COS committee members determined the "condition" and social status of the applicant and the cooperating charity, if the applicants were deemed worthy. Condition held three categories denoting the applicant's state of need and worthiness: "cases worthy of relief; cases needing work rather than relief; and cases not requiring, unworthy, or not entitled to relief." Of the 1,070 cases that year, the Indianapolis committee evaluated the applicants as

worthy of relief: 379
worthy of work: 314
unworthy: 374
not classified: 3

Put another way, they judged 65 percent as worthy poor and 35 percent as unworthy paupers.[27]

The Indianapolis COS further divided these three categories to identify different causes of poverty. For instance, "worthy of relief" included four subcategories of those beset by circumstances beyond their control: children with no living parents or one parent unable to support them, the aged, the incurable (presumably referring to a permanently disabling condition), and those incapacitated by temporary illness or accident. In the 1883–84 report, the 379 cases worthy of relief contained only one case listed as an orphan and six as incurable. Of the remaining 372 cases, 50 were aged and 322 had temporarily fallen ill or experienced an accident. Those were persons who, as the unknown author of the report put it, "belong to the poor whom it is a privilege to help." Among those persons in need of work, 170 were listed as out of work, 102 with insufficient work, 22 were infirm or had family cares to attend to, and 20 were identified as shiftless, improvident, or intemperate, but, in the eyes of the investigator, not hopelessly so.[28]

The 374 cases in class three—those not requiring, not entitled to, or unworthy of relief—fell into eight subcategories:

- Not requiring relief
- Owning property
- Having relatives able to support
- Shiftless or improvident, Hopelessly so
- Vicious, Hopelessly so
- Prefer to live on alms
- Tramps
- Confirmed Inebriates

The first three subcategories evaluated an applicant's means, and the last five, his character. Collectively, 115 of the 374 cases fell into the first three subcategories, and the remaining 259 into the other five. From an-

other perspective, the COS denied relief, on the grounds of poor character irrespective of their financial resources, to 24 percent of all cases
that year: 259 out of 1,070.[29] Other annual reports from the period all
show similar proportions.

The COS's statistics also classified the types of people who applied for
relief. For 1883–84, the COS grouped cases into ten social states:

- Families with both parents living
- Widows
- Widowers
- Divorced wives
- Deserted wives
- Deserted husbands
- Single men
- Single women, with illegitimate children
- Other single women
- Orphans

Reportedly 39 percent of all cases (419) involved families, followed by
widows (24 percent or 256), deserted wives (14 percent or 153), and single
men (13 percent or 141). Only 4 cases dealt with orphans, and the deserted husband category held a single lonely soul.[30]

The results from November 1883 to November 1884 give a fair portrait of the Indianapolis COS operations in its earlier years. Although
the members collected and published such statistics annually, the information that has survived to the present contains gaps. The annual report issued in 1890 summarizing the results of a decade of work reveals
similar proportions to the 1884 report. Of 9,255 applications for relief investigated covering 33,469 persons, the COS secured relief for 36 percent
of the cases, offered work rather than relief for 23 percent, and declared
no relief to be necessary for 41 percent.[31] A national tabulation of 28,000
cases reviewed by COS in 1887 produced results comparable to those
found in Indianapolis: 36.9 percent were worthy of either continuous or
temporary relief, 40.4 percent needed work rather than relief, and 22.7
percent were unworthy.[32]

Viewed in their entirety, the quantitative data available for the 1880s
indicate that the Indianapolis COS members appear to have hardened

the division they made between the worthy and unworthy poor, identifying a growing percentage of persons as unworthy. Over the course of the decade, the percentage of people that the COS committees judged worthy of relief remained relatively constant. The 1884 report indicated that 35.4 percent of all cases were worthy of relief; for the year 1890 the value stood at 31.5 percent. Cases that the investigators decided deserved work but not relief, however, dropped from 29.3 percent of all cases in 1884 to 11.8 percent in 1890. As the number of cases in this category declined, cases judged to be unworthy or not requiring any form of relief leaped from 34.9 percent of all cases in 1884 to 56.6 percent in 1890. The middle ground between situations warranting outright relief and situations warranting nothing appears to have disintegrated.[33]

The internal breakdown of cases within the "not requiring or unworthy of relief" category further suggests this development. Of cases where the COS committee judged an individual unworthy of or not requiring relief, they did so on the grounds that they were "vicious, hopelessly so" in 19.3 percent of cases in 1884, but only 2 percent in 1893. Related, those judged to "prefer to live on alms" crested at 43.8 percent in 1885 and declined to just 17.1 percent by 1893. The declines in these two categories would seem to indicate that investigators moved away from judgments concerning moral character. A closer inspection, however, reveals that the number of cases falling into the "tramps" category moved from 4.5 percent in 1884 and 5 percent the next year to 46.7 percent in 1893.[34] It appears that "tramp" became the new lump category for those who might earlier have been judged vicious or preferring to live on alms; the popular conception of the tramp certainly included both of these elements. With Indianapolis's central position on the railroad lines, it is likely that both the actual number of tramps riding the rails through Indianapolis and the already high level of public concern increased over time. There is little in the data to suggest that members of the Indianapolis COS suffered from blurred moral vision.

Standardizing Worthiness in the Statistical Blank of 1888

A telling example of visitors' struggles to gather and objectively evaluate data on the poor, and subsequent interest of the NCCC to impose guidelines for proper investigations and statistical forms upon the diffuse COSs, comes from the travails of Anna R. She visited the Indianapolis COS's office in March 1880 to explain how her husband had died thirteen years earlier working on the railroad, and she said that she did not "think this a good city for the poor. They don't look after the poor enough." The record of her encounters with the trustee and then the COS suggests as much. The COS's investigation into her history with the Center Township trustee revealed that in December 1876 her family was sleeping on a "pile of rags on the floor" and lacked "enough clothing to cover themselves." Anna went barefoot in the snow. She had five children from the ages of thirteen to eighteen, one of whom at the time of her trip to the COS had typhoid fever, chills, and "lung disease." Only two or three times had she asked for relief from the trustee, and she "had always worked" while her oldest daughter worked whenever possible. Further examination of the trustee's records revealed that she had been shipped to Indianapolis from Greencastle in 1874, where the local trustee had furnished her with a pass out of town.[35] Such passing of the poor from city to city had been commonplace for decades and continued to be practiced in Gilded Age America. Indianapolis's solution for many hopelessly poor people was to pay for a one-way ticket to the city of their nearest relatives and hope the destination point's trustee did not send them right back.[36]

These tragic circumstances might suggest an immediate need for charitable relief, and indeed the report concluded that Anna R.'s family was destitute. The responsibility, however, was in their own moral and biological failings. "This old Irish fraud depends on public charity for a living," which "has made her chronic," explained the trustee's initial report from 1876. She was a "professional liar and beggar." No amount of help could make the family "live any other way than like hogs. They are stable bred and cannot rise above their breeding." When the COS took up her case in March 1880, its review of the trustee's report resulted in an initial decision to deny Anna's family any relief.[37]

Deeper investigation into her circumstances, however, belied the claims of an easily identified distinction between worthy and unworthy cases of need. When a COS visitor first called on Mrs. R. at her home at the end of May, she noted that Anna's thirteen-year-old son, Johnny, worked when he could but had "typho-malarial fever," while her oldest, Mary, similarly was too ill to work. She wrote, "This combination of circumstances has made it necessary for her to solicit aid from the benevolent to support her family and pay her rent and in my opinion, under these circumstances, with which I am reasonably well acquainted, I think she is deserving." In the same entry where the visitor declares Mrs. R. deserving appears an addendum noting the contrary opinion of Father Bessonies, a member of the COS committee that ultimately determined who would receive relief and in what kind. He found one of the daughters to be a "bad girl" and that "not much could be said in her favor."[38]

Was Anna R. the undeserving hog, a pauper feeding from public and private troughs alike with ill-behaved children inheriting her manners as their birthright, or was she the deserving poor, afflicted by death and disease and old age? The vagaries in investigators' evaluations of the poor confounded both the leadership of scientific charity and the poor who sought relief. The former earnestly thought that poor relief could and must be brought under proper scientific scrutiny and that by doing so they could easily sift out the pauper from the poor. The poor, meanwhile, both struggled to present themselves as they imagined the investigators desired and resented and resisted the intrusions, the moral condemnations, and outright coercion. The difference between relief and rejection often might depend on which visitor knocked at the door.

Scientific charity's leading thinkers noticed these inconsistencies in visitors' assessments and went through a regular cycle at the National Conference of decrying the paucity of reliable statistical data, expressing hope that better data would lead to the discovery of social laws that might end poverty, reforming the statistical surveys, or "blanks" they recommended for use by the charity organization societies, reporting on the causes of poverty discovered by the new blanks, and then returning to the issue a few years later to decry once again the inadequacy of the data. This pattern provides a window into the reformers' changing analysis of poverty, pauperism, science, and worthiness and the place of volunteer friendly visitors and investigators in their work. The creators of these statistical blanks inscribed their belief in a pauper/poor dichotomy onto the investigative surveys they created, hoping to find single-cause explanations for poverty that they could easily categorize as either misfortune or misconduct. However, as members of scientific charity moved toward a more nuanced view of poverty that stressed the interrelation of hereditary and environmental, individual and social factors, and simultaneously grew more wary of the objectivity and qualifications of their visitors and investigators, they also altered the design and intent of their surveys.

As they began accumulating and interpreting the data collected by individual COSs, scientific charity reformers tended to conflate symptoms of pauperism—especially ones suggesting moral weakness—with causes, and used data on the presence or absence of a symptom as proof that the symptom could directly induce pauperism. Intemperance in particular leapt off the pages of tabulations as a common feature and therefore a cause of pauperism. Dr. Diller Luther, secretary of the Board of Charities of Pennsylvania, noted at the 1880 conference that the board's survey of poorhouses in the state had found that half of the inmates were intemperate.[39] The 1881 chairman of the Standing Committee on Organization of Charities in Cities, Dr. Charles E. Cadwalader of the Philadelphia Board of Guardians, declared that the results of a survey sent by the NCCC to COSs throughout the nation indicated that a majority of those seeking aid were poor due to intemperance: 75 percent of seekers in Newport, 80 percent in New Haven, 60 percent in Poughkeepsie, 50 percent in Portland.[40]

Even those who typically expressed the most caution in what conclusions could be drawn from simple tabulations accepted the data as proof of alcohol's pernicious influence. Frank Sanborn issued a critical report in 1885 on behalf of the NCCC's Committee on the Prevention of Pauperism that condemned the sorry state of the census and of data from particular states pertaining to paupers. Even so, Sanborn felt confident enough in the data and the commonly known habits of the poor to conclude that intemperance caused pauperism.[41] W. L. Bull's report the next year on results of a survey on tramping condensed its causes into forty-seven specific and eight general causes of trampery, with drink second only to laziness in frequency; lack of employment followed in third.[42] Both men assumed that intemperance alone was sufficient for producing pauperism and was the cause, not the effect, of dependence.

Such results seemed promising, but the deluge of raw data produced by the COSs quickly brought forth two objections by leaders at the NCCC: they lacked uniformity and, to a lesser extent, they lacked analytic complexity. Efforts to address these concerns eventually brought scientific charity's elite to reevaluate their stances on intemperance and other personal failings as causes of pauperism and the fitness of friendly visitors. Frederick Wines, like Sanborn a founder of the NCCC and also a member of the U.S. Census Bureau, gave the sharpest critique of scientific charity's statistics in 1886. His criticism centered on his belief that charity workers confused the conditions of poverty with its causes and arbitrarily picked single factors out of a wide array of possible culprits as accounting for poverty when in truth "these causes lie much deeper than anything which we are able to see." He declared that statistics on crime and pauperism, particularly those concerning intemperance, were "not worth the paper they are printed on." Of the COSs' friendly visitors, investigators, and relief committees, he warned that there was "nothing more dangerous" than statistics "in the hands of a man who does not know what he is talking about." Their ignorance brought misapprehension in regard to the true, complex nature of the causes of pauperism, crime, and insanity and an ill-conceived belief that those causes could easily be ended. "There are many who do not seem to have the slightest idea of the complicated organization of society," he complained. "They do not understand the springs of human action nor its historical relations." Wines capped his remarks with a bitter critique of the efficacy of the National Conference and of charity workers' pretensions to scientific rigor, scoffing:

> I would give more for the opinion of some good motherly woman as to the best methods of meeting some of these evils than for all the learned papers read before this Conference by learned men who think they understand it all. . . . I do not think that we should call that scientific which is not. Here are these people [charity workers], who know little or nothing of social anatomy or physiology or pathology or hygiene, but they say, "Here is my little pill. . . . Put out your tongue and take it, and you will be all right."[43]

Wines singled out W. L. Bull's report on "trampery" as a particularly telling example of statistical illiteracy. A survey sent by the NCCC to charities, public officials, and "prominent philanthropists" nationwide in 1886 asked the institutions to identify the causes behind the "Tramp Problem." Of the 116 answers among the 130 returned surveys, Bull distilled 47 causes of tramping. Those causes and Wines's criticisms vividly expose the diversity of opinions on the causes of pauperism and scientific charity reformers' struggle to standardize subjective reporting into coherent data and causes. Bull noted with bemusement that the responses he received from the survey ranged from "existing type of civilization and its estimate of wealth and resulting conditions" to "pure cussedness." Bull's list of the causes "most generally acknowledged as well as the most unique and suggestive" comprised:

> Drink, lack of employment, laziness, war, example, ignorance, lack of home training, dime novels, tobacco, discontent, poverty, shiftlessness, vice, love of roving, heredity, indiscriminate almsgiving or false charity, inability, dishonesty, strikes, depravity, disappointment, worthlessness, immigration, existing type of civilization, improvidence, force of habit, low wages, loss of self-respect, fees made by officers and magistrates, aggregation of capital in manufactures, the use of machinery in agriculture and manufactures, socialistic ideas, overpopulation, lack of manhood, lack of a trade, our jail system, imbecility, defective system of education in our public schools, hospitality of jails and almshouses, uncomfortable homes, high temper, industrial causes, ex-convicts, specialization of Labor, lack of Wayfarers' Lodges, Chinese, the Devil.[44]

The list is as amusing today as it was to Bull and Wines, but it also illuminates the movement's understanding of dependence, the limits of its data, and the desire of national leaders to rein in and standardize the data generated by the individual COSs. At some risk of not giving dime novels or the Devil their due, generally the reformers of the 1880s focused first on the inherent depravity of the individual and the related issue of intemperance as the causes of pauperism, with the maladministration of charitable and public relief and hereditary forces as the circumstances most responsible for sapping a pauper's moral strength. Bull's tabulation of causes revealed the following frequencies:

1. Laziness	69
2. Drink and vice (36+10)	46
3. Lack of employment	32
4. Depravity and worthlessness (8+4)	12
5. Roving disposition	12
6. Indiscriminate almsgiving	10
7. Lack of home training	9
8. Immigration	8

Although historians typically place the origins of widespread American awareness of unemployment as a factor in poverty in the 1890s, due es-

pecially to the 1893 depression, Coxey's army, and renewed fears of social
unrest, Bull's survey indicates that scientific charity reformers were at
least half-awake to unemployment's importance a decade earlier. When
compared with changes in reformers' analysis of other forms of dependence and social deviance, evaluations of poverty and pauperism hewed
more closely for a longer period of time to an internal analysis of the
subject's moral failings, with less interest in the importance of external
causes.[45] While discussions among scientific charity enthusiasts at the
National Conference suggest this, Bull's list also shows that the scientific charity community considered a host of systemic, societal explanations for pauperism and tramping that ran the gamut from industrialization and urbanization to the growing concentration of wealth and the
very construction of civilization. Also running contrary to a common
historical claim, that charity reformers saw their effort as intimately tied
to the need for immigration restrictions, Bull's list demonstrates that
outside of New York City and perhaps Massachusetts, scientific charity
reformers did not see immigration as one of those external factors relevant to their battles with pauperism and tramping, a point further documented in chapter 6.

Bull's report also included results of the proposals suggested by the
surveyed charities, revealing an equally far-ranging list of suggestions
for personal and social reform. The suggestions compiled from individual COSs by the NCCC in this report demonstrate an interest described by one historian as "strengthening the individual against financial disaster," suggestions that then circulated out from the NCCC to
new charities who picked up on the ideas from the conference's proceedings. The New York City Charity Organization Society, for instance, established a Penny Provident Fund in 1889 and established "the first important Provident Loan Society in the United States to loan money at
low rates of interest upon pledges of personal property" in 1894. These reforms and others, like the Indianapolis COS's creation of a Dime Savings
and Loan, "follow the proposals published in the proceedings of the National Conference of Charities and Correction" in Bull's 1886 report.[46]

To address the great variance in quality and detail of statistics generated by charity organization societies and their different forms for evaluating the poor, the NCCC empanelled a committee to create a statistical
blank that participating COSs could choose to use in their investigations

of relief applicants. The committee's report to the 1888 conference in Buffalo recommended a statistical schedule based on one that the Buffalo COS had used in compiling 6,197 cases in the previous ten years. Curiously, the editor of the conference's proceedings chose not to include any mention of the committee's work on the new statistical blank. In its place the most detailed account came from Stanford economist and former Baltimore COS agent Amos Warner's 1894 textbook of scientific charity, *American Charities.*

By endorsing the schedule, the committee also accepted an analysis of pauperism and poverty that addressed only, as Warner put it, "the chief cause of destitution, and not the tributary causes."[47] The statistical blank gave physical form to a mono-causal analysis of poverty, very much in keeping with the common understanding of statistics at the time. This "case-counting" method, Warner noted, indicated that those who recommended it prioritized determining whether a case of dependence was the result of personal fault or of misfortune, meaning pauperism or poverty.

The standard blank adopted in 1888 divided the causes of poverty into two categories: those "indicating misconduct" and those "indicating misfortune." With the advantage of hindsight, Warner explained that the blank tended to describe the personal circumstances of dependents as much as the actual cause of dependency.[48] In dividing causes into "misfortune" and "misconduct," the authors of the blank wrote their own assumptions about the causes of poverty into the document designed to discover those causes. Misconduct included the subheadings "Drink, Immobility, Laziness, Shiftlessness and Inefficiency, Crime and Dishonesty, and Roving Disposition." Misfortune comprised three subdivisions, each featuring further subdivisions.

Misfortune
- Lack of Normal Support
  - Imprisonment of Breadwinner
  - Orphans and Abandoned Children
  - Neglect by Relatives
  - No Male Support
- Matters of Employment
  - Lack of Employment

- Insufficient Employment
- Poorly Paid Employment
- Unhealthy or Dangerous Employment
- Matters of Personal Capacity
  - Ignorance of English
  - Accident
  - Sickness or Death in Family
  - Physical Defect
  - Insanity
  - Old Age

Finally, a "Not Classified" category served as a grab bag for other causes, including "Large Family, Nature of Abode, Pauper Associations and Heredity, and Other or Unknown."

Despite the simplicity of the new standard blank—or perhaps because of it—the conference members quickly discovered that the generations-old habit of charity workers blaming much poverty on drunkenness had in fact grossly overstated intemperance's importance. Warner believed that the data gathered from the blanks in 1892 and 1893 would surprise readers when they learned that intemperance figured as the chief cause of destitution in only one-fifteenth to one-fifth of cases, depending on the given city. In another 28.1 percent of all cases, no evidence could be found of intemperance operating as either a primary or contributing cause. Warner speculated that this was because "the ravages of intemperance are most plainly to be traced in classes distinctly above the pauper class," and the pauper likely was too poor and dissipated to purchase alcohol. Oscar McCulloch likewise had noted with surprise the general absence of drunkenness in the Ishmael tribe.[49]

For scientific charity's leaders, the 1880s ended with iron laws describing the causes and relief of poverty and pauperism further off on the horizon than they had been at the start of the decade. The relative importance of indiscriminate alms, economic conditions, intemperance, and

Facing. Chart of causes of poverty as ordered in the 1888 statistical blank. Samuel McCune Lindsay, "Minutes and Discussions: Second Session Meeting," in *Proceedings of the National Conference of Charities and Correction at the Twenty-sixth Annual Session Held in the City of Cincinnati, Ohio, May 17–23, 1899*, ed. Isabel C. Barrows (Boston: George H. Ellis, 1900), between 370–71.

City	Ratio New York New Haven Boston	New York 1889	1891*	1892*	1893**	1895/96	1896/97	1897/98	1898/99	Boston 1889/90	1890/91	1891/92	1892/93	Baltimore 1889/90	1890/91	1891/92	1892/93	1893/94	1894/95
Drink *Intemperance*	15.28	11.70	10.70	13.65	12.20	13.43	12.44	12.00	12.56	23.00	19.30	22.20	23.00	22.43	9.53	9.00	7.00	6.00	6.00	5.00
Shiftlessness and inefficiency	.44																			
Crime and dishonesty	7.51	6.90	7.22	6.54	7.00	4.73	5.26	5.14	5.36	6.00	7.60	7.00	6.40	6.47	10.30	44.00	12.00	8.00	8.00	5.40
Roving disposition	.68		1.41	.76	.60	.58	.45	.57	.53		1.55	1.40	6.00	.52		.70	1.00	1.00	.50	.55
	1.19		3.26	2.14	1.40	.74	.23	.10	.45		.60	1.00	1.00	.32		1.50	1.50	2.00	2.00	.35
Imprisonment of Breadwinner	.76	1.00	.57	.50	.40	1.00	.70	1.20	.97	2.00	1.70	2.00	1.00	1.57	.65		.60	.60	.40	.25
Orphans and Abandoned Children	.34		.14	.23	.17	.10	.05		.65		.60	4.00	.30	.67			.30	1.00	.60	
Neglect by relatives	.91	.50	.50	.57	.40	.63	.05	.12	.28		.60	1.00	2.30	1.42		2.00	1.55	2.55	1.10	1.00
No male support	4.30	6.00	7.22	4.06	5.70	3.66	4.26	6.19	4.65	5.50	7.20	6.00	3.30	6.05	4.00	4.00	5.00	6.00	3.60	4.00
Lack of Employment	23.16	32.80	28.96	30.76	34.20	37.67	37.66	35.57	19.55	14.10	14.10	14.00	14.00	14.00	30.20	13.00	12.00	22.00	37.50	36.00
Insufficient "	6.51		6.09	6.07	8.00	10.54	14.35	14.47	2.55		6.00	5.00	4.00	5.11		8.00	9.00	7.15	10.00	11.00
Poorly-paid "	1.81	10.55	2.48	2.65	2.55	1.27	.99	.84	1.00		.50	1.00	1.00	.85	8.90	6.00	4.00	4.00	4.60	4.25
Unhealthy and dangerous "	.09			.08		.05		.12	.06			.10	.10	.06		.40	.25	.50	.30	
Total — Employment	31.57	53.30	37.53	39.57	44.70	49.08	53.01	47.08	49.68	23.00	21.20	20.20	19.10	20.04	40.30	27.40	25.25	33.00	52.40	57.25
Ignorance of English	.41		.35	.46	.30	.37	.35	.06	.26		.70	1.00	.40	.67		.30		.50		.75
Accident	2.86	1.20	3.33	3.29	2.60	1.70	2.04	2.78	2.01	1.60	3.60	2.30	3.00	2.96	1.30	4.00	5.00	2.00	2.80	3.20
Sickness or death in family	22.27	17.80	18.48	17.05	17.00	18.41	14.66	17.11	16.78	26.50	23.40	25.00	25.20	25.44	25.20	19.52	21.00	18	13.75	18.00
Physical defects	3.69	3.50	2.76	3.21	4.70	1.38	1.48	2.00	1.63	1.55	2.56	2.30	3.00	2.55	6.20	5.40	5.00	7.00	6.50	4.10
Insanity	.85	1.00	.71	.61	.40	.69	.68	.96	.74	1.00	.70	3.00	1.00	1.05	.70	.60	1.00	1.00	3.60	.25
Old Age	4.00	4.00	3.33	3.29	3.40	2.23	3.97	3.54	3.21	4.00	4.00	4.00	3.40	3.87		5.00	7.00	4.60	3.10	3.20
Large Family	.73		.57	.53	.50	.32	.35		.22			.40	.40	.45		4.50	2.00	2.00	.80	.60
Nature of Abode	.12		.50	.37	.27	.16	.18		.11		.30			.09		.70	.60	1.00	.25	1.00
Other or Unknown	2.00	2.40	.99	1.11	.50	.42	.66	.46		4.50	2.40	2.40	3.61	2.80	1.65	2.25	1.50	.75		.60
Total number of cases.	7225	1700	1412	2641	1850	1884	1712	1664	5262	902	985	1092	1043	3120	712	724	774	773	811	1220	1377

* Probably 1891–92. Taken from Table VII in Warner's American Charities. ** Six months. † Average for three years. †† Fiscal year begins June 1st.

° Fiscal year begins Nov 1st.

other factors remained unclear. Like their assessment of heredity and environment's effect on the pauper, reformers' deliberations about surveys and statistical forms show their struggle to integrate their growing appreciation of social complexity with traditional notions of individual autonomy and moral worthiness. The statistical tools available to them certainly did not lend themselves to complexity. Victor Hilts observes that the "statistical method amounted to nothing more than the presentation of tables and charts," and "no really distinctive method of statistics in fact existed" before the 1890s.[50] Simple tabulations like those done by the Indianapolis COS or described by Bull earlier in the chapter generally were seen as tantamount to the discovery of laws of society, Wines's objections notwithstanding.

A More Scientific Charity: The Friendly Visitor Goes to School

By the late 1880s, scientific charity faced new criticism on several fronts, and its primary expression, charity organization, faced new competition. Those challenges and the movement's response are fully examined in the next two chapters, but the criticism of the friendly visitor's use of statistics and doubts regarding her value in scientific inquiry also help to illustrate her contested role in charitable relief and investigation. Frederick Wines's frustration over the negative stereotypes popularly associated with the movement fueled his harsh criticism of scientific charity workers' statistical methods. Commenting on the poor status of charity work in general and the battered reputation of scientific charity in particular, he joked that "there seems to be a general impression that any one who is deeply interested in charitable work is more or less of a crank, and it is a common belief that our conference is composed largely of long-haired men and short-haired women."[51]

To inoculate charitable workers of all hair-lengths against such criticism, the movement's leaders drew closer in the 1890s to professional social scientists. Organizers of both the National Conference and local charity organization societies sent members out for scientific training and invited sociologists, economists, statisticians, and psychologists in for lectures and discussions. The partnership in what has been described as the "honeymoon" stage of sociology and social work served the interests of both groups well.[52] The late nineteenth century was a period of "major reorganization in scientific activity in the United States," which included the introduction of statistics across the social science disciplines as part of their efforts to establish credibility as disciplines. Several academic institutions, including Johns Hopkins, Yale, Harvard, Wisconsin, and Columbia, that demonstrated their friendly disposition toward scientific charity by hosting the National Conference, sending faculty as participants, and collaborating with its charity organization committee or local COS were also among the institutions first to distinguish themselves in their commitment to statistics.[53] Since the production of most statistical data came from sources outside of the universities until World War I, social scientists benefited from gaining access to massive amounts of raw data obtained by the COSs' investigations of relief applicants and citywide economic conditions.[54] Scientific charity workers in turn won access to scientific credentials and training that advanced their claim to represent the vanguard of charitable reform and an ability to influence the direction of sociology toward coursework concerning practical social problems, often taught by part-time faculty from backgrounds in charitable work.[55] The collaboration helped to shore up scientific charity and charity organization's waning credibility in the face of the 1893 depression, but widespread collaboration began a few years before then. This suggests that scientific charity reformers' interests in attaining objective, rigorous data preceded their most dire challenges or their precipitous decline in public support. By the mid-1890s the collaboration had brought forth training schools in scientific charity, university courses in sociology and charity, and the establishment of a permanent committee of sociology within the National Conference.

In one of the first and most important partnerships, social scientists and scientific charity members established social science training classes for COS volunteers. The scientific charity elite—those serving on or conversant with the NCCC's Committee on the Organization of Charity, local COS executives, and authors of treatises on the principles of scientific charity—constantly fretted that they could not replace sympathetically and indiscriminately given alms with an objective, systematized plan of relief without well-trained visitors capable of rigorously interviewing and objectively categorizing the poor. The resulting classes at first grew outside of the university setting as extension courses, summer

classes, or independent study groups, and they varied wildly in orientation. Some held minimal scientific content and were designed to address
practical techniques for identifying the character of relief applicants and
appropriate courses of treatment, while others taught the principles of
sociology and statistics as they applied to charity. Each class, however,
shared one belief in common: the COS investigators and visitors needed
greater training and standardized methods in order to realize the movement's claims of conducting rigorously scientific social reform.[56]

Because of McCulloch's concern for improving the place of his church
within Indianapolis society, the Indianapolis COS's friendly visitors had
access to one of the first and most extensive courses in sociological training available to charity workers in America. Workingmen's absence from
church distressed McCulloch; at one point he sent out a questionnaire
asking why they did not attend and what might be done to address it.[57]
To that end McCulloch transformed Plymouth Church into one of the
first two or three of the "institutional churches" in America. Plymouth
and similar churches followed an "open door" program in which, true
to the slogan, the church would be open to the public every day of the
week. McCulloch envisioned Plymouth serving as a "people's college,"
offering classes on sewing and literature, bringing in guest lecturers, and
generally ministering to congregants in not just their spiritual needs but
practical ones as well.[58] McCulloch sought to build Plymouth Institute's
adult educational program using the university extension movement in
England as his model. His shift in interest from programs for children to
ones for adults occurred as Indianapolis expanded its public school system, and he was further stoked by his correspondence with the Working Men's College in London. The 1890–91 courses included "General
Literature," "Emerson," "Browning," "Dante," "Civil Government, for
the Study of Bryce's American Commonwealth," "Modern History, for
the Interpretation of the Events Beginning with the French Revolution,"
and the "Study Class in Social Science in the Department of Charity and
Correction."[59]

Alexander Johnson offered the Study Class in Social Science to COS
volunteers and the general public for free.[60] First a friendly visitor and
then general secretary of the Cincinnati COS and, following that, of the
Chicago COS, Johnson moved to Indianapolis in 1888 at McCulloch's

request. The two had collaborated in relieving victims of a Cincinnati flood in 1884, and McCulloch eventually persuaded him to come to Indiana, where he quickly rose to become the first secretary of the Indiana State Board of Charities. His later activities included unsalaried work as the secretary and editor of the *Proceedings*, a year as the president of the NCCC, and finally positions at the Vineland training school for the feebleminded in New Jersey and the American Red Cross.[61] Students met twice a month at Plymouth Church, where Johnson lectured on the latest theories of social science and their application to charitable work. Johnson complemented the lectures with an extensive course syllabus that prescribed large doses of Herbert Spencer's writings. One of the few figures in American scientific charity to express such interest in the archetypical social Darwinist, Johnson also assigned selections from Amos Warner, McCulloch, and journals devoted to charity and social reform. Early lessons focused on the economic, historical, and ethical treatment of poverty, pauperism, and charity, while later lessons focused on more pragmatic matters of charitable organization at different levels of government.[62]

Training courses thrived in Indianapolis for at least twenty-five years. In 1898, the COS sent its volunteers to an "American Charities" class at Butler College, beginning a period of collaboration. Starting in the winter of 1904–1905, friendly visitors who did not have such a strong predilection for learning could attend thinner courses in charity and science. The COS's annual report for that winter noted that U. G. Weatherly, professor of economics at Indiana University, had delivered six lectures on the following topics:

- Historical Evolution of the Family
- The Man of the Family
- Female Workers, Married and Unmarried.
- Economic Aspects of Childhood
- Housing and Home life
- Social Ethics of the Family and Divorce

The notice concluded by advertising the coming winter's course, at which Weatherly proposed to "introduce results of investigations showing local conditions."[63] This lecture series continued at least into the 1910s, attracting several professors from Indiana University to lecture on diverse topics.[64]

Outside of McCulloch and Johnson, members of the Indianapolis COS rarely hinted at what they thought about the interplay of heredity and environment. Where qualitative evidence does exist, it suggests that COS members believed in the reality of hereditary pauperism. The COS file opened in 1880 on Andrew G. included a quotation from a recent Indianapolis *Herald* article that warned readers of his children, who allegedly supported the house by begging, and observed that Andrew was "a victim of hereditary pauperism and bad whisky. He is a good workman spoiled by public indulgence." His family was "dirty, slothful, and vicious."[65] In an article published in the COS's 1890 *Year Book of Charities,* Margaretta S. Elder advocated removing girls from homes described as "the gens [dens] of vagrancy and vice" where they inherited "ignorance, filth and disease." Such situations produced girls "whose hereditary taints are unrestrained . . . and who develop into paupers, liars and confirmed thieves."[66] Similarly, the 1893 yearbook listed a seventh objective of the COS not seen in early editions: "to prevent children from growing up as paupers."[67]

The study group created by the Brooklyn COS suggests how diverse the training courses and the aspirations of the friendly visitors could be. In a report to the 1892 NCCC, Mrs. S. E. Tenney recounted how friendly visitors from ward twenty in Brooklyn had expressed their "need of more knowledge of defined principles, methods, and means for use in working out the problems" that they encountered in investigating the poor. When others also expressed interest, the Brooklyn COS established a study group. With a visitor from each of the Brooklyn COS's districts, some office workers, and church representatives, the class met for an hour each Tuesday afternoon over the course of twelve weeks. Students brought written questions to place in a drop box, some of which would then be discussed in class while others were used to form lessons for future weeks. The group circulated the topic for the coming week, with accompanying page citations to the relevant books in the COS's library. At the meeting, a member would be called on to summarize the lesson from the previous week. Half an hour would then be spent "in noting the slowly enunciated statement of the [week's] subject, its relation in the general field of sociology, and especially its relations, applications, and uses in the daily work of the Friendly Visitor."[68] Little in her syllabus suggested a growing scientific orientation among Brooklyn's friendly visitors, but the existence of programs like Johnson's or Tenney's prove that opportunities for advanced practical and theoretical training in charity work existed at least ten years earlier than the opening of the school commonly cited as the origin point, the New York COS's Summer School in Philanthropy.[69]

Historians identify the Summer School as the first program of charity training because it eventually grew into the Columbia University Graduate School of Social Work, which often is hailed as the institutional birthplace of modern social work. In its own day, the Summer School in Philanthropy served scientific charity workers looking for more advanced training in social investigation. Leaders of the New York COS and sociologists from Columbia University initiated a plan in 1894 to train charity workers in a combination of sociology, practical statistics, and fieldwork. As Mary Richmond explained the Summer School's rationale, charity would never attract "young people of high character and unusual attainments" unless it offered benefits and prestige comparable to professional work. The secretary of the Baltimore COS, later director of the Charity Organization Department of the Russell Sage Foundation and author of one of the seminal books in social work, Richmond proposed at the 1897 convening of the NCCC a two-year course beginning with general principles and an introduction to "other forms of charity," with more specialized study in the second year.[70]

Richmond's paper to the NCCC has been cited as the immediate stimulus for the creation of schools of social work.[71] The Summer School in Philanthropy came into existence a year later, with twenty-seven students attending the six-week session of lectures, field trips, and fieldwork. Another course was added for the winter afternoons of 1903–1904, after which John S. Kennedy endowed the school so that it could function on a permanent basis. The school's affiliation with Columbia University strengthened the following year, as Edward T. Devine was appointed to the newly endowed Jacob H. Schiff Chair of Social Economy. This made the influential national leader both the general secretary of the New York City COS and a professor at Columbia, the university at the vanguard of academic research in the social sciences at the turn of the century.[72] The program expanded to a two-year course in 1910, and by 1919 it was known as the New York School of Social Work before finally becoming the Graduate School of Social Work. Chicago, Harvard, Ohio State, Indiana, Minnesota, and other universities soon followed suit in establishing their own schools, while the Russell Sage Foundation offered the schools funds supporting research from 1907 to 1912.[73]

As the training courses developed outside of or in association with the university setting, coursework on scientific charity increasingly found its way within the university curriculum as well. At Chicago and elsewhere, the study of scientific charity or "applied sociology" grew out of existing programs in sociology. At Johns Hopkins University, President Daniel Coit Gilman offered a course on social science focusing on charity and poverty. The 1889 syllabus included readings from Richard Dugdale and Oscar McCulloch as well as an examination of the local work of the Baltimore COS, which had built close ties to Gilman.[74] Daniel Fulcomer reported to the 1894 gathering of the NCCC that a survey of 422 universities revealed 29 offered sociology courses that included matters of charities and correction in their content.[75]

These lectures and courses, their content, and the qualifications of the teachers indicate that leaders of scientific charity took the friendly visitor's role as objective investigator quite seriously. It is more difficult to establish whether or not the visitors shared that concern. Friendly visiting was one of a growing number of available avenues into the social sciences, social investigation, and social reform in late nineteenth-century America. As visiting became a paying position, it also became more attractive to young, unmarried women looking to begin careers.[76] Several motivations may have brought a visitor to attend a training course. One person may have sought access to a scientific education or to education in general, and another may have hoped to make new acquaintances. It is equally hard to ascertain how this scientific training influenced friendly visitors in their work or in their attitudes toward the poor without knowing specific persons who took the course or how closely they paid attention. Most friendly visitors cannot be identified with confidence and did not remain long enough to track any evolution in their thinking, anyway.

Sociology's Reintroduction to the NCCC

The changing composition of the National Conference of Charities and Correction in its choice of presidents, venues, and committees further indicates the strengthening personal and institutional ties between charitable work and academic sociology. Fulcomer's 1894 report inaugurated a permanent new committee within the conference, "On Sociology in Institutions of Learning," whose members included President Seth Low and Franklin Giddings of Columbia University, Francis Peabody and John G. Brooks of Harvard, William F. Blackman and the Reverend Arthur Fairbanks of Yale, Charles Henderson of the University of Chicago, and Graham Taylor of the Chicago Theological Seminary. Underscoring these new institutional ties, in 1895 the National Conference gathered at Yale University. The dean of Yale Law School, Judge Francis Wayland, headed the local committee responsible for welcoming the conference, while Low chaired the committee on sociology.[77]

Low is illustrative of the intricate connections between charity organization, academic sociology, and the NCCC. Low first appeared at the NCCC in 1879 to deliver a paper on how organized charitable work could obviate the need for outdoor public relief and better distinguish between paupers and the worthy poor.[78] Shortly thereafter he won election as mayor of Brooklyn while also helping to form and serving as president of the Associated Charities of Brooklyn, another expression of scientific charity similar in essence to a COS, and continuing his regular attendance at the NCCC. From the mayoralty, Low moved to the presidency of Columbia College, which he helped transform from a teachers' college to one of the new research-oriented institutions, a prominent part of the larger late nineteenth-century transformation of American higher education into a competitive network of research institutions dedicated to producing highly skilled professionals capable of methodically examining each other's work addressing complex, often controversial questions. Historians consider Columbia's emergence as a research institution to be among the most dramatic successes, and a significant part of that success is found in the department of sociology.[79] Columbia was "at the academic center of New York's dynamic social science activist net-

work."[80] Low and president William Rainey Harper at Chicago established departments of sociology that matriculated more than 90 percent
of all sociology PhDs in America before the Great Depression.

At each university, the development of sociology reflected a "dual
constituency" that the new discipline struggled to satisfy: skeptical academics from more established fields like political economy and from
more polite, genteel backgrounds, and civic-minded reformers who expected practical investigations into pressing social issues.[81] At both Columbia and Chicago, the departments were established with the in-
tention of synthesizing issues of social welfare with data-driven social
science to create "practical" or "Christian" sociology. The NCCC had
been among the many groups lobbying for the inclusion of sociology in
higher learning, efforts that historian of social sciences Hamilton Cravens notes were "quite successful" by the early 1890s. The universities of
Illinois, Wisconsin, and Missouri, to name a few, pursued similar lines
in the development of departments of sociology.[82] Especially at Chicago,
the coursework in sociology stayed closely linked to questions of social
welfare, and Low, Harper, and much of their sociology faculty met regularly at the NCCC to work in conjunction with the leaders in charity organization. An examination of articles published in the *American Journal of Sociology* found that more than a quarter from 1895 to 1900 were
written by members of the NCCC or the American Prison Congress. The
NCCC similarly constituted 30 percent of the American Sociological
Association membership in 1905.[83]

Collectively the training schools, the university courses, the sociology
committee of the NCCC, and the individuals who populated each of
them show the extent to which members of the scientific charity movement and academic sociology moved toward each other for support in
the 1890s. They did so at a moment that was crucial to sociology's development as a distinct profession and to scientific charity's evolution and
survival, and in so doing they defied many historical narratives about the
steady divergence of professional academic social science from amateur
social reform projects. Several factors help explain the partnership. First,
considerable ambiguity remained over where charity or applied sociology ended and social science began, and the two groups' memberships
shared a common profile. Many of the era's best sociologists shared the

liberal Protestant ministerial background typical of the scientific charity workers, or indeed came to sociology out of charity work, and as several historians have noted, the two groups strengthened their contacts in the early 1890s.[84] This made boundary crossing relatively easy. Second, sociologists desired access to the rich and relatively unprocessed data collected by local charity organization societies, as well as access to the large pool of eager volunteer labor. Third, scientific charity suffered a severe decline in social prestige and credibility and stiffer competition from other charities at the start of the 1890s, which made urgent the need for new blood and new respectability. Finally, it is worth considering the possibility that movement leaders in fact took seriously the original professed mission of the movement: the pursuit of more objective and systematic methods for distinguishing between types of poverty and identifying optimal treatments.

The controversies surrounding the lower-level charity volunteers in general and visitors in particular, the nature of their work, methods employed, and data produced reveal a movement that entered the 1890s in a state of flux. Leading figures fit their analysis of dependence into a sharp dichotomy of worthiness and unworthiness, while they simultaneously demanded analytic fluidity and shunned simplicity or mechanized methods of treatment. Through the visitor the scientific charity movement sought to reestablish the ideal relations across social classes that supposedly had existed in a simpler and shared past, yet they employed a medical and scientific outlook that began to transform individual poverty into a social disease that had symptoms and prescribed courses of treatment in the hands of experts. Conflicting understandings of what it meant to synthesize individualized and systematized, feminine and objective, moral and scientific understandings of pauperism first appeared in discussions from the 1880s about the friendly visitors. While few if any claimed that the visitor's primary role was as the scientific investigator, her unreliability as an objective judge and gatherer of data raised alarm among movement leaders.

That concern helps explain why scientific charity and sociology defied the historical narrative of a growing distance between professional social science and amateur social work at the end of the nineteenth century. As public criticism of their methods mounted around 1890, scientific charity leaders both at individual charity organization societies and within the National Conference renewed institutional and informal ties to academic sociology in order to bring new rigor and credibility to their profession. But again, more was at work than a calculated decision to draw upon the prestige of science. As crude as they may appear in retrospect, the statistical blanks sought to bring standardized, scientific precision to the causes of poverty while fitting those categories into traditional notions of worthiness. It was a tall order. The distinction between deserving and undeserving had always been at least slightly troubled by disagreement over their precise meanings. Conference members got further bogged down in distinguishing causes of poverty and pauperism from conditions found in those already afflicted. As disagreements over the proper approach to investigation and the meaning of the data gathered multiplied in the 1890s, scientific charity could boast of incredible success at mobilizing charitable volunteers nationwide, of a voluminous collection of theoretical treatises on the proper relationship of science, charity, and investigation, and precious little consensus about the true causes of pauperism and the best methods for its relief.

4

OPPOSITION, DEPRESSION, AND
THE REJECTION OF PAUPERISM

The Tarnished Image of Scientific Charity

Scientific charity's leaders directed almost as much scorn at other charitable institutions as they did at the paupers who supposedly benefited from those institutions' misguided generosity. They advertised scientific charity as a corrective for the ill-conceived and poorly executed work of the entrenched charities that engaged in indiscriminate, unscientific, and counterproductive almsgiving. Belying the effusive overtures of friendship and camaraderie with more established charities, scientific charity's advocates spoke in stark terms of the old and the new in a manner that assumed that the public could not help but accept the self-evident correctness of their new methods, even though topics like distinguishing the worthy from the unworthy, renewing social bonds, and improving the suspect behaviors of the poor had been of interest to charitable reformers for decades. Although charity organization often succeeded at bringing Protestant, Catholic, and Jewish charities into cooperation, religious tensions also regularly surfaced, since many leading authors tended to be religiously liberal or unorthodox Protestants who wrote critically of the misguided application of biblical enjoinders to aid the poor. Protestant charities often were suspicious of scientific charity's avowed secularism. Catholic charities worried that the often overwhelmingly Protestant orientation of the COS's leadership and of the charities cooperating with the COS might make it a Trojan horse for assimilation and evangelism. Churches in general and Catholic ones in particular were reluctant to turn over lists of their poor to an outside source. It also did not help that in New York City, Josephine Shaw Lowell and fellow scientific charity stalwart Homer Folks led the fight to curtail state support for Catholic charities under the auspices that it promoted indiscriminate outdoor relief.[1] While some cities, like Indianapolis, enjoyed support from or even were founded by the highest social circles of the city, in New York City and elsewhere the same social fragmentation that motivated the growth of scientific charity also ensured it would not find broad-based support from the highest rungs of the philanthropic class, who were themselves no longer homogeneous and might prefer any of several charitable approaches.[2]

Most antagonizing of all to the established charities, the charity organization societies threatened their autonomy. The COSs existed to coordinate all charitable relief in a city; their investigators told cooperating charities which poor they could relieve and what sort of relief should be given. While many charities readily cooperated for the sake of streamlined and efficient relief, others spurned the COSs' entreaties as threats to their independence. As the New York City COS gained influence in city hall, reluctance to cooperate could also prove a threat to a charity's independence. By 1898 the city had spent over $3,130,000 in public subsidies to private charities, money that the COS fretted would weaken efforts to sustain private philanthropy and result in redundant services. Attempting to rein in this system, the city comptroller turned to the COS for help. Of the 114 private charities in Brooklyn that had received public subsidies from the city to support their work in 1898, 40 had their payments suspended by the comptroller the following year. The official publication of the New York City COS explained, "Their alleged charity work is of vague and doubtful character."[3] While this may have boosted the COS's reputation as a force for responsible and cost-effective government, it also undermined efforts to secure cooperation and trust between charities. Frank Bruno described how "the society could not without bad grace set itself up also as a commentator and critic of its peers. . . . It was an assumption of superiority—to some extent pushed upon it—on the part of the charity organization society that fatally handicapped its substantial success."[4] While the New York

COS eventually adopted the Russell Sage Foundation's suggestion that it divest the responsibility for evaluating and improving the work of other charities to a new agency, more typically a COS struggled to both investigate and provide services to the poor while also coordinating work with other charities. The COS's unwillingness to give up direct oversight also motivated its opposition to community chests that would centralize fund-raising for charities.[5]

These aggressive tactics and rhetoric merged with the incongruous image of a charitable movement dedicated to not giving out charity, producing a backlash that surprised no one save those hit by it. "The callous and presumptuous charity worker," observes Dawn Greeley, "was a stock character in late nineteenth- and early twentieth-century popular literature."[6] Alarmed charity leaders gave particular attention to the inability of the New York State Charities Aid Association and the New York City COS to win over the press or to challenge the newspapers' caricatures of their work. To great fanfare, in 1887 Bertram Howell sued the New York City COS for libel due to it having labeled him a "professional beggar."[7] Worse yet for the COS, New York City newspapers including the *Herald, World,* and *Tribune* set up charitable programs during the depression of the mid-1890s at least in part to express their frustrations with the deliberative and discriminating policies of scientific charity.[8] Joseph Pulitzer's *World* provoked the worst of the bad publicity; it established a free bread line with the declaration "that you are hungry is credential enough" for relief, a thinly veiled indictment of the COS's investigations of worthiness.[9] The paper went so far as to track the results of seven applicants who called upon the COS for relief and published sensationalized reports of its obstructionism and tight-fisted ways. In response, the COS tepidly issued a private memo to its members regarding the seven cases.[10] Nationwide, labor unions and the settlement house movement added to these complaints, as unions challenged the assumption that it was the poor, and not the organization of industry, in need of reformation. Settlement and scientific charity workers also struggled to stay on friendly terms. COS members uneasily observed the greater popularity of settlement houses among the poor.[11]

In spite of these setbacks, perhaps the gravest problems facing scientific charity organizers were the consequences of their success at influencing social policy. By the late 1890s, most major American cities had severely curtailed public outdoor relief; San Francisco, Baltimore, Brooklyn, Philadelphia, New York City, Memphis, Atlanta, Denver, Washington, D.C., and Kansas City abolished it entirely.[12] The New York City COS successfully lobbied against the city's dispensation of free coal, then targeted free school meals and free eyeglasses to poor children. The COS grounded its objections to free coal as part of a broader effort "to take public welfare provision out of . . . the grip of the patronage-oriented political parties," and by 1871 the Tammany Hall political machine had extended to include New York City's Department of Charities and Correction.[13] Unlike its position toward coal, the COS opposition to free meals and glasses for the poor could only be seen as an ideological opposition to any form of broadly construed public relief. Thus in the 1890s the scientific charity movement wound up alienating potential allies in charitable relief as well as many of the intended recipients. With sources of public welfare disappearing, the needy grew ever more dependent on charities for relief. Numerous charities developed in response, and many of them practiced charity with a generosity and lack of method that scientific charity advocates abhorred. Disaster relief charities generally did not inquire about the worthiness of a survivor of flood or fire or earthquake.[14] The urban missionaries of new evangelical groups like the Salvation Army deliberately rejected sorting out the poor into categories of worthiness. Its membership and scope of efforts grew rapidly.[15] The charity organization societies, however, as a rule did not spend any of their own funds on relief except in cases of dire, immediate need; instead, members referred applicants to the appropriate cooperating charity. As a result, many harped that the COSs took money without actually doing anything to relieve distress. One contemporary critic griped, "That Organized Charity, scrimped and iced, / In the name of a cautious, statistical Christ"—a couplet that has proven irresistible to historians, as historians have correctly (and perhaps ironically) observed.[16] When a prospective donor asked chairwoman Josephine Shaw Lowell how much of his contribution to the New York City COS could be expected to go to the relief of the poor, she famously replied, "Not one cent." Money instead would be spent on investigation and coordination with the proper relief-giving charities. Her declaration echoed the spirit of a sign that hung on the front door of the first American COS in Buffalo: "No Relief Given Here."[17] Such instances suggest how the societies earned a reputation as miserly and standoffish.

In the midst of these controversies and setbacks arose an unprecedented economic panic in 1893 and subsequent depression lasting most of the decade. Its convergence with the criticisms from traditional charity, labor, settlement work, and sociology, as well as an introspective process of reevaluation among scientific charity leaders, brought about a reevaluation of the movement's aims and methods. The national movement responded to internal complaints about the reliability of its friendly visitors and their data by reestablishing ties with academic sociology, as the previous chapter discussed. In conjunction with external criticisms of their scientific pretensions and tin-eared approach to charity, the barrage culminated in a reinterpretation of poverty and pauperism that was significantly more generous and sympathetic toward the poor than the scientific charity position of the early 1880s. By the century's end, the leadership of the movement had abandoned the most overtly judgmental terminology they had once used to describe the poor, and in growing numbers they denied the social and biological reality and analytic utility of the term *pauper*. While the depression propelled that transformation, historians tend to cite it as the most significant or even exclusive cause rather than one of many factors in the changing charitable practices. Scientific charity leaders and their critics initiated these changes well in advance. In questioning their assumptions about worthiness, however, the movement elite also drifted further from the understanding of poverty held by the local volunteers staffing the COS.

Doubts about the Indianapolis COS

Oscar McCulloch possessed a better sense of the importance of good public relations than most of the first leaders of the scientific charity movement, but the former traveling salesman still struggled to persuade Indianapolitans that they should cooperate with the COS's work. While virtually everyone connected to charitable relief in the city agreed that something needed to be done to stop the pauper and to reduce public and private relief, no one could agree on how best to go about it, and the COS's pronouncements often antagonized existing charities as much as they persuaded. COS advocates believed that most charities adhered to outdated and inefficient methods that did more harm than good, and they asked these more established charities to relinquish their autonomy to what amounted to an upstart charitable movement advertising new ideas and methods. In Indianapolis, moreover, the minister who established and ran the COS had arrived less than three years earlier, had a reputation for theological and political irregularity, and professed that an organization housed inside his own church was secular. Given this message, why would existing charities listen with open minds?

McCulloch knew the COS's success depended on winning the cooperation of Indianapolis's Protestant charities. The city's Methodist ministers discussed the new organization's plans at their weekly meeting the morning of 26 January 1880. There the Reverend T. G. Bebarrel agreed that agencies relieving the poor overlapped too much in their work. He suggested that either the churches tend to their own poor and leave the state to care for the remainder, or that private charities or the state assume responsibility for all cases. The ministers, however, also complained that they did not clearly understand the missions of the IBS and COS, that the organizations were active only in that part of the city north of Washington Street, and that the IBS had paid an $800 salary to one office but distributed only $300 to the needy.[18] The allegation that charity organization spent far more on administrative overhead than on actual relief had considerable clout. The town's pro-labor newspaper, the *Indianapolis People,* already had made such complaints against the IBS. Years later, a letter to the editor at the *Journal* sniped, "So the poor—the deserving poor, the superlatively, double-distilled, deserving poor—get only fifty cents out of each dollar collected. It is a beautiful work."[19]

The day after the ministers' meeting, the COS-friendly *News* carried the response of the IBS secretary, Henry D. Stevens. Stevens pointed to the two reports published in the city papers earlier that year documenting the IBS's expenditures, which indicated that they had paid $378 in secretarial and clerical wages and given out $437.85 in relief. Stevens chose not to respond to criticisms about the wisdom of the IBS's methods, saying it was "not seemly" to do so. Finally, he explained the geographical confinement of their work as due to their cooperation with the ladies' relief society, which supervised operations on the city's south side, thus preventing any confusion or overlapping relief. Responding to the per-

ception that charity organization wasted too much money on administrative costs, Stevens responded with a barb about the "false idea" that
charitable work should be judged only by dollars and without regard to
the wisdom of its distribution.[20]

Methodist and Baptist ministers voiced the most persistent and spirited objections. In both 1883 and 1886, a committee of the Union Association of Ministers convened to examine the practices of the IBS and COS
and their relationship with Plymouth Congregational Church. Much of
the motivation for the conferences seems to have come from the ministers' concern that they might be perceived as having abdicated their
charitable duties to an unorthodox minister. The *Journal* remarked of a
meeting on 1 March 1886 that they "were embarrassed in their endeavor
to do charitable work by the common remark that the charities are under
the control of Rev. O. C. McCulloch, who is not regarded as orthodox."
The ministers additionally claimed that the public did not understand
the COS's work. Newspaper reports suggest, however, that the ones lacking understanding were in fact the Union ministers. The Reverend R. V.
Hunter, a regular attendee of the Union Association of Ministers, acknowledged that perhaps some of the fault lay in his peers' ignorance
of the charitable goings-on in the city and that he had grown more impressed with the COS the more he learned of it.[21]

McCulloch and three members of the COS executive board met with
the Evangelical Ministers Association the following month to address
questions similar to those raised by the Union Association of Ministers.
The meeting, described as "informal in character," began with McCulloch once again explaining distinctions between the IBS and COS, with
the gathered ministers expressing in turn their confusion and skepticism. They asked "scores of questions" about the IBS and COS, institutions "with which the ministers were evidently not before acquainted.
The impromptu discussions which incidentally sprang up . . . were al-
together spirited and interesting."[22]

"Spirited" probably understated the conversation. The Reverend Dr.
James McLeod, a frequent charity organization critic, expressed several
of the most common objections and misconceptions regarding charitable work in Indianapolis, especially the relationship between the IBS,
which administered relief, and the COS, which evaluated applications

for relief and advised the IBS on whom to relieve. McLeod thought the division between the two societies was "an illusionary distinction and really does not exist," and he considered McCulloch the executive officer of each, ideas McCulloch dismissed as a "misapprehension." The religious affiliation and the administrative overhead of the COS similarly came in for close scrutiny. McLeod further expressed his regret that "there was not a closer bond of sympathy between the churches and the charities, for an impression existed that the ministers had nothing to do with the organized benevolence of the city." He charged, "It was generally believed that if a business man should give $50 to the canvasser that $25, or even more of it, would go toward the expenses of administration while less than $25 would go to the poor. In other words, it took about 50 per cent of all the money collected to expend the other 50 per cent." McCulloch bluntly dismissed the statement as "false in spirit and in fact."[23]

At the close of this exchange, the Reverend Dr. Joseph S. Jenckes of St. Paul's Cathedral tried to ease tensions by offering a resolution, stating that "we cordially approve of the present management of the associated charities of this city, and recommend to all charitable people that they take a more active interest in the same, both by their attendance and contributions." The text of an unmarked newspaper clipping found in McCulloch's diaries describes the reaction to the offer as if "a bombshell had been thrown among the brethren."[24] A long wait ensued before the resolution gained a second. Still the resolution did not pass, and another minister raised an objection "on the ground that the ministers of the city had no business to either approve or disapprove an organization that was purely secular."[25] Another unidentified member of the Ministers Association inquired, "Are these organizations civil or ecclesiastical?" McCulloch answered, with some verve, "Civil; nothing ecclesiastical until this morning." In the same vein, when McCulloch invited the Association to attend the COS's executive meetings, Jenckes asked if he extended the invitation to them as ministers or as subscribers. McCulloch replied, "I ask you as citizens. There are no ministers in this organization."[26]

Even a compromise resolution offered by Jenckes thanking McCulloch and the others for their appearance and noting that it was not the association's place to pass judgment on the status of a secular organization failed to win approval. Members rejected it on the grounds that their association's rules did not grant the authority to endorse individuals. In adjourning, Jenckes tried to put the best face possible on what must have been a difficult morning. He gushed: "There was not a single one of the ministers present who might not have been in generous rivalry with Brother McCulloch in his good work if he had seen fit to be. But Mr. McCulloch has done the work better than we could. I recognize in his ability the law of the survival of the fittest, and also that he is the best fitted for it by the amiability with which he submits to this prodding." Jenckes finished with the declaration that there was no better way to show their respect for McCulloch's work than to attend the COS's next meeting, and he passed a five-dollar bill across the table to McCulloch.[27]

More motivated the ministers' disagreement with the COS than denominational rivalry, their interest in protecting traditional divisions of charitable work, or ignorance of COS methods. Although they did not stress the differences, the ministers also occasionally objected to COS policies. At one meeting of Methodist ministers, the Reverend J. W. Duncan read prepared remarks on pauperism that lauded the good work of the associated charities, but argued that more must be done. In a session that also saw the ministers unanimously condemn the card game euchre, Duncan advocated that the city raise sufficient money by taxation to support all the poor, with nonpartisan officers in charge of oversight. The theological conservatism of the Methodist ministers should not be confused with an inability to think expansively in regard to pauperism.[28]

The Indianapolis COS also faced occasional resistance from the Center Township trustee. A thankless position responsible for dispensing relief to the poor, trustees or their equivalent positions nationwide seemed always to give out more aid to more people than what the taxpayers wished. Nineteenth-century critics in cities across America accused the trustee of being a partisan appointment used to patronize the base of the controlling political party. The Indianapolis trustee, Mr. Kits, defended his work from such attacks levied at him by both the COS and the Union Association of Ministers. In an 1886 report, Kits objected to the COS's work on the grounds that worthiness could not practically be determined, and that while certainly many paupers won relief, little could be done to stop them. He appreciated the need for investigation, but thought that the COS's methods produced unfair skepticism in the face of real distress. The *News* described Kits's objection as that "he can't compel a starving man to prove a good pedigree before assisting him, but each new applicant for aid must present evidence of his distress and . . . must have a home and a family." The trustee reminded his critics that he too employed inspectors "to visit every applicant and report his or her true condition." Finally, Kits suggested establishing a public works system and the setting aside of $30,000 annually for a park beautification program employing "men who are now paupers in the eyes of the law and of the public, and yet who profess themselves willing to work."[29] The trustee's and the ministers' criticisms indicate that established relief agencies accepted the distinction between the unworthy paupers and worthy poor used by scientific charity reformers. Instead, disagreements arose over how best to define and identify pauperism, if it could be done at all, whether private agencies or public officials could best manage and coordinate relief, and whether the COS had any business trying to dictate how other organizations conducted relief work.

The Indianapolis COS Confronts the 1893 Depression

Charity organization leaders launched their work with great confidence in their ability to distinguish between poverty and pauperism, to affect the end of mendicancy, and perhaps even to end poverty itself. While many cooperated, other charitable groups challenged or simply mocked their confidence and methods. But that alone would not have sufficed for scientific charity reformers to reevaluate the efficacy of their work. At the moment that their work came under the closest and most critical scrutiny by other charities and the press, scientific charity reformers saw their scientific pretensions challenged by settlement workers, sociologists, the poor, other charitable groups, and some within their own ranks. Compounding the upheaval, economic circumstances undermined core assumptions about the place of individual agency and worthiness in an advanced industrial economy. From 1893 through 1897, a severe depression gripped America, resulting in drops in productivity and wages, more than 800 bank failures, 15,000 businesses bankruptcies, and 156 railroads responsible for about 30,000 miles of track placed in receivership.[30] The depression occasioned the growth of widespread civil and labor unrest across America. Strikes brought violence against workers and authorities alike, sparking riots and fears of socialist revolution or general social disintegration—not unlike the fears that first prompted the development of the scientific charity movement in the late 1870s. The interclass bonds that were to be strengthened through visiting, investigation, and judiciously administered relief seemed more tenuous than ever. At local and especially national levels, the depression brought movement leaders an opportunity to test their assumptions about charity and pauperism. The results generally accelerated their shift in interest from pauperism to poverty, from ending indiscriminate relief to providing adequate relief.

The Indianapolis COS received attention from scientific charity reformers nationwide for its response to the depression. At its annual meeting at the end of 1893, Benjamin Harrison challenged fellow members to "let Indianapolis be known by the whole country during the winter of this year of terrible depression as having the best organized and most liberal benevolent organization of any city in the land; let it be known by the whole world that we take care of our own."[31] But where Harrison described their work as "liberal," other accounts indicate that he must have meant the term to denote thoroughly organized charity, not generous charity. The depression hit Indianapolis with a relatively feeble punch, offering to COS members less rationale that it did nationally for expanding their work beyond the traditional efforts to prevent pauperism and strengthen interclass bonds.[32] The society worked in conjunction with the city's influential Commercial Club, a group established by chemical manufacturer Eli Lilly in 1890 to promote social responsibility by business owners and good governance in the city. The alliance of private charity and business continued to insist that recipients of relief earn it through some form of labor, coupled with "leniency toward worthy persons known to be unable to meet their obligations for rent" and access to "a place where substantial food could be bought at a nominal price."[33] The club appointed a committee led by COS chairman H. H. Hanna to administer the new work-for-food program that aided 1,889 persons with more than 9,000 days' worth of work costing $18,717.68. As a COS publication from 1909 described the plan in retrospect, they had designed it in the belief that "the great majority of helpless people would prefer to pay for what they got, and that above all things the self-respect of the applicants would be preserved." Tramps, beggars, and persons who refused the COS's work arrangements were arrested.[34]

The society and club representatives lacked no confidence in their ability to manage the depression through the coordination of private businesses, charities, and churches, without resorting to extraordinary measures like public relief. They counted thirty-six charities officially allied with their work, which in addition to the COS and IBS featured groups serving many of the most significant ethnic and religious communities in the city. These included the Flower Mission, Children's Aid Society, Indianapolis Orphan Asylum, Catholic Orphan Asylum, German Protestant Orphan Asylum, German Lutheran Orphans' Home, Home for Friendless Colored Children, Board of Children's Guardians, Indiana Humane Society, Girls' Industrial School, Hebrew Aid Society, Home for Friendless Women, Alpha Home for Aged Colored Women, Home for Aged Poor, German Ladies' Aid Society, Hebrew Ladies' Benevolent Society, Society of St. Vincent de Paul, Jewish Aid Society, and the township trustee, city hospital, and dispensary, among others.[35] Including the sympathetic churches with which they regularly communicated brought the count of cooperating organizations closer to fifty. Businesses similarly lined up to fund the COS's work. Beyond its work with the Commercial Club, a list of COS subscriptions in 1897 included Indiana National Bank, Merchants National Bank, Hide, Leather and Belting Company, Indianapolis Chain and Stamping Company, Indianapolis Water Company, Eli Lilly and Company, National Starch Manufacturing Company, Parry Manufacturing Company, Pettis Dry Goods Company, and several smaller contributors including breweries, foundries, publishers, pavers, clothiers, insurers, and furniture companies.[36] McCulloch, whose increasingly critical view of business is discussed in the next chapter, passed away in 1891, an event that likely facilitated businessmen's renewed interest in working with the COS. The strength of the charity web inspired the Reverend Henry A. Buchtel, pastor of the Central Avenue Methodist Episcopal Church, to claim that their circle of charities was "so complete" and provision "so adequate" that no one in their city "need ever suffer for food or shelter or proper attendance when sick." With six friendly visitors and a capacity to field ten if needed, Buchtel boasted, "In our present emergency, business is transacted with a dispatch never before necessary in our city."[37] Personal visiting remained the surest method for avoiding "mechanized" charity or the "wholesale relief" that they believed fostered pauperism. As one anonymous COS author explained, "The value of its services lies largely in the prevention of pauperism. . . . Prevention is always better than cure."[38] As they always had, the COS framed the visitors' work as part of the search for "complete knowledge of the circumstances we are asked to improve, and the causes that have given rise to them" and as part of the fight to save children from pauperism.[39]

In spite of their self-confidence, one has to wonder just how far $18,000 went or just how well six investigators could supervise and learn about the poor when asked to cover the city between them. Frank Watson and Edward Devine monitored the Indianapolis situation closely, and each noted that only one-fifth of all applicants received temporary employment. In his history of the scientific charity movement, Watson singled out the Indianapolis COS for "some of the most efficient relief work" conducted in the first winter of the depression, yet still insisted that the initial response remained "inadequate."[40] Devine included in his sharp critique an unattributed quotation that observed that the "dependent class was largely composed of persons who were the first to be discharged when labor was not required, and the last to be employed when it was needed."[41]

The Indianapolis COS's response to the depression indicates that in many ways its leadership and friendly visitors sought to maintain their traditional work at thoroughly investigating the poor so as to classify them by their moral worthiness. A flow chart on "Causes of Indigence and Remedies" produced for the COS's 1893–94 yearbook graphically displayed the COS's understanding of poverty by categorizing all forms of indigence under three general causes: unemployment, handicaps, and demoralization. Each category contained more specific causes of indigence, with appropriate remedies.[42] Descriptions like "demoralization," "vicious habits," "extravagance and ignorance," "low efficiency," and "unwillingness to work" show no divergence from the moral terminology used at the Indianapolis COS's founding more than a decade earlier.

General causes	Specific causes	Remedies
Unemployment	Unwillingness to work	Correctional action opportunity
	Out of work	Finding employment Giving relief
	Physical incapacity	Medical service Giving relief
Handicaps	Low-efficiency	Training
	Large family	Utilization of wage earner
	Extravagance and ignorance in home	Instruction Friendly visitor
	Debt	Friendly help
Demoralization	Intemperance	Correctional medical treatment
	General discouragement	Friendly visitor
	Vicious habits	Correction

The reports filed by the friendly visitors further indicate philosophical continuity as Indianapolis endured the economic downturn, augmented perhaps with a growing interest in the COS for the environmental conditions affecting poor children. Often the visitors functioned as truant officers for poor families; at times this seems to have commanded most of their attention. Virtually every case entered into the Indianapolis COS's casebook in 1894 and 1895 involved children, and most of those children frequently stayed at home to help support the family. Often the poor family would protest that their children did not have adequate clothing and shoes to attend school. Visitors almost always responded to this point by bringing around some used shoes and clothing deemed suitable for school, and then insisted that no reason remained for keeping the child at home.

The several entries concerning Ira G.'s family are a useful guide to the visitor's daily work. A visitor first called upon Ira and her eight children at her residence on Pearl Street on 1 October 1894, and observed that she was "extremely dirty." She took a particular interest in ten-year-old Ivy G., whom Ira kept at home to do housework and help rear the younger children. The visitor insisted that Ivy attend school the next day and lectured that "Ira must make some sacrifice for her children." After being sent home from school the next day on account of "her head being so badly inhabited," presumably with lice, Ivy successfully attended on the third. No visits were recorded until the following March, when the visitor dropped in at another address on Pearl Street to call on Lula G., presumably a relative of Ira's, who was "out of school some weeks because she had frozen her feet and were too sore to wear shoes." The visitor concluded they "seem to be 'shiftless' people, house and people very dirty." Still she agreed to send an old pair of shoes for Lulu. A few weeks later in April, she returned to check on Ira and the family's clothes and shoes, promising to send more if needed.[43] The reports on the G. family were atypical only in their larger than average number; most families only appeared one to three times in the casebooks. The judgmental tone, emphasis on filth, relief in the form of used shoes and clothes, presumed untrustworthiness of the parents, and seemingly genuine concern for the children all were characteristic of Indianapolis's friendly visitors.

Efforts made by the visitors to keep kids in school graduated from friendly advice, to pressure, to coercion. One entry from 1894 observed that the "majority of chronics are keeping closer to school for they feel they are being watched and I do make certain rounds every day or so." Later that year, a visitor, likely the same person, remarked, "Their attendance in general is quite good. I have explained to the parents that at any time they are absent the teacher sends me a note and I am sure to make them a visit at once."[44]

If this sounds intrusive to modern readers, the poor agreed. One of the most revealing entries indicating how the poor viewed Indianapolis's visitors comes from a visitor's entry in December 1894. In it she related her experiences of trying to mend fences with several poor families who did not appreciate her work on their behalf.

> Spent most of this month visiting those that were placed in school through visits made, and trying also to make friends with those where I had been "findin' to other folks business" [presumably those who had accused her of meddling in their private affairs]. Mrs. A. says she only keeps her children in school because she has to. She told the police officer she wished she had never seen Mrs. Moore [presumably the visitor, referring to herself in third person]—that she had given her more sorrow than she had ever had in all her life. As this was vacation week I made her a friendly call but had to

push open the door to gain an entrance. My excuse for calling was to find the whereabouts of a family but she did not know. Told her I thought her children would be sure to know. She finally led the way to the kitchen where the whole family were. Artie had broken his arm two days before but was sitting up. I hope I have made them feel a little differently after this visit than after former ones.[45]

The visitor's role as moral exemplar and watchful eye changed little over the years in Indianapolis. Her language likewise stayed comfortably within the frames of individual worthiness and chronic dependence, cleanliness and dirtiness, reformable and hopeless, although she rarely expressed the concern for pauperism, especially its biological component, which was so commonly found in pronouncements from the COS leadership. It is little surprise that Mrs. A. accused the visitor of having "given her more sorrow than she had ever had in all her life." Children typically were no more impressed with the visitors. Other reports remarked at how frequently children playing in the streets would scatter when they saw visitors coming near or lie to visitors in order to avoid punishment.

The argument that Indianapolis's charity organization members remained steadfast in their view of poverty throughout the depression, however, requires important qualifications. Mirroring national developments discussed later in this chapter, Indianapolis's scientific charity leaders adjusted some of their terminology and categorization schemes and found greater numbers of poor whom they judged worthy of relief. The annual reports for the years 1894 through 1897 are unavailable, and the 1898 report reveals that the charity organization members had replaced the terminology and organizational system that they had used in their investigations of the poor from the COS's founding through 1893. The members replaced the original tripartite division of case decisions—those that deserved "relief," "work rather than relief," and the "unworthy/not requiring," with a new, more specific classification of the type of relief a case needed. The new categories included:

Should have continuous relief (not in-door)
Should have temporary relief (not in-door)
Should have intermittent relief (not in-door)
Should have in-door relief

Not requiring
Work rather than relief
Unworthy

The categories still mapped very well onto the earlier relief, work, and unworthy/un-needing distinctions, but without knowing for certain the reasons behind the change, there is some uncertainty as to whether COS members still thought they were measuring the same things they were in the 1880s.

Adding to the difficulty in making comparisons in charity organization members' attitudes toward relief immediately before and after the depression, at some point between 1893 and 1898 the society also separated its evaluations of the circumstances of the applicant, or the cause of poverty, from its decision on whether and how to relieve the applicant. In the 1880s and early 1890s, the COS placed four circumstances within "cases worthy of relief": orphans, the aged, the incurably sick, and those temporary ill or impaired by accident. By the late 1890s, however, the COS chose to use one table for classifying the condition of the applicants and a separate, independent table for relief decisions. A person whose circumstance the COS categorized as falling under "sickness" conceivably could be assigned to any category, from earning continuous relief to being told he did not require any relief.

The separation suggests that during the depression, COS members came to desire a more flexible system where the circumstance of a person's poverty did not predetermine the relief decision. How much difference this made in practice is uncertain. The annual reports still listed a few morally judgmental categories like "worthless husband" and "roving disposition" as causes of poverty, and it is unlikely that the few cases thus classified by the COS received a positive decision on relief, just as it is doubtful that a person in need due to sickness found himself judged anything other than worthy.

Two major developments stand out when comparing the data provided in the reports from before and after the 1893 depression, and each suggests a gradual liberalization of relief policies and softening of attitudes toward the poor within the Indianapolis COS. Most notable, the new format separated "unworthy" and "not requiring" into distinct categories, and COS members labeled virtually no one as unworthy. Only 2 out of 752 people warranted the label in 1898, 19 out of 942 in 1899, and no one in 1900. Other morally evocative categories like worthless husband, shiftlessness and inefficiency, and roving disposition contained similarly small numbers. Over three years and 2,331 cases, the COS committee found only 5 worthless husbands and only 149 shiftless and inefficient persons. Even the category "prefer to live on alms," which held 86 cases in 1898, 23 in 1899, and none in 1900, lacked the denigrating edge of previously used terms like "vicious, hopelessly so" and "tramps," neither of which appeared in the new classification scheme.

Second, the COS withheld relief from a much lower percentage of applicants after the depression than it had previously. Again, reports for 1891 and 1892 are unavailable.

No relief necessary:

1880–90	41%
1893	51%
1898	22%
1899	9%
1900	23%

Work rather than relief:

1880–90	23%
1893	16%
1898	17%
1899	26%
1900	9%

The cases from 1898, 1899, and 1890 that did not fall into the "no relief" or "work rather than relief" categories instead warranted some amount of material relief; the COS found that most of those cases needed relief on a temporary basis. Temporary relief constituted 50 percent, 38 percent, and 44 percent of all cases in the three-year period. Finally, a handful of cases needed either continuous or intermittent relief. Adding together the percentage of cases from the new categories that indicated a person warranted any type of outdoor relief and comparing that result with the "worthy of relief" category that the COS previously had used shows a considerable trend toward granting relief.

Relief:

1880–90	36%
1893	33%
1898	57%
1899	48%
1900	57%

In addition to indicating changing attitudes toward relief and worthiness during the depression, the data from the Indianapolis COS also reveal glimpses of its members' attitudes toward poverty and race. COS policy had always held that members would investigate all cases of poverty regardless of race or ethnicity; the dividing line between the worthy poor and unworthy pauper concerned scientific charity organizations far more than did racial or religious lines. Poor whites did not hold monopolies on either the trait of industry or of idleness. Similarly, persons of any race might pass on the hereditary taint of pauperism. To ensure that charity was not stolen from the industrious by the idle, and to combat the rising tide of biological paupers, all must be investigated. But the already complicated dynamics between charity investigator and applicant that often resulted in idiosyncratic and arbitrary decisions were compounded when the all-white COS volunteers investigated requests from Indianapolis's black citizens. Unsurprisingly, examples found in the Indianapolis COS 1880 casebook did not always meet the movement's stated ideals. Nancy H.'s request for groceries included the positive recommendation of her doctor, who thought her "a sober and industrious woman" who was too poor to help her sick son. An inspection of the trustee's records of previous relief, however, indicated that the white man she had brought to "add force to her statements" was in fact "blacker in character than she is in color." Her oldest boy was a "hoodlum too lazy to work" and the family was "a bad crew."[46] The COS file does not record any decision either for or against Mrs. H. The brief record of Charles and Milbry B.'s application includes the trustee's earlier evaluation that Charles "appears an industrious darky," but even that typically relief-winning term *industrious* did not motivate the COS to follow up or to record the verdict of their final decision regarding relief.[47]

Through some combination of choice, alternative sources of relief, and white racism, African Americans tended not to go to the COS for help. A tabulation of the number of follow-up visits conducted by COS visitors in the 1880 record book reveals that the society revisited 20 of 37 African American applications, 54 percent, compared with 104 of 160 Caucasian applications, 65 percent. Entries in African American cases also appear more commonly to be truncated, with perfunctory statements of decision like "no relief" or "no more aid." John F.'s case indicates only that he was "Col'd," had lived in the city for three months with his wife, Hester, and their four kids, and that the COS had made a decision: "No more aid needed."[48]

Similar conclusions can be drawn from examining the 1898 COS annual report, which for the first time included data on the racial composition of aid applicants. White applicants constituted 84 percent, 78 percent, and 78 percent of all applicants from 1898 to 1900, while "colored" composed 15 percent, 22 percent, and 20 percent with a small fraction of cases described as "unknown." Ideally, the COS volunteers also would have published data on the racial breakdown of relief decisions in the annual reports. The 1898 report at least subdivided new and old cases by races. While the table only listed the raw number of old and new cases, a quick calculation shows that only 34 percent of all African American cases were old ones. In comparison, 44 percent of white cases were old. This suggests that fewer African American citizens felt encouraged by their experience to return to the COS for help, and instead looked elsewhere if need persisted. An 1886 report from the Center Township trustee further supports this hypothesis. It stated that "negroes" accounted for 60 percent of applicants for public relief, followed by the Irish at 20 percent, "Americans" (most likely referring to native-born whites) at 15 percent, and Germans at 5 percent.[49]

African Americans, like German and Irish immigrants, also chose to found their own relief societies with different degrees of cooperation in the COS plan. The Colored Orphan Asylum long had participated in the COS's circle of charities, and African Americans founded the Colored Benevolent Society in 1897 to help put organized charitable giving under their own control.[50] At the same time, the COS launched a project first proposed by McCulloch to establish settlement houses throughout Indianapolis's neighborhoods. Flanner House, founded in 1898 by the donation of a building owned by COS member Frank Flanner, became the city's second settlement house and the first to serve the black population.[51]

Even as the COS's leaders claimed to organize charitable giving through-out the city, the society remained first and foremost a private, voluntary association of like-minded citizens. Since the COS only investigated cases that were brought to its attention by alert townspersons or the applicants themselves, and since a small and close-knit group of white middle-class men and women ran the COS, their social networks and those of poor African Americans likely did not have many points of in-tersection. There also is no reason to believe that the average friendly visitor held a less racist worldview than her peers or was less likely to tol-erate the de facto segregation of charitable work within the city. What is surprising is that a group of white Hoosiers who founded an organi-zation fifteen years after the Civil War with the expressed purpose of maintaining social order and strengthening social bonds would put what amounted to an antisegregation and discrimination clause in their so-ciety's founding document and then, evidently, at least make some oc-casional attempts to follow it. The original programmatic statements of scientific charity all emphasized investigating every case regardless of race, ethnicity, or creed because they supposed the temptation to live off of alms was universal and dangerous, no matter the color of a malinger-er's skin.[52]

The numbers do not present an entirely clear picture, but suggest that while COS volunteers continued working to identify the truly needy and the nature of assistance they required, they felt less inclined to explain the withholding of relief in terms of individual failings like moral or bio-logical unworthiness. The data collected by the Indianapolis COS vol-unteers show the growing presumption that a growing number, perhaps even all of the poor, were in some sense worthy and that more and more could benefit from material relief. In a milder and more cautious man-ner, this transition resembled national developments.

Competition and Cooperation with the Settlement House Movement

The Indianapolis COS's response to the depression mostly kept true to the original conception of scientific charity, responding once again to fears of labor violence, poverty, and social upheaval with efforts to ration a limited amount of temporary relief on the basis of moral worthiness, albeit now with a more generous attitude concerning worthiness. But at the national level, leaders charted a new course. The confluence of economic and social upheaval, an influx of new perspectives from settlement workers and sociologists, as well as new data from the COS, brought scientific charity's elite to reconsider the balance between moral and scientific, atomistic and systematic explanations of poverty and pauperism. In their new synthesis of science and charity, the national leaders in scientific charity rejected their previous concern for identifying and suppressing pauperism in favor of a more politically progressive and potentially even radical analysis, one that first expanded the pool of poor persons considered worthy while keeping a moralistic analysis and then, for a brief time at least, eschewed that analysis for a social one that nearly erased the division between worthy and unworthy.[53]

Few outside groups so vigorously challenged scientific charity advocates to reevaluate their assumptions as the settlement house movement. From the 1889 establishment of Hull House in Chicago by Jane Addams, the movement grew to where about one hundred settlement houses dotted American cities by 1900. In addition to their similarly prolific rates of growth, historian Mina Carson observed that both the settlement and scientific charity movements shared a commitment to wedding Christian humanitarianism with social science to address poverty, and both came to America via English reformers.[54] Beyond this common starting point, however, the two movements initially took different approaches to poverty. Compared with scientific charity workers, settlement workers tended to have greater formal education and academic connections. Most of the early settlement workers had extensive college training in the social sciences.[55] Additionally, the typical settlement worker came from a higher socioeconomic background and was politically more progressive and personally more sympathetic to the plight of the poor as well as to labor unions. Whereas charity organization societies' friendly visitors merely visited the poor, settlement workers lived with them. Residents of the settlement houses typically made decisions democratically, while charity organization, as the name itself suggests, employed a hierarchical structure. Finally, while scientific charity in the 1880s concentrated almost exclusively on the problem of charitable relief, settlement workers emphasized from the movement's inception the importance of environmental conditions on poverty and were among the first to demand social justice for the poor, including immigrants. Carson observes, "The settlement philosophy emphasizing the multifaceted richness of human life and social interaction had a built-in bias against the negative and one-dimensional concerns of organized charity."[56] Similarly, historian Paul Boyer describes settlement houses as the most significant challenge to charity organization societies.[57]

The initial, strained tone of the encounters between settlement workers and charity organizers at the National Conference of Charities and Correction belied the fruitful exchange of ideas and methods that took place. Daniel Fulcomer, a lecturer in social science at the University of Chicago, invited Julia Lathrop, one of the founders of Hull House, to speak to the 1894 conference. In addition to her settlement work, Lathrop also kept active in areas more familiar to scientific charity reformers; the previous year she had become the first woman appointed to the Illinois State Board of Charities. Lathrop's address, "Hull House as a Laboratory of Sociological Investigation," inaugurated a succession of talks by settlement workers critical of scientific charity reformers' pretensions to scientific rigor.[58] In an 1896 talk she asserted that settlement workers were "trained to look for causes" and warned her audience against charity based upon the "goodness of individual sentiment, unguided by science and exact knowledge."[59] Criticizing scientific charity reformers' pretensions more forthrightly, Lathrop argued that the conventional notions of political economy and causation used by conference members were too simple to capture the complex nature of poverty.

Another co-founder of Hull House, Mary McDowell, announced that settlement work was the new mediator between the fields of science and traditional charity, essentially appropriating that title from the scientific charity reformers. Settlement house workers felt entitled to make such claims not only in light of their academic credentials but also because of the knowledge they gained from living in direct contact with the poor and ministering to the needs of the community. Whereas the scientific charity workers remained prone to treating the chronic poor as free moral agents who were seduced into lives of idle degeneracy by the temptation of alms, the settlement workers generally viewed poor people more in terms of their relations and degree of adjustment to the surrounding community. With their up-close knowledge of the poor, settlement workers claimed they were in a position to see causes of poverty that were invisible to the friendly visitor. McDowell explained, "The residents of a settlement, because of their constant and close touch with the needy... are able to give to the scientific charity worker inside knowledge and keep a fresh, vital flow of life into the veins of the organization, and thus prevent fossilization."[60]

McDowell mounted a second critique of the scientific charity movement's ability to truly understand poverty. In their fight against overly sympathetic and therefore indiscriminate charity, the scientific charity workers had created a system too mechanized to let them really know the poor. Their conception of scientific inquiry, she insisted, needed another infusion of sympathy and understanding. Scientific charity's first theoreticians had expressed faith that they could at once systematize and rationalize charitable relief while also reconnecting the middle class with the poor in personal and sympathetic bonds of understanding. Now McDowell argued that they had failed to meet their goal and that only the settlement workers who lived with the objects of their concern were "able to judge of the character and needs of the poor in that neighborhood." In the houses "they may find the inside knowledge of facts which are more often encouraging than discouraging because of the everyday neighboring together." An individual's drunkenness might appear chronic to the occasional friendly visitor; the settlement worker might know that it was an aberration.[61]

Her comments encapsulated a popular criticism of the day, that scientific charity was a cold and calculating, emotionally distant form of relief, but McDowell also forcefully rejected the "hysterical" and chaotic charity guided only by sentiment. In a presentation laden with gendered assumptions similar to those applied to friendly visiting, she instead positioned settlement work as the mediator between an austere, spiritually impoverished scientific charity and haphazard sentimental charity. McDowell, Addams, and many other settlement workers presented their efforts as a feminine hand guiding the instruments of science. Proper reform of the poor was too complex to be left to untrained women, too delicate to be given to men.

In spite of the tough words, settlement workers soon gained acceptance among charity organization supporters within the National Conference and in individual COSs, as each moved toward a more environmental analysis of poverty.[62] Their rapid growth in popularity and numbers and the scientific charity movement's momentary vulnerability probably necessitated some of this development. Not be overlooked, however, is that ultimately the conflict amounted to a "family spat," as Boyer described it, within a very particular subset of social reformers.[63] Both groups shared an upper-middle-class Christian and scientific outlook on poverty and the poor. Each engaged in "a widespread exchange of personnel" as charity organization men like Devine and Frederic Almy spent periods of residence in settlements, part of the larger "proliferation of reform organizations, often with interchangeable memberships."[64] Lathrop's 1896 talk inaugurated a full conference session on "Social Settlements and the Labor Question," and from there the level of settlement house workers' representation in the NCCC only grew. One quick indication of their growth is that in 1910 Jane Addams became the first woman to serve as president of the NCCC.

The changing composition of the NCCC suggests the changing set of influences, social concerns, and interests of those involved in scientific charity. From its beginning in the 1870s as a meeting place for people connected to public institutions, the NCCC quickly evolved into the de facto home for scientific charity in the 1880s, with the old stalwarts of the state boards of charity openly wondering if they ought to leave the NCCC as they had the ASSA. At the end of the nineteenth century, when scientific charity reformers confronted the most pointed skepticism toward their claims of being either scientific or charitable, the influence of the state boards of charity within the National Conference waned; instead, the conference invited in academic sociologists and settlement house advocates.[65] The integration of the settlement workers and academic professionals with scientific charity advocates at the conference ignited the most creative period in the history of scientific charity.

The Reinterpretation of Worthiness

Josephine Shaw Lowell made one of the most remarkable adjustments. A founder of scientific charity in America and one of the most outspoken critics of outdoor relief, Lowell began to turn away from her "not a cent" approach in the late 1880s. As her most recent biographer observes, Lowell embraced "a markedly different agenda." Her interests moved away from considering the moral failings and moral uplift among the poor and a corresponding social Darwinian analysis of charitable relief, in favor of studying the environmental, structural causes of poverty.[66] Lowell "expected government action" in order to release the full potential of the poor from "a social order that destroyed life choices." She gave particular interest to labor relations and class antagonisms and came to view a raise in wages, brought about by unionized workers, as the best way to fight poverty.[67]

In reconsidering the mission of scientific charity, Lowell worked to reorient the New York City COS and by extension the entire movement. In 1895 she announced that a study conducted during the first two winters of the depression compelled her to change her position on material relief. The data collected in New York City showed that despite having distributed emergency material relief in the depression's first winter, surprisingly few applicants had returned for further assistance the next winter. This indicated that relief had produced no pauperizing effect. Lowell remarked on her surprise and sense of relief:

> During the winter of 1893–94 we were forced by the emergency to do many things which seemed to us dangerous, and we dreaded to meet in the winter of 1894–95 the evil consequences of our actions; but from all the cities comes the same report,—the evil consequences have not ensued. This means that we did the good we meant to do and did not do the harm we feared we were doing. It means that our earnest desire to not hurt the souls of those in need, while we helped their bodies, was so strong and so genuine that our influence upon them was good; and it may well give us renewed faith both in human nature and in the spirit in which we have tried to do our work.[68]

Lowell further observed that in the most recent winter of 1894–95, only 6 out of 500 relief applicants at the University Settlement of New York had requested help the previous year. Likewise, the United Hebrew Charities, Association for Improving the Condition of the Poor, and the New York City COS all reported a decline in raw numbers of applicants that winter. She exclaimed, "It has been most remarkable that the people, hard pressed as they have been again this winter, have not succumbed to the temptation to turn for help where they got it so freely last year."[69]

In light of the unexpected good news, Lowell proposed a new plan of relief to the conference by which the poor "may be helped physically without being hurt morally" and without inviting tramps or the rural poor into the city. The only public relief available to the poor would remain indoors, in state institutions. Lowell proposed a three-stage system of public institutional relief. First, a system of lodging houses should be made available for men and women to stay for up to a week, "where cleanliness and strict order and discipline should be enforced." Second, she endorsed the establishment of a "Farm School" for training inmates for agricultural work and, third, "an asylum for moral idiots where men and women who have proved themselves incorrigible shall be shut away from harming themselves and others."[70]

That statement fit well with her announced position on public relief, but in her remarks on private charity Lowell broke from her earlier beliefs. She listed three functions that private charity must perform: providing a "knowledge of the facts," "adequate relief for the body," and "moral oversight for the soul."[71] The first and third functions had always been tenets of scientific charity, but Lowell turned "adequate relief for the body," which had been an on again, off again topic in scientific charity, into a central issue for the next two decades of the movement. She claimed that if the private charities succeeded in abolishing all overlapping relief, they could then give adequate relief "in every case." Lowell rhetorically asked:

> Yet can any one really approve of inadequate relief? Can any one really approve of giving fifty cents to a man who must have $5, trusting that some one else will give the $4.50, and knowing that, to get it, the person in distress must spend not only precious strength and time, but more precious independence and self-respect? Is it not a pity that all relief societies give to so many people, and give so little to each? Would it not be far better if each were to concentrate upon a smaller number of persons, and to see that each one of those was really helped, that the relief given to them really *relieved* them?[72]

Her remarks were extraordinary in the history of scientific charity and in her own work to that date. Asking "how much relief does this man need" expressed an optimism toward the person's redemption and utility of material relief, whereas the prior questions of "does this man need relief, and what is the least amount that we can provide without corrupting him" expressed far more ambivalence toward the efficacy of both the poor and charity. While Lowell's comments indicate that she continued to believe that a class of the poor existed which could not be helped by charity, she had been a steadfast opponent of charities giving out material relief of any sort to any person, save for cases of urgent necessity. Heretofore she had insisted that not even the worthy classes benefited from financial aid, which soured even the most industrious person toward thoughts of labor.

Lowell's remarks coincided with a deemphasizing in the scientific charity movement of pauperism and deservingness and a liberalizing of relief. The selection of Edward T. Devine to serve as general secretary for the New York City COS in 1896 catalyzed these trends. A part of the exodus of Americans pursuing advanced education in Germany in the 1880s, holder of a PhD in economics from Johns Hopkins, and one of the two or three most influential figures in twentieth-century scientific charity, Devine promptly secured an amendment to the COS's constitution removing the distinction between deserving and undeserving cases.[73] He explained the basis for this change at the 1897 National Conference. The investigation of relief applicants was "not for the purpose of labeling him worthy or unworthy, deserving or undeserving, to be helped or not to be helped," he said, "but solely for the purpose of ascertaining whether and in what way help can be given." Devine noted that this goal clashed with the public perception of their work, and this discrepancy needed to be corrected immediately. Concerning the public's belief that scientific charity evaluated moral worthiness, he lamented:

> We receive letters asking if we will please ascertain whether such and such a family is worthy, and I never read such a request without regret that the question has been asked. Who are we, that we should attempt to decide it, at any rate negatively? Sometimes a caller in conversation will bring in the word "worthy "or "deserving," doubtfully, as if not exactly accustomed to use it when talking of the neighbors, but as if thinking that no other classification would be quite in place in a charity organization office, just as we half-unconsciously drop into the use of such semi-technical words as "acute" and "chronic," when speaking to a physician. . . . Is it not time for us to let the public understand that we do not make any such classification at all, and that our decision as to our own action in any given case is determined partly by the resources available, but chiefly by the attitude of the applicants toward their own future?[74]

Devine helped turn both the policy of the New York City COS and the discussion of the National Conference toward a more inclusive definition of worthiness, a lower threshold for obtaining relief, and a more liberal interpretation of adequate relief. The new emphasis on adequate relief did not necessarily compel greater disbursements; Devine described as "inadequate" the provision of "groceries from a visitor on the first visit" to a family with "four generations of dependency caused directly by the character of the persons."[75] In practice, however, it amounted to greater generosity in evaluating the poor. In New York City, a caseworker wrote Lowell in 1898 with news that only 32 percent of families in his district suffered poverty as "the result of their own faults, while 68 percent was due to causes beyond their control."[76] Other intellectual leaders of the movement including Mary Richmond and Amos Warner also distanced themselves from the worthy/unworthy dichotomy during the depression.[77] To address how much relief constituted adequacy, members of the NCCC produced some of the earliest formulations of a poverty line and of family food budgets in America.[78]

The change in the most prominent reformers' perspective is borne out in local practices of relief giving, which echo the changes found in Indianapolis, discussed earlier. As the specter of pauperism subsided, charity organization societies loosened the purse strings and ended their prohibition against giving direct monetary relief. A 1901 survey of seventy-five COSs found fifty-one gave relief from their own funds, and only five seemed totally to rely on external sources to furnish relief. In 1922 Frank Watson, a sociology and social work professor with deep involvement in scientific charity, observed in his history of the movement that by 1904 about half of all COSs gave direct relief for all cases. The Atlanta COS founded in 1905 was the last to be established on a no-relief platform.[79] These changes match larger trends in American charity in the 1890s in favor of liberalized relief policies as the number of alternate options for surviving periods of unemployment dwindled.[80]

In blurring the lines that divided worthy from unworthy and accepting that material relief could serve the best interests of the poor, scientific charity's elite began to abandon the idea of pauperism. The simplest way to measure scientific charity's move away from pauperism is to count the frequency of the root *pauper* as it occurs in the National Conference's

Proceedings. A full-text search shows a precipitous decline in usage at the turn of the century. From 1893 to 1898, the yearly occurrence of the root *pauper* was 221 times, 92, 164, 164, 172, and 149. But then in 1899, the frequency dropped to 80, followed by 64, 50, 58, and stabilizing around 30 uses per year until 1921, when it disappeared almost completely. Members of the conference noticed the development as it occurred. Homer Folks, commissioner of public charities in New York City, observed in 1903 that "dependence is not a problem by itself, but one aspect of a very much larger question of social well-being" and that "the pauper is about to disappear."[81] Lee Frankel of the United Hebrew Charities and the chairman of the conference's committee on needy families, reported in 1906 a "slow but marked change in charitable nomenclature" with "less frequent use of the terms 'pauper' and 'pauperism' and a more frequent acceptation of expressions such as 'needy families,' 'impoverished families,' 'poverty' and 'dependents.'" Similarly, the term "adequacy of relief" had replaced the categories of "no relief," "work rather than relief," and "unworthy of relief," all of which had been commonly used in the previous decade. Finally, Frankel noted the increasing usage of the phrase "social uplift" and a decline in "individual degeneracy" and "hereditary tendencies." Frankel claimed that this change had emerged due to the gradual rejection of both religious and secular assumptions that poverty must be endemic to society. Citing recent studies conducted by "a number of the more important charitable organizations" and data on institutionalized dependents found in a recent report by the Census Department on benevolent institutions, he concluded that the data indicated claims of pauperism had been greatly overstated. In fact, there was "no material persistence of dependency," and what dependency was found proved to be of "a temporary character."[82]

    This change came concurrently with a declining emphasis on "demoralizing influences within the family" as causes of poverty, as well as greater study of environmental forces and living standards. A careful study of dependence, said Frankel, revealed that much of what had been identified as causes of poverty had actually been the effects of poverty and that the only obstacle that stood between Americans and the complete abolition of poverty was the country's sense of fatalism.[83] Edward Devine, the incumbent conference president in 1906, echoed these re-

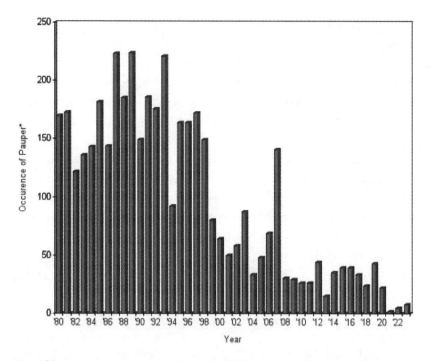

Use of the root *pauper* in the *Proceedings of the NCCC* over time. Based on a full-text search of the entire run of the *Proceedings*, available at http://www.hti.umich.edu/n /ncosw/. The search includes all forms of the root *pauper*, such as *pauperized, pauperization,* and *paupers.*

marks by arguing that pauperization long had been recognized as "a conjunction of some inherited or acquired weakness in the individual and an overt temptation or an unfavorable condition external to him," and he recommended that modern philanthropy deal "by radical methods" with the conditions, not the man.[84]

The pauper's disappearance near the turn of the twentieth century coincided with much broader trends in which "almost all varieties of reform thought . . . retreated from moral classifications of the poor into two groups on the basis of their 'worthiness' for relief."[85] At the same moment that the pauper menace began to diminish in the 1890s, historian Kenneth Kusmer has documented "an appreciable decrease in the number of stories appearing in the papers about aggressive tramps."[86] As these two incarnations of public fear of the poor receded, the newly jobless pressured city and state governments to address involuntary unemployment, not willful idleness, as the key problem of poverty. Alexander Keyssar notes that before the 1893 depression there was "little historical precedent" for offering public aid to the able-bodied poor; if anything, there were generations of resistance to it based on the fear that it "could only weaken the social fabric by undercutting the self-reliance of working people." These "deeply ingrained preconceptions" about the poor and poor relief "collided with a changing social reality," a world filled with large numbers of able-bodied poor desiring work, unable to find it, and suffering.[87] Pauperism and tramping were simultaneously incorporated into the broader problem of poverty and diminished in importance relative to common poverty, while suspicion persisted that even the worthiest of the poor would find their moral fiber weakened by the temptation posed by a community committed to generous or open-ended poor relief.

Worthiness Reconsidered: The "Statistical Blank" of 1899

Scientific charity leaders at the NCCC inscribed their concepts of the causes of poverty in the forms used to gather data on the poor, and like the Indianapolis COS, the NCCC also reworked its categorizations in light of the depression, indicating underlying changes in scientific charity leaders' analysis. In 1888 the committee members charged with producing a uniform document that cooperating COSs might use for classifying cases of poverty affirmed, after some disagreement, their commitment to a mono-causal and generally moralistic analysis of poverty. Field workers and academics alike greeted the "statistical blank" with immediate criticism, arguing that it failed to capture the complexity of individual cases. Mary Birtwell of the Associated Charities of Boston asked whether the survey required that intemperance be marked as the cause of poverty in the case of a widow and her six children, since her intoxicated husband had quite literally fallen off of the wagon and died. Birtwell further inquired as to the cause of poverty that should be ascribed to a young man who, as a boy, had received "no proper training because his father was a drunkard."[88] Was this a failure of morality, a failure of education or the economic system, or just a case of bad circumstances? The statistical blank of 1888 could not answer such questions.

The criticisms prompted the formation of a committee at the 1898 conference to revise the form, which then would be deposited at the New York City COS and a copy made available to any COS writing to request one. University of Pennsylvania sociology professor and noted social reformer Samuel McCune Lindsay presented the new blank to the 1899 conference, in a discussion that included several of the most prominent leaders in scientific charity, including Edward Devine and Mary Richmond. Lindsay cautioned that charity workers must not confuse causes with conditions and must avoid constructing another blank that reduced poverty to single causes. Instead, the charity worker must appreciate how "most real causes so interact on each other that, to be accurate, we must speak of groups of causes rather than single causes." A truly scientific study must also appreciate the complex nature of causation, accounting for both indirect and directed causes of poverty.[89]

But what were indirect causes, and just how much account of them must an investigator take? Committee members worried that revising the form to permit a more nuanced approach to causation would conflict with the need for one simple enough that individual COSs would adopt it and the charity volunteers could use it in thousands of investigations. Warner's *American Charities* recounted one example of this conundrum in the story of a man who was so committed to identifying chief and contributing causes of poverty that, at the 1888 meeting where the statistical blank first was constructed, he suggested requiring all friendly visitors to describe each case they investigated in terms of ten causal units in order to show the relative influence of difference factors that caused poverty. The committee rejected the system on the grounds of its impracticality.[90]

At the 1899 meeting, Lindsay and the committee again grappled with how best to represent multiple causes of varying influence without creating an unwieldy document. For a time the committee considered designing it so as to indicate both a "chief cause and a subsidiary cause" in each applicant's poverty. They rejected the proposal ultimately, but not on the grounds that it was too complex. Lindsay agreed that poverty resulted from a variety of interrelated causes, but opposed writing multicausality into the form due to his misgivings about the investigators who would be charged with using them. Such an instrument "relieves the investigator who catalogues a case from the necessity of coming to a full decision, and enables him, when in doubt, to distribute the responsibility for the particular case in question among several causes, according to some fixed rule in the investigator's mind." While he supported "making provision on the blank for indication of subsidiary causes," Lindsay insisted "upon the importance of stating as completely and accurately as possible the chief cause."

If the committee members did not fully trust the investigators' skill at identifying objective causes of poverty, they had even less faith that the poor might accurately explain their condition. Mistrust of the poor's intentions and honesty underlay many of the calls for systematic investigation and registration, but rarely was it given such explicit expression as in the discussion of the new statistical blank. Commenting on the poor's ability to tell investigators what they wanted to hear, Lindsay warned, "Undoubtedly, the first impression as to cause of poverty is often not so good a measure of the cause as it is a measure of the intelligence and ability of the applicant to measure the district agent." He dismissed a first impression as "of more interest to the psychologist than it is to the sociologist or statistician," and advised that it was of use only if the visitor corrected it later in light of other information.[91]

Lindsay directed members' attention to work done in this area by Franklin Giddings. Giddings first appeared at the NCCC in 1894 as a member of the new National Conference Committee on Sociology in Institutions of Learning and subsequently the Committee on Organization of Charity, where his colleagues included Edward Devine. A college dropout and journalist by training, Giddings had just been hired by Seth Low to be the first professor of sociology at Columbia. Giddings held a precarious position in a fledgling discipline. To shore up both his own credibility and his field's, Giddings aggressively presented his work as inductive, based in statistics, and comparable to hard sciences such as biology, from which he frequently drew analogies and lessons for human society.[92]

Giddings quickly developed a productive collaboration with the New York City COS. He had lobbied for Devine to get the appointment as executive secretary to the COS; in return, Devine offered a seat on the COS central council dedicated to a Columbia political science faculty member, held by Giddings.[93] Giddings used the partnership to study

800 cases received by the New York Charity Organization Society, in which he compared the cause of poverty as reported by the poor person with the final, true cause as determined by himself. He first classified the cases according to the cause initially given to an investigator by the applicant, then had each applicant's case history read out loud to him and reconsidered the cause in light of the history. His results proved to him that the poor were not reliable witnesses to their poverty. Of the 800 cases Giddings studied, 313 applicants claimed poverty due to unemployment, 222 to sickness, and 25 to intemperance. The causes as reevaluated by Giddings revealed only 184 due to unemployment and 164 due to sickness. Intemperance leapt up to 166 instances. Shiftlessness now appeared in 101 cases, although none of the 800 applicants had thought of identifying this as the cause of his or her poverty. An additional 121 cases were dismissed as not having any real need to begin with.[94]

Giddings both motivated and represented several important developments in scientific charity's study of pauperism and dependence. By using the New York City COS's records as part of his larger project to secure the reputation of his own field and his position at Columbia, he represented the interdependence of sociology and scientific charity. Students in the department at Columbia received similar assignments to gather and evaluate data from the COS as part of their training.[95] Giddings in turn offered a professional, scientific critique of the work of the friendly visitors and the methods of data gathering found in the charity organization societies, enhancing their scientific credentials in the short term while potentially undermining their long-term hopes for preserving autonomy and authority in interpreting the meaning of data.

Shifting from his discussion of Giddings's findings of the unreliability of the poor, and somewhat in tension with those findings, Lindsay's next criticism of the 1888 form was that it also had slighted the importance of economic factors. The old blank separated employment-related causes of poverty into three divisions: lack of employment, insufficient employment, and poorly paid employment. A method that better grasped the underlying problem, Lindsay suggested, would be to group these causes together as a single "matters of employment" category. Recalculating the data gathered from the blank adopted in 1888, Lindsay observed that the new, inclusive category on employment showed more variance from year to year than from city to city. This suggested that national economic forces were at work in causing poverty and were of greater consequence than local circumstances.[96]

Further indicating the shift away from pauperism and some softening of the worthy/unworthy divide, the committee members replaced the 1888 blank's division between causes of poverty "indicating misconduct" and ones "indicating misfortune" with two new types of causes: those "within the family" and those "outside the family." Causes within the family included "disregard of family ties (desertion, neglect to contribute by children, by brothers, sisters, or other natural supporters); intemperance (abuse of stimulants or narcotics); licentiousness; dishonesty or other moral defects, lack of thrift, industry, or judgment; physical or mental defects (blind, deaf, crippled from birth, insane, feeble-minded, etc.); sickness, accident, or death." Causes of poverty from outside the family included "lack of employment, not due to employee (change in trade, introduction of machinery, hard times, strike or lockout, partial or complete shut-down, removal of industry, etc.); defective sanitation; degrading surroundings; unwise philanthropy; public calamity."[97] Although explanations of poverty rooted in individual moral failure endured, especially in the "within the family" category, moral failure no longer claimed its own analytic category. The poor might still be mendacious, their poverty due to drunkenness or laziness or stupidity. But like the Indianapolis COS's recategorizations, the new divisions untangled some of the association between individual causes of poverty and presumed moral guilt. The 1899 form categorized "blind, deaf, crippled from birth" on the same side of the ledger as "dishonesty or other moral defects." Both were causes of poverty found "within the family," and this mattered more than the moral comparison between the blind man and the drunk. Poverty had subsumed pauperism in the 1899 blank.

The statistical blank finally arrived at by the 1899 committee was a compromise. It was not credulous of the self-diagnoses of the poor or of the evaluations of undertrained investigators. It reflected the growing importance that scientific charity workers placed on systemic, social causes without walking very far down the slope of a wholly environmental explanation of poverty or abandoning the belief that lapses in individual moral responsibility caused some important amount of poverty. The division between causes within and causes beyond the family, though erasing the formal divisions between pauperism and poverty and giving greater credence to interdependent, systemic forces, also continued to correspond quite well with the idea that investigation would discover two distinct sorts of poverty: that which belonged to individuals and that which belonged to society.

The Progressive Transition of Scientific Charity

Responding to growing unpopularity among other charitable associations and the poor, a changing economic landscape that unmistakably signaled the importance of factors beyond the individual in causing poverty, and criticism that their work had not in fact produced scientific laws governing the origin and relief of pauperism, the scientific charity movement's intelligentsia refashioned their work in the 1890s as more scientifically credible and more concerned with relieving the sufferings of the poor. They began a period of often contentious but fruitful collaboration with university-based sociologists and with members of the settlement house movement, and revised their position on material relief in the light of a newfound interest in the environmental and economic causes of poverty. Only recently have some historians of social welfare considered the seriousness with which scientific charity's leading figures adhered to this scientific optimism or noticed the extent to which they transformed the movement in the 1890s. Historians of science have not. Instead, most historians hold that by then intellectual rigor mortis precluded scientific charity's thinkers from addressing the economic and social challenges of an industrial economy with the compassion and efficacy characteristic of more socially attuned groups like the settlement house movement. This interpretation misses the moment of greatest controversy, vitality, and physical growth in the history of scientific charity. Beset by critics on all sides, scientific charity's leadership refashioned their movement as a more scientifically engaged and ideologically flexible enterprise.

The infusion of new blood, the challenges of the 1890s depression, and a host of other factors brought great changes in how scientific charity's elites understood pauperism. For the first ten to fifteen years of their movement, the reformers tried to arrange these diverse causes so that they fell onto one side or the other of a sharp divide that separated the

so-called worthy, honest, or deserving poor from the unworthy, dishonest, and undeserving pauper. But attempts to categorize the causes of
pauperism as compared to poverty faced grave difficulties. The distinction between deserving and undeserving had always been troubled by
disagreement over their precise meanings, and conference members got
bogged down in distinguishing causes of poverty and pauperism from
conditions found in those already afflicted. Upon further investigation,
fewer and fewer cases seemed due to single events or conditions, and statistical surveys struggled to reflect the growing sense of complexity that
lay behind poverty and pauperism. The concept of scientific charity expressed nationally at the conference evolved away from treating poverty
as an aggregate of individual free agents, deemphasized the moralistic
nature of charity as a private gift, and moved from moral paternalism toward social paternalism, with calls for comprehensive social reform to
ameliorate poverty.

5

"I SEE NO TERRIBLE ARMY": ENVIRONMENTAL REFORM AND RADICALISM IN THE SCIENTIFIC CHARITY MOVEMENT

The Conversion of Oscar McCulloch

On 18 May 1891, a gravely ill Oscar McCulloch released his final and definitive statement on scientific charity and poverty, "The True Spirit of Charity Organization." The moving prose expressed an almost complete abandonment of his earlier positions regarding biology and pauperism. The man who had helped launch the scientific charity movement and inspired the eugenics movement by comparing paupers to parasites and warning of "armies of vice" now wrote:

> I see no terrible army of pauperism, but a sorrowful crowd of men, women and children. I propose to speak of the spirit of charity organization. It is not a war against anybody. It is not an attack against any armed battalions. It is the spirit of love entering this world with the eye of pity and the voice of hope. It sees in men and women, despairing, disfigured as they may be, . . . simple fragments of humanity. They show the incompleteness of men, the partial losses of life. It is, then, simply a question of organization, of the best method for the restoration of every one. . . . Therefore, I say, we look upon men, women and children, whom we call paupers, or now distinguish into paupers and poor, pitifully, but hopefully; for not one but may be brought back by persistent effort. . . . Always try again. It is never too late. There is always a chance for a man or a woman.[1]

McCulloch's statement is extraordinary in at least three respects. First, McCulloch rejected the biological pessimism that a decade earlier had led him to believe that a pauper could only be rehabilitated if he were removed from his family's debased environment while still a small child, before it activated his hereditary predisposition. Second, the statement implicitly rejected the biological and social distinctions between the potential pauper, actual pauper, common poor person, and "normal" human being. Whereas much nineteenth- and early twentieth-century American commentary treated the poor as essentially different from normal people, and paupers as distinct from the poor, McCulloch here suggested that the so-called pauper, though presently abnormal, also was potentially normal. Third, no historian has sought to square this McCulloch with the McCulloch who compared paupers to parasitic barnacles in the Tribe of Ishmael. McCulloch did not abandon his early speculation that the family might "be made something of, by changed surroundings," for "a more strictly hereditarian perspective" on poverty, as Nathaniel Deutsch recently argued in his history of the family.[2] Instead, McCulloch expanded his liberal social gospel theology and increasingly socialistic politics and synthesized each with a new assessment of biology. In doing so he became one of the first and most prominent scientific charity advocates to bring all of the poor population within the parameters of normalcy, to decouple biology and poverty, and to deny the reality of a pauper class. He would not be the last. At the turn of the twentieth century, the movement's national leaders distanced themselves from biological explanations of poverty, even as biological determinist thinking gained its strongest influence in American thought.[3]

As they collapsed the pauper into the larger category of the poor, the NCCC's presidents, committee chairs, and lay members all spoke with a renewed optimism about eradicating not just pauperism but poverty. Unlike earlier predictions of the imminent end of want, in which change could come simply from proper registration, investigation, and classification of the poor, the new scientific charity advocates envisioned systemic social reconfiguration and worked for its accomplishment. Some, like Edward Devine and Charles Henderson, became key figures in the early twentieth-century drive for compulsory universal health insurance; a survey of members of the National Conference of Charities and

Correction and American Economic Association indicated overwhelming support for the idea.[4] Robert W. de Forest and John M. Glenn, two former NCCC presidents and the respective president and chairman of the executive committee of the New York City and Boston COSs, served on the board of trustees of the Russell Sage Foundation, from which they dispensed millions of dollars in grants to philanthropic projects dedicated to social reform, especially as it pertained to environmental conditions afflicting the poor.[5] Other conference attendees, even conference presidents, declared they were socialists; a few participants professed to being revolutionaries, although few socialists or radicals held positions of influence in the charity organization societies. In arguing that poverty did not belong with the tangle of failings explained by biological and moral degeneration, the affiliates of scientific charity work also began to blunt the arguments for eugenic solutions to poverty that their own movement had once helped advance.

The evolution first in McCulloch's thinking and then in much of the scientific charity leadership becomes sensible by considering their changing use of science. As labor unrest pushed McCulloch toward political radicalism in 1885 and 1886, he rethought his analysis of biology's role in creating paupers and the criteria for evaluating worthiness. By the end of 1886 his interests had moved away from biological pauperism and gravitated toward the environmental factors that brought about chronic and intergenerational poverty. McCulloch's thinking evolved to the point where he abandoned his concern for the pauper almost entirely, focusing instead on systemic economic and social causes of poverty that required comprehensive reform, but that held promise for permanently ending all poverty. Pauperism increasingly became for McCulloch and other leaders in scientific charity a remedial condition, a misdiagnosis of poverty that was due not to bad biology but to larger social and economic factors that could not be blamed on the poor.

The mantle of science also gave scientific charity's leading proponents rhetorical cover for their occasional dalliances with radicalism. By the turn of the century, scientific charity reformers felt compelled to defend their mission as not revolutionary. In arguing that their new, far-reaching critique of the social and economic factors that caused poverty was radical but not revolutionary, they pointed to their use of science.

The scientific basis of their work ensured that rational, objective reform would result. Science was both the engine of progress and the brake against revolution.[6]

The earliest evidence that McCulloch considered the possible influence of environmental conditions on poverty and even pauperism comes from the January 1878 diary entry in which he described the impoverished, semi-nomadic Ishmael clan as "hardly human beings." At the end of his account, however, McCulloch changed his tone and opined, "But still they can be made something of by changed surroundings. The children ought to be taken from them and brought up separately."[7] Similarly, the cryptic last sentence to his "Tribe of Ishmael" report insisted, "We must get hold of the children."[8] In these comments McCulloch almost certainly intended to refer to the practice popularized by Charles Brace of the New York Children's Aid Society and found in several cities, where private charities enjoyed the legal authority to remove children from families deemed "unfit," often Catholic immigrants, and find them more acceptable adoptive parents.[9] Although the practice risked abuses of authority and was a source of great controversy between charities in its own time, in the context of McCulloch's evolving analysis it is important to recognize that this recommendation required a belief in some plasticity in human nature and a hope for personal improvement via environmental improvement, if the intervention occurred early in the child's life.

A sermon McCulloch delivered a few days after the founding of the Indianapolis COS further reveals an analysis of chronic dependence more complex and potentially radical than any pronouncement he made in these first years of his scientific charity work. The sermon described the "very deep impression" made upon him by his investigations into the causes of poverty and "the conditions of various classes of society." The first half revisited the bitter lessons McCulloch drew from his research on the Ishmael family. He explained how the circumstances of education, birth, power, and ability cause a natural "crystallizing" of men into "various classes." The dictum that in America there is "no man who is born poor who may not become rich" did not diminish his belief that the well-off and poor-off were of "two very distinct classes." While some of this classification came from social circumstances, McCulloch also explained it as the natural separation between the "well-born" and "ill-born." The former possessed "a faculty to get on in the world" and to practice thrift, explained McCulloch. The latter were "constitutionally incapacitated for success in the struggle after wealth." In the absence of thriftiness, a person turned shiftless, which necessitated in turn a descent into improvidence and dirtiness, followed by pauperism and crime.[10]

In the remainder of the sermon, however, McCulloch deemphasized the moral and biological failings of paupers in favor of considering chronic dependence as a problem of social and economic organization. In so doing he directly addressed the defining political issue of the 1880s, the "Labor Question," squarely on the side of labor. What might cause a man to lose his sense of thrift? Laborers might work ten hours a day for ten years in a row refining a single skill and become "unfitted for anything else." If and when a new invention made the laborer's skill obsolete, such a man faced "great difficulty in finding his place in society again." Possessing only one specialized skill, the man could not create his own business, and the capital needed to begin one obviated that possibility, anyway.[11] Monopolists dispatched those few remaining displaced laborers fortunate enough to start their own business. Turning from the laborer to the housewife, McCulloch noted that the woman so poor that she only has one dress to wear all week "must necessarily become untidy." With no time or money to attend to appearances, McCulloch asserted that she "soon fails to recognize any difference between tidiness and untidiness." These conditions, McCulloch told his congregation, could wear down even the most resolute family until it fell into pauperism.

McCulloch called not for repressive measures against the pauper but for personal understanding and justice. He preached, "We have talked too much about Christian love and benevolence. Christian justice is of much more importance." The poor "insist that they have rights and they demand that these rights shall be taken into consideration. It is no question of benevolence, but of justice—justice between employers and employes [sic]."[12] The scientific charity movement could help facilitate economic justice, McCulloch hoped, by worrying not so much about discovering the unworthy but concentrating instead on assisting the worthy. While others also stressed that the movement's first priority lay with helping the worthy, McCulloch may have been the first in the movement to suggest that the industrial economy should be faulted for converting worthy laborers into unworthy paupers. Although his critique did not yet challenge the assumption of worthy and unworthy classes, McCulloch suggested earlier and more exactly than other scientific charity reformers that environmental conditions might absolve some paupers of personal responsibility for their state. The Indianapolis *Saturday Herald* speculated, "If there were any close-fisted capitalists present, they must have been driven, for once, to introspection and self-hatred."[13]

McCulloch's shift in perspective accelerated in the economic and social upheaval of the mid-1880s. Indianapolis's Center Township trustee reported that in January 1886 he saw more applications for aid than at any point in his four years in office.[14] Nationally, conflicts between labor and management grew more frequent, massive, and violent. All of the Indianapolis newspapers gave detailed and regular attention to the Knights of Labor, the movement for an eight-hour workday, and especially strikes in St. Louis against the Gould railroad lines that led to deputy sheriffs in East St. Louis killing six innocent bystanders in the midst of a strike-related riot. The *Journal* editorialized that the strikers were to blame.[15]

Witnessing the rise of labor unrest, McCulloch began calling for economic and social justice for all of the poor. Not one to wade gently into new waters, he invited Henry George to speak about his land value tax proposal to audiences at Plymouth Church on 8 and 10 April 1885. In introducing the author of the wildly successful *Progress and Poverty*, McCulloch described George as a man "who had started up more thought than any man of his time, excepting, perhaps, Charles Darwin."[16] The event heralded McCulloch's entry into a larger world of economic and labor issues. In a letter from 11 July 1885, a member of the Department of the Interior's Bureau of Labor wrote McCulloch asking him to contribute to a report on the causes and remedies of economic depressions.[17] If McCulloch replied, it has not been found, but the request itself signaled a change in interest from moral or biological failings to economic ones. A sermon in June defending organized labor drew considerable attention from the city newspapers. July saw the *Journal* cheer his "conversion from the darkness of free trade to the wisdom and justice of protectionism" as he took "a manly stand against the pernicious fallacy of buying in the

cheapest market, the corner-stone of the free-trade heresy."[18] Stephen
Hall speculates that the failure of the business community in 1885 to
support a public bathhouse that McCulloch had endorsed prompted
this break between McCulloch and the businessmen of Indianapolis.[19]
McCulloch increasingly directed his ire at employers who sought to sell
the cheapest garments by paying the lowest wages, again anticipating
larger trends in national reform. Josephine Shaw Lowell helped found
the New York Consumers' League a few years later, to organize local efforts in support of businesses that supported fair labor practices, and the
National Consumers League was founded in 1899.[20]

McCulloch's new interest in economics included support for organized labor and favorable references to socialism; a choir of socialists serenaded him at the start of the new year in order to "show him that they
appreciated his work in favor of the poor and the laboring classes, and
his kind and unbiased expressions in reference to Socialism." McCulloch reportedly said that "he considered the serenade the greatest com-
pliment he had received in his life," and he saved one of the newspaper
clippings in his diary.[21] A March 1886 sermon in favor of the unions won
him the approval of Indianapolis's pro-labor newspaper as well as the local socialist party.[22] Although he had delivered sermons in Sheboygan
concerning the rise of labor unions, riots, and communism, at that time
he had explained them as social evils that came about from the abuse of
workingmen, growing levels of economic inequality, and the lack of assimilation of immigrant labor. As his biographer noted, "This viewpoint
toward the laboring classes . . . changed radically as he studied laboring
conditions and the relation of capital to labor."[23]

The newfound interests drew McCulloch into two acidic exchanges
in the autumn of 1886 as he defended first the Knights of Labor, then the
Haymarket anarchists. On Sunday, 19 September, between 3,000 and
10,000 people representing all of Indianapolis's unions gathered for a
parade organized by the Knights of Labor. Thousands more thronged
the streets along the route, "to witness the largest procession of organized labor ever seen in Indianapolis." The parade concluded at the Ex-
position Grounds, where attendees heard speeches, danced, and played
baseball. The *Journal* characterized the public response as "favorable."[24]
Similarly, the *News* reported that the event had been orderly, with no

liquor sold on or near the grounds and "no disturbances nor quarrels of any kind." This happy state, explained the *News,* "can be attributed to the vigilance of the management."[25]

Keeping the Sabbath, however, had emerged as a national issue by 1884 with the publication of the popular *The Sabbath for Man,* part of the larger swath of moral reformation projects driven by Protestant theologians, often out of dislike for Catholic immigrants with more lax approaches to the Sabbath or other expressions of Protestant virtue. An 1885 petition drive to Congress requested an end to "military parades, mail, and interstate trains on Sunday," and resulted in a bill based on these petitions introduced to the Senate. Several labor unions, including the Knights of Labor, endorsed the bill.[26] Such controversies over observance of the Sabbath could be found in Indianapolis as well, and the church sermons delivered by Indianapolis's ministers the following Sunday described the parade as a desecration of the Sabbath and a violation of the rights of others to worship undisturbed. The Reverend J. Albert Rondthaler of the Tabernacle Presbyterian Church proclaimed that all Christians "must keenly feel the disgrace put upon the city." The Reverends James McLeod, R. V. Hunter, and E. A. Bradley likewise weighed in with condemnations.[27]

McCulloch addressed the controversy in his next sermon. Defending the parade, he reminded his listeners that the Knights had aimed to hold the festivities on a Monday but could not secure the grounds. Since the factories would not accommodate any other day, Sunday remained as the only possible choice. Furthermore, the Knights had scheduled the parade to conclude before church services began, but rain pushed back the starting time. McCulloch then defended both the workers' overall conduct and the theological appropriateness of holding the event on a Sunday.[28] His words inspired the Central Labor Union to offer him a formal vote of thanks and to attend his 10 October sermon as a body. The *Sentinel* impishly remarked, "The workingmen owe it to themselves and to the cause of labor to sustain Mr. McCulloch in his work, as the advocacy of humanity's cause is sure to gain for him the ill-will of other ministers."[29] Indeed, McCulloch received much criticism for his defense of the Knights' parade, but a stronger expression of his new views and a larger dose of attendant controversy lay ahead when McCulloch weighed in on the trial of the Haymarket anarchists.

The labor demonstration held in Chicago's Haymarket district on 3 May 1886 had turned into a riot when police fired into a crowd of battling strikers and strikebreakers, killing four. The next day, a peaceful, city-authorized gathering turned into a calamity when, as a riot squad began forcefully dispersing the crowd, someone threw a bomb into the scrum. The explosion killed a policeman, and police responded again by firing into the crowd, injuring at least a hundred spectators and several of their fellow officers. In all, the bombing, shooting, and mayhem claimed the lives of eight policemen and an uncounted number of civilians. Newspapers quickly convicted immigrant radicals for the carnage.

The incident seemed proof that the decade of simmering tension between workers and management and associated questions about the place of immigrants, socialism, anarchism, and other radical doctrines in America had erupted into low-level war. Three days after the bombing, McCulloch wrote in his diary, "The one thought on my mind is the Labor Trouble. I wish that I could speak on that and nothing else. When I read of the anarchists in Chicago I said, 'They know not what they do.' The law and order of society must be preserved, but they have suffered much." While most Americans demanded swift justice, McCulloch speculated about the iniquities and injustices he might find in the biographies of the alleged bomb-throwers. "What was their history, first at home?" he asked, and "What had they suffered?" McCulloch wrote that the immigrants likely came to America with the feeling of hope and "with the idea of liberty." Imagining how they must have felt upon waking up to their impoverished situation, McCulloch empathized, calling the immigrant radicals "frankensteins of modern society."[30] As was true of many Americans, McCulloch saw assimilation as the goal for immigrants. In Sheboygan he had observed that unassimilated food spoiled the body; unassimilated immigrants or, for that matter, the unassimilated pauper Ishmaels he found in Indianapolis poisoned the body politic.[31]

Considering the hang-them-all mentality pervading Indianapolis, McCulloch wisely kept his thoughts to himself for six months. Not until his post-Thanksgiving Sunday sermon did he speak out, arguing that the death sentences recently given the anarchists were unjust and that they deserved a new trial.[32] The *Journal, News,* and *Sentinel* all carried McCulloch's sermons, editorials, and COS announcements regularly, and all chose not to publish the text of this sermon. McCulloch's editorial response to an article appearing in the Monday morning edition of the *Journal* represents his views:

> I have a horror of all methods of violence. I believe in obedience to law and in enforcement of law. I have no sympathy with the . . . methods employed by these men. I feel that freedom of speech has its limits. I believe that these men should be punished for the consequences of their words, even if they were not directly concerned in throwing the bomb. But a nation is great by reason of its capacity to forgive.
>
> So I say of these men, "They know not what they do." They are misguided men. They are in the midst of human sorrows and sufferings. They see hundreds of men out of work. They hear the cry of many thousand children who work in the mills, factories and foundries of Chicago. They see young girls who work without wages sufficient for life. They see women sewing for thirty cents a day. They see machinery displace men who then go about asking vainly for work. They see all this and then denounce. They denounce the rich without distinguishing good from bad. They denounce the factories and mills, the system, the civilization. They cry, "Hang them! Burn them!" They cannot understand the law of political economy.[33]

The *Journal*'s editorial reply condemned McCulloch's "gospel of gush," anarchists, and immigrants in general. Conceding the minister's right to defend the "bloody wretches," the editor then asserted that there was no such right "to use a pulpit of a leading and intelligent church in which to utter unmitigated hogwash." McCulloch's quotation of Jesus's words on the cross was "a gratuitous insult to common intelligence," his rationalizing of the bombing "unadulterated trash, which would be simply foolish were it not dangerous in the mouth of a man of standing and influence."[34] The criticisms diminished McCulloch's esteemed position in the community. In a diary entry from early December, he wrote, "It was report'd that my church was broken up."[35] The controversy, followed by an extended bout of illness, kept McCulloch from engaging in such heated public controversies in the future.

With a new appreciation for avoiding controversy, McCulloch turned his attention to stretching the scientific charity mission to fit his expanding interpretation of the causes of poverty. Among the earliest and most

illuminating examples, the Indianapolis COS sponsored the establishment of the Indianapolis Dime Savings and Loan Society in 1887, quite
possibly modeled on the paper W. L. Bull presented the previous year at
the NCCC recommending just such measures. According to a flier announcing the society's first meeting, "much of the suffering of the poor
is due to a lack of habit of saving small amounts, and to a lack of opportunity for laying by small amounts weekly."[36] Contributing to that
lack of opportunity, said the flier, the city's deficit of savings institutions
gave small wage earners no opportunity to learn the habits and virtue
of thriftiness, while high fuel prices ate into what little income they did
possess.

The Indianapolis COS intended for its savings and loan to function
more as a community resource for the poor than as a normal bank. To
help inculcate the habit of thriftiness, the society sold $25 shares, bought
incrementally through small dues. Collectors inspired, or perhaps enforced, the saving habit by calling on members at their homes for their
ten-cent dues each week of summer "when work is more plentiful," and
permitting withdrawals only during the winter. By 1890 the Savings and
Loan counted 1,174 members owning 3,654 shares of stock, with receipts
at the bank totaling $24,148.12, "and no small part of this has been paid in
nickels and pennies"; $10,025 had been loaned at 6 percent interest.[37] The
Savings and Loan collected an average of $350 per week, added twenty
new members "without solicitation" each week, and paid an astounding
750 weekly visits. A report from 1897 similarly claimed the Savings and
Loan's staff made 40,000 visits during the year.[38] That number jumped to
63,579 the following year, with collections totaling $17,749.51.[39] The sav-
ings and loan additionally sold its members coal and other goods that the
COS had purchased at bulk rates.[40] It is unclear how many people participating in the Dime Savings and Loan program possessed the means
necessary for buying a home, but the COS noted that the city's current
home-building associations did not "reach down far enough, nor do they
reach those whose need of them is greatest."[41]

The claims made by the Savings and Loan's directors ran from the
modest and practical—saving members fifty cents on each ton of coal or
escaping from the installment plan—to more dreamy notions of home-
ownership and financial independence. One report even claimed that

"among a class more or less dependent," the Savings and Loan had "rescued many from pauperism and helped to keep others independent." Such claims can only be swallowed with a healthy dose of skepticism, but they fit well with the philosophy of scientific charity. Said the report, "The best aid to the poor that we can give is not the dole, the crust or the dime, but the opportunity to help themselves. The salvation of the poor is through economics."[42]

The Savings and Loan served as a vessel for teaching self-help, but its work must also be seen in the larger context of the evolving attitudes toward poverty among scientific charity reformers. The emphases on personal savings and frugal bulk purchasing as well as the presence of collectors making weekly calls for the dimes all set comfortably within the moralistic emphasis that characterized the first decade of scientific charity both nationally and in Indianapolis. But the savings and loan's directors also expressed concern about the usurious interest rates of installment plans and the absence of home associations for the poor, indicating a concern for larger issues of economic opportunity and justice. Two years after the establishment of the Indianapolis COS, the influential New York City COS created its own Penny Provident Fund and, a few years later, a Provident Loan Society.[43] Groups dedicated primarily to the suppression of the pauper do not create savings and loans or fight for fair credit practices for the poor. McCulloch brought his change in perspective with him to the NCCC. At the 1889 meeting of the NCCC, he reiterated the six objectives of scientific charity that he had first listed in 1880, all of which focused on detecting paupers, elevating the morality of the poor, and restricting charitable relief. To these objectives McCulloch now added a seventh, which called for "the reform of abuses in existing laws, the securing of justice, and the modification of conditions which make for poverty and crime."[44] In a book review of Jacob Riis's *How the Other Half Lives* the following year, McCulloch again affirmed that environment was the cause of vice and depravity; if vice were to be combated, it must be done through reform of the environment.[45]

McCulloch's investment in the Indianapolis COS and NCCC also increasingly affected the public administration of charitable institutions in Indiana. McCulloch had endorsed the creation of a state board of charities at least since 1881. After seeing a bill die in committee in 1887,

McCulloch successfully lobbied for the founding of the Indiana Board of State Charities in 1889. As his biographer chronicles, McCulloch worked tirelessly to move the bill forward. Working with the Society of Friends in Indiana, McCulloch helped bring in the secretary of the Ohio State Board of Charities, the Reverend A. G. Byers, to address the Indianapolis COS. Copies of his speech, "On the Organization of State Charities," then circulated throughout the city. The NCCC almost certainly was the vehicle by which he and McCulloch came to be acquainted: Byers had attended it annually since its creation, and his 1880 paper to the conference on Ohio's care of its dependent children was cited by Governor Hendricks in the Big Moll trial.[46] McCulloch additionally "worked through COS committees, . . . spoke before the legislature, and mailed information on the subject to the newly elected legislators. When the bill . . . was referred to the Committee on Benevolent Institutions, McCulloch lobbied extensively, talking with each of its members."[47]

The resulting Indiana Board of State Charities "was an epochal event in the development of public welfare in Indiana."[48] Before the creation of the board, institutions were under the control of political patronage. Like most state boards, Indiana's could investigate and supervise state institutions, but not compel changes in their operation. Its efficacy instead came from the savvy political work of its board members, a group dominated by associates of the Indianapolis COS and NCCC. McCulloch served on the board, and Alexander Johnson became its first secretary. Four other members of the board were elected president of the NCCC.[49] McCulloch had worked for years to coordinate the establishment of local boards that would have the power to remove children from bad homes as he recommended in his writings about the Ishmael family. In addition to establishing the Board of State Charities, in 1889 the state legislature also enacted a bill that McCulloch had drafted earlier in the year, establishing such boards in all Indiana towns with populations greater than 75,000—meaning Indianapolis. McCulloch exclaimed, "It is the most radical bill ever passed" and predicted it would save 550 Indianapolis children from a fate of pauperism in the next five years.[50]

The board engaged in arguably more radical work in the years after McCulloch's death, and again his imprint and the broader influence of charity organization is unmistakable. Amos Butler served as the board's secretary from 1898 to 1923 and is credited with "changing the politically dominated handling of outdoor relief by the thousands of township trustees to a well-organized and carefully supervised distribution of assistance to the needy comparable with the method used by the private urban charity organizations."[51] In so doing he demonstrated a point argued by scientific charity and NCCC stalwarts like Frederick Wines and Frank Sanborn that, given the proper personnel and philosophical approach, public outdoor relief could indeed be conducted in a satisfactory manner. Butler explained, "Indiana has applied the principles of charity organization to the whole state."[52]

The Board of State Charities led the effort to pass a series of laws in 1895, 1897, and 1899 that required trustees to keep full records of their relief and mandated that they cooperate in sharing records with local charity organization societies or similar charities operating in their towns, along with the county commissioners and the state board. In this way the board gained data on poor relief administered across the state. An 1897 law ended the system that had been in place since 1852, when the trustees first were granted responsibility for poor relief, in which they had submitted their relief expenditures to their respective boards of county commissioners, who generally paid the bill without question—potentially a source for much inefficiency and corruption. After 1897, instead of being able to distribute relief knowing that someone else had to pay the bill, public relief in a township would be funded by a property tax levied by the trustee.[53] Obligating the disburser of relief also to pay for it had an immediate effect on the amount disbursed. In five years the state's expense on outdoor poor relief dropped from $630,168 to $209,956. Over a ten-year span, the number of people relieved by outdoor relief declined from 71,414 to 45,331, while the value of aid per person grew modestly, from $4.97 to $5.51 per recipient.[54] The year 1897 also saw passage of a law that ended the placing of children in poorhouses. No longer would children find themselves mixed in with the likes of Big Moll. In 1899, eighteen years after McCulloch wrote in his diary that putting Dr. Culbertson on trial would let "the authorities [know] that they are watched," the state passed regulations on the proper management of the asylums and procedures for appointing superintendents and physicians.[55] Finally, beyond legislation that most distinctly reflects the charity organization agenda, Butler also approvingly noted the passage of several other reform-oriented laws that the board had recommended or endorsed, ranging from prohibiting work in the coal mines for all boys under fourteen and for all women, to compulsory education and impeachment of public officers.[56]

The Open Door Sermons: From Competition to Cooperation

As McCulloch reevaluated the economic and social forces at work on the poor, he also reconsidered his exegesis of the relationship between biology, religion, and poverty. The Open Door, a collection of Sunday sermons from the last two years of his life, 1890 and 1891, contains several theological commentaries on the place of poverty in the modern world. Many emphasize his belief in the potential for all to be forgiven and saved, for poverty itself to be abolished through concerted action, and for the moral necessity of charity projects. In the sermon "Abundant Life," for instance, McCulloch expressed a new understanding of the plight of Indianapolis's poor: "Most of them live so close to the line of actual want that a week out of work, or a month's sickness, brings hunger and cold, or debt." He also evinced a new optimism, going on to say that "to all these a fuller, happier life is possible. Nature is kind."[57] The use of the word all and the omission of any distinctions between poverty and pauperism are noticeable.

When McCulloch looked at the poor in 1891, he saw that "lying dormant in these souls are capacities for art, music, intelligence, skill, success." The same point is expressed most explicitly in "The Ideal in Man," where McCulloch argued that an "Ideal Human" exists in all souls. He cited an experiment by a New York City newspaper that chose "a chance tramp" from the streets and offered him "a new suit of clothes, a bath, and a week's board in a good hotel." This man, whom McCulloch once would have classed as an irredeemable pauper, is described as having "a new seriousness . . . in his face and a new light in his eyes, like the recovery of one who is lost and regained." "Here is a man," McCulloch told his parishioners, "who says he will try to live a better life. I myself think the experiment would be a hopeful one."[58]

Further evidence of McCulloch's reinterpretation of pauperism comes in his discussion of intemperance. Proponents of the scientific charity movement of the 1870s and 1880s had, like previous generations of charity workers, regarded drunkenness among the poor as indisputable proof that such individuals were unworthy. Since the worthy poor would not dissipate their bodies or savings with drink, drunkenness must be a sign of the moral and now also biological weaknesses that characterized pauperism. Yet McCulloch had found little evidence of intemperance among the Ishmael family, and years later he began to reconsider the causal relationship between poverty and drink. In his sermon "The Mission of the Son of Man," McCulloch turned to argue that "the causes of intemperance are other than the individual will" and that "the greatest cause of intemperance is poverty, absolute misery of life." His change in perspective led him to see traits like chronic poverty and intemperance as consequences of broader social failings, which suggested to McCulloch a new understanding of charity. In "The Discontent of the Fortunate," he explained how charity was changing: "It used to be pity. It is not pity now. It is the equalization of opportunity. The new religion takes the social as well as the individual into its life." In "The New Vow of Poverty," McCulloch exhorted all Christians to hate poverty and work to end it, arguing that the environmental effect of poverty "starves life" and soul.[59]

In these last sermons McCulloch described all poor people as worthy and capable of redemption, given the proper social organization. But what of the biological basis of pauperism? In his sermon "The Law of Mutual Aid," McCulloch rejected the scientific premises of his "Tribe of Ishmael" work in favor of a new interpretation of biology. Here he sought to harmonize Jesus's "intense sympathy" and "intuition of love" with recent discoveries "being made known by the sympathetic reading of science." Human sympathy is the "essential quality of Christ" found in the practice of modern Christianity. The monuments testifying to Christian sympathy are modern facilities "for the protection of the weak . . . the recovery of the lost . . . the enlargement of the life of the unsuccessful."[60]

The Christian obligation for the better-off to tend to those in need had "encountered a certain obstruction," however, in the face of "what is believed to be the revelation" of Darwinian evolution. McCulloch agreed with the Darwinian belief that a struggle for existence "is nature's chief factor in the progress of the species" and that it pervaded not just nature but also industry and commerce. If this was the full extent of the law of evolution, he conceded, it would trump the Christian's moral warrant for saving and reforming the weak and for exercising human sympathy through the gift of charity.[61]

But McCulloch also believed that a new law coming to light, the law of mutual aid, held implications for Christian charity. He noted that "a Russian zoologist," Petr Kropotkin, espoused a view of evolution as a co-operative venture. The "Anarchist Prince," feted in the literary and sci-entific circles of London where he lived in exile, had recently begun an extended confrontation with Darwin's associate, Thomas Huxley, over the social implications of evolution. In the English monthly magazine *The Nineteenth Century*, Kropotkin wrote that his study of animal so-cial behavior suggested to him that the "prime factor in nature" was not the "struggle for existence," as Huxley had claimed, but the "law of mu-tual aid."[62] Sociable animals such as bees, ants, and ducks struggled to-gether against their environment, allowing evolutionary advancement on a group, not individual, level.

McCulloch had a long-standing interest in social cooperation, hav-ing given sermons on how ideas like the Rochdale weavers' coopera-tive grocery store worked for financial and moral uplift among labor-ers while creating social solidarity at least since 1881.[63] Such interests increasingly characterized several strands of American thinking as the 1890s approached, and biological explanations and justifications for co-operative human associations appealed to leaders in the labor and So-cial Gospel movements, Christian Socialists, social scientists, and so-cial reformers. One of the nation's most esteemed scientists, John Wesley Powell of the Geological Survey, explained that social institutions me-diated human evolution, making it a cooperative process.[64] A founder of academic sociology and equally prominent progressive intellectual, Lester Frank Ward, similarly explained that competition could not ex-plain the evolution of humanity's higher mental functions; social insti-tutions had guided that development.[65] Kropotkin toured America in 1899 and 1901, visiting Jane Addams at Hull House and lecturing at the University of Wisconsin as the guest of progressive economist Richard Ely.[66] To McCulloch, Kropotkin's lessons indicated "the struggle for ex-istence is not as between man and man . . . so much as between every-thing and its exterior circumstances."[67] McCulloch declared that science now vindicated the "sacred instincts" of compassion and cooperation that the heart had always known to be true. By implication, science also vindicated his changing analysis of scientific charity and poverty.

McCulloch marked a lifetime's involvement in social reform and science by serving as president for the 1891 meeting of the National Conference of Charities and Correction, held 13–20 May at Plymouth Church. There he proposed a national scientific survey of philanthropy patterned after the recent geodetic survey, as well as a national register of dependent, defective, and delinquent persons.[68] The proposal has been viewed by historians as a precursor to efforts by the Eugenics Record Office, and indeed decades later the ERO did use the Tribe of Ishmael in its pro-sterilization propaganda.[69] McCulloch, however, died just six months after this proposal without having the opportunity to fully flesh out the function or purpose of this register. The *Open Door* sermons and the exhortation from "The True Spirit of Charity Organization," published the same week as the conference, indicate that he was heading in a direction far removed from the eugenics movement.

The NCCC Reconsiders Heredity, Degeneracy, and Eugenics

Scientific charity's decade of upheaval and reevaluation in the 1890s coincided with larger changes in American attitudes toward heredity and environment. Historian Charles Rosenberg identified the mood of Americans toward heredity in the middle third of the nineteenth century as one of "optimism and activism," of "confidence that man's most fundamental attributes could and should be manipulated." To scientifically minded reformers, heredity provided a mechanism for improving both the individual and the society. The influence of heredity did not end at conception; at least through weaning and perhaps for several more years, a child's hereditary constitution continued to settle. Humans supposedly inherited wide swaths of behavioral tendencies that could be activated, exacerbated, or mitigated by the experiences of early childhood. Therefore, social deviants like criminals, the insane, alcoholics, and paupers inherited their behaviors not only in the womb but in the nursery as well. The general mood toward heredity, however, darkened near the century's end, favoring an outlook that was more "tenaciously aggressive, nativistic" as well as more deterministic and pessimistic than the mood of the 1870s.[70] Historians of American eugenics identify the end of the nineteenth century and the first two decades of the twentieth century as the pinnacle of "hard" hereditarian theories united with repressive measures designed to prevent the "unfit" from reproducing.

A closer look at the scientific charity movement reveals a complex set of beliefs that diverged from the trend toward hard hereditarianism and eugenics. Scientific charity's leading proponents disassociated poverty from the cluster of socially deviant behaviors considered "degenerate" and open to eugenic solutions. The more deterministic stance that characterized hereditarian thought in the 1890s and early 1900s actually lessened where poverty was at issue, as charity reformers gave increasing weight to the importance of environmental reform in shaping individual behavior of the poor. While those attending the National Conference met a growing number of sociologists, psychologists, and physicians who spoke strongly about the need for eugenic solutions for the feebleminded and insane, those who came to the meetings from the field of charity generally avoided linking eugenics to their work with the poor. Although they still mentioned degenerate paupers occasionally, charity and social workers greatly contracted the scope of what counted as pauperism, almost to the point of defining the matter out of their field of study. Heredity even became a way for some to absolve the poor of responsibility for their condition, making them part of the ever expanding category of worthy poor. Many if not most conference members shared a basically hereditarian outlook, reinforced by the influx of professional social scientists and the unrelenting presence of the poor and dependent in spite of reformers' best efforts at ending poverty. Nevertheless, scientific charity workers sought to remove pauperism and chronic poverty from the list of dependent groups subject to hereditarian analysis.

Albert O. Wright, the secretary of the State Board of Charities and Reform and former inspector for the State Board of Control in Wisconsin, gave a bruising presidential address in 1896 that marked one of the last, most thoroughly hereditarian analyses of pauperism given by a close associate of scientific charity. Wright interpreted the "New Philanthropy" to mean the study of causes of dependence and delinquency at the group and individual levels. As the application of sociology raised charity to "the rank of a science," the new charity would fight social and individual pathologies alike through preventative measures and new medical cures. Like many of scientific charity's early leaders, Wright thought most social ills flowed from the same source of biological degeneration. "The criminal, the pauper, the tramp, the neglected child, even many of the insane and the idiotic, are all interrelated with one another, and are mutually exchangeable." Echoing social Darwinian principles more characteristic of the scientific charity movement's first decade, he alleged that "our very efforts to improve the conditions of the defective classes have tended to increase them," since charity sheltered the weak from the law of "survival of the fittest in the struggle of existence." Worse, the unfit would "propagate their weakness and wickedness, and entail them on future generations."[71]

Categorized as parts of the same tangle of degeneracy, the problems of delinquency, insanity, and pauperism were open to the same cures: institutional segregation and more severe reproductive limits. Wright claimed that the new philanthropy was "cutting off the entail of hereditary pauperism and crime and insanity and idiocy in a very large degree by keeping defectives in institutions, which resemble heaven in at least one particular, because there is neither marrying nor giving in marriage in them." Since the only alternatives to institutionalization and marriage prohibition were "wholesale death or equally wholesale castration," "wholesale imprisonment" stood as the only viable option for ending a defective line and removing children from their parents' corrupting influence. Wright rejected needless sympathy toward the poor as unscientific and counterproductive, the product of "imperfect knowledge" that "pities . . . the pauper rather than his posterity."[72]

Alexander Johnson became the second charity organization figure of national prominence to fully endorse eugenics as a solution to pauperism when in 1897 he used his president's address to argue the merits of state paternalism. The address, "The Mother-State and Her Weaker Children," envisioned a state that doled out tough love to its degenerates by informing them:

> My child, your life has been one succession of failures. You cannot feed and clothe yourself honestly. You cannot control your appetites and passions. Left to yourself, you are not only useless, but mischievous. I have tried punishing, curing, reforming you, as the case may be; and I have failed. You are incurable, a degenerate, a being unfit for free social life. Henceforth I shall care for you. I will feed and clothe you, and give you a reasonably comfortable life. In return you will do the work I set for you and you will abstain

from interfering with your neighbor to his detriment. One other thing you will abstain from: you will no longer procreate your kind. You must be the last member of your feeble and degenerate family.[73]

With his authoritarian rhetoric, Johnson gave the most full-throated endorsement of eugenics among scientific charity leaders. Considering how much of the movement's early support originated in complaints about the scale and corruption of government spending, the need to reform public institutions, and the defense of laissez-faire capitalism, Johnson's assumption that state intervention would be necessary to fight the forces that produced poverty and dependence was equally interesting.

Wright and Johnson's consecutive presidential addresses heralded not the beginning but the conclusion of a eugenic approach toward pauperism among the scientific charity leadership that gathered at the National Conference. Scientific charity leaders removed pauperism from the group of related degenerate behaviors while simultaneously positioning the few remaining hereditary paupers beyond the pale of scientific charity work. Their hereditarian analysis also reflected a broader trend among charity workers toward abolishing or at least greatly blurring the worthy/unworthy dichotomy, as heredity became not a mark of irredeemable unworthiness but an issue beyond moral judgment.

Agnes Maule Machar expressed that point most cogently in her talk to the 1897 conference, where she argued for a broad view of worthiness that included even those considered hereditary degenerates. The teachings of science demanded that charity workers "must judge others relatively to the circumstances of their lives,—their heredity and environment." For Machar, this absolved the poor of blame for their condition and removed any sort of eugenic solution from consideration. She argued at length that what had been known as the hereditary pauper really belonged within the category of the worthy poor. Machar first conceded to the eugenicists the power of degeneration, saying, "Evolutionary science teaches us that all living beings are subject to a law of degeneration or reversion to a more primitive type." America included many degenerate families where "the degrading influence of their environment for generations has sent them into the world with weakened physiques, enfeebled minds, relaxed energies; and they are, in consequence, of an inferior moral type."

After accepting the premises of biological degeneration, Machar then departed from Wright and Johnson's conclusion and argued instead that these biological defects were not markers of unworthiness. "Such unfortunates can no more help these characteristics than they can help the color of their eyes or hair." Instead, their behaviors were "the result of their deteriorated constitutions" brought about by "the influence of unsanitary surroundings, precarious employment, seasons of semi-starvation, and too generally badly prepared food." These families were "pauperized by nature" and therefore deserved "our earnest sympathy and uplifting aid. Shall we dare to stigmatize these degenerates as unworthy, when they are simply what heredity, environment, and our social system have made them?"[74]

As Machar reinterpreted degeneracy to be within the realm of worthiness, scientific charity workers also pared the issues linked to degeneracy. With the pauper category evaporating and the dividing line between worthy and unworthy challenged, chronic poverty and dependence began to disappear from the list of linked degenerate social behaviors. Wright's 1896 address is the last use of the phrase "hereditary pauperism" found in the conference proceedings that does not amount to a dismissal of the concept.[75] Some papers simply failed to list chronic dependence as a degenerate trait. Charles Faulkner's presidential address in 1900 and Alexander Johnson's in 1903 both failed to mention dependence in their review of dysgenic ailments. Others held that heredity affected human physiology but not social deviancy.[76] Some argued for a conservative approach of institutionalizing only the "most manifestly unfit for parenthood," as University of Chicago sociologist and longtime charity organization enthusiast Charles Henderson did in his presidential address to the NCCC in 1899, while cautioning that public opinion would not sanction anything more, at least not yet.[77] The 1899 statistical blank discussed in chapter 4 also had removed heredity from the list of factors that could directly cause poverty.

Scientific charity's leaders did not forget about hereditary pauperism; they abandoned it. The 1901 conference offered two of the most striking examples of the shift in outlook among this cohort. Jacob Riis, the photographer who in 1890 famously documented the poor's living

conditions in *How the Other Half Lives,* delivered one of the two introductory addresses. Riis's remarks are instructive, given that he had accepted most of the distinguishing traits of paupers characteristic of the
first years of the scientific charity movement. In *How the Other Half Lives*
Riis portrayed them as sustained by ill-conceived acts of charitable generosity, fundamentally and hopelessly unworthy and duplicitous, as well
as clannish and proliferating. One passage even referred to "professional
beggars, training their children to follow in their footsteps—a veritable
'tribe of Ishmael,' tightening its grip on society as the years pass."[78] In
1901, Riis arrived at the National Conference to profess a new optimism.
After recounting his years despairing of ever reforming the hopelessly
poor and criminal, Riis explained how he had found new hope among
young criminals and troublemakers who, given the opportunity, had
surprised him with acts of generosity and compassion. The aptly titled
address, "A Blast of Cheer," challenged the conference's members to join
him in rejecting the "specter" of heredity as "a doctrine of despair." What,
he asked, was heredity "but the sum of the environment that should have
been mended generations back?" Riis issued a challenge to his audience,
demanding that "if they cast up heredity against you, you fling it back in
their teeth, and tell them that our real heredity is this: that we are children of God. So we can do everything. There is none to make us afraid.
No: give me the other doctrine, that of environment."[79]

The other opening address, delivered by the Reverend Samuel G.
Smith of the State Board of Corrections and Charities of Minnesota,
complained about the recent overuse of the word *degenerate* and insisted
that this was not the proper study of the conference. Smith insisted that
their material "does not consist of the abnormal classes, but of the misguided classes." The problem of the abnormal classes belonged to physicians, and Smith dismissed this concern as irrelevant to charity, exclaim-
ing, "Kill them off if you will, if you can find hangmen enough; but that
is not our problem. Our problem is to lift people with human love and
patience."[80] Smith's severe remarks illustrate a trend among conference
participants toward medicalizing degeneracy as a topic best left to psychiatrists and physicians, while leaving children and the poor within the
domain of charity. The development is crucial in explaining why the sci-

entific charity organization movement stayed on the periphery of eugenics in the 1910s, when their closest cousins in social reform became key actors. Much of the poverty that once had been attributed to pauperism was now explained by charity reformers as secondary effects of feeblemindedness, insanity, and criminality, areas out of their purview.

The change in hereditarian outlook also is found in a comparison of Alexander Johnson's pronouncements in his 1897 "Mother-State and Her Weaker Children" address with the report he penned for the Committee on Colonies for Segregation of Defectives in 1903. Johnson, then serving as the superintendent of the Indiana School for the Feeble-Minded, headed the committee and wrote the majority report. That there were majority and minority reports speaks to the contested status of degeneracy and heredity in the conference; it is the only instance of contending committee reports in the conference's first fifty years. Johnson even began the majority report by telling his audience to note that the title should not be taken to suggest agreement on the issue within the NCCC.

The report was one of the last and most forceful statements made at the NCCC by an associate of the scientific charity movement to link pauperism and degeneracy. In it Johnson proposed segregating "those who, either physically or morally, are so far below the normal that their presence in society is hurtful to their fellow citizens, or that their unhindered natural increase is a menace to the well-being of the state." The groups "often classed as degenerates" included "many habitual paupers, especially the ignorant and irresponsible mothers of illegitimate children, so common in our poor houses; many of the shiftless poor, ever on the verge of pauperism and often stepping over into it." Each was "related as being effects of the one cause . . . degeneracy." Segregation should be preferred over sterilization, he said, as the proposition "is a dreadful one," "far in the future" and out of step with "belief in the infinite value of the individual."[81]

But upon closer inspection, Johnson's language betrays a deeper agnosticism toward the biological basis of pauperism. Johnson included paupers in a list of "those who are often classed as degenerates," but he avoided a definitive pronouncement. Whereas scientific charity advocates once spoke of *hereditary paupers,* Johnson now chose the term *habitual paupers.* He acknowledged that no one would argue for the complete segregation of all the groups listed, saying instead that certain classes certainly warranted segregation "who are either truly, hereditary degenerates or whose condition resembles this so much that they may be treated like them." Among those that Johnson said could be treated as tantamount to hereditary degenerates were the chronically insane, feebleminded, idiotic, and epileptic. He did not place paupers on that list.[82]

The majority report also needs to be assessed in reference to the stridency of the minority report, which advocated sterilization. The author, Mary Perry of Boston, appears to have had no affiliation with a charity organization society, a state board of charity, or the NCCC beyond her participation in that 1909 committee report, and she made no mention of pauperism or chronic dependence as degenerate problems or ones open to sterilization. Instead, she rebuked those who thought that "the millennium must come before we are able to put a stop to the fast increasing population of the epileptics and feeble-minded," and she recommended the "assistance of the surgeon's knife" to end the "curse" through sterilization.[83]

The conflicting reports were the final efforts from scientific charity practitioners at the NCCC to claim that chronic poverty was de facto proof of degeneration and to argue for sterilization. Edward Devine in *The Family and Social Work* gave at once one of the most forceful yet nuanced explanations for charity and social work's attitude toward eugenic measures. First, he vigorously defended the obligation of the community to support all its members, regardless of any eugenic conclusions that might be drawn from biology.

> We who are strong are to bear the burdens of the weak, even if in so doing we go down together. We do not expect to go down, but if that should be the last word of current biology, we can only say in reply: Here we stand, we cannot do otherwise. A community in which the strong deliberately crush the weak for the sake of having still stronger descendants does not appear to us worth saving.[84]

Typical of the scientific charity reformers, Devine accepted the proposition that some people were defective and of bad biological stock. He sought to distinguish, however, between the judgment and proposed solutions offered by charity or social workers toward the defectives and those that biologists might prefer.

> We come to care for the unfortunate defective girl, not primarily because she may become the mother of illegitimate children who will in turn become public charges, prostitutes and criminals, but for her own sake, as one who needs all our sympathy and our tenderest care. It is not so much that healthy stocks are to be protected from her taint, as that she is to be protected from criminal assault. She is our handicapped sister, a daughter of man, not less but more certain of our warm human sympathy because of her affliction.[85]

Devine cautioned that Mendel's genetics presently held "very limited applicability to human heredity." "How far our actual burden of pauperism, crime and disease are actually due to the perpetuation of degenerate breeds, and how far they are due to bad economic and social conditions which we could more quickly and directly affect by appropriate action, is the open question." Having posed the question, Devine left no doubt in his belief that social action would and should be the answer. Although he supported "the permanent segregation, during the reproductive years of life, of the feeble-minded, the insane, the incorrigibly criminal, and the hopelessly ineffective," Devine left paupers or the chronic poor off this list of eugenic targets, just as Johnson had. He likewise did not include paupers or the chronic poor among those "diseases and defects which have demonstrable hereditary consequences ... [that] might properly be made a legal bar to marriage." Sterilization, furthermore, for any person was "a policy of very doubtful expediency." Devine argued that those whose poverty was not a consequence of feeblemindedness ought to be considered not abnormal but subnormal, with the potential to be lifted into normalcy. "They are not degenerate, but they are nevertheless in need of regeneration. They need not be eliminated" if society would instead work toward their transformation.[86]

Progressivism, Radicalism, and Science in the National Conference

Scientific charity volunteers of the 1910s and their professional offspring, social workers, conducted their discussions at the National Conference in the presence of an increasingly voluble radical minority. As leading thinkers in the movement elevated environmental and economic causes

of poverty, more radical calls for social justice found space in the conference agenda. The composition of new voices defies easy generalization,
but it included pacifists, socialists, scientific utopianists, and critics of
science's seemingly sterile and dehumanizing objectivity and neutrality.

Once more, the changing composition of the conference's membership and leadership signals broader changes in scientific charity's mission, its sources of support, and the extent of its reach within the broader
community of American reform. Robert Treat Paine Jr., president of the
Associated Charities of Boston and in 1895 the first conference president
to come from outside the state boards of charities, declared himself a socialist in its "noblest meaning." A term as nebulous as it was controversial in the Gilded Age, Paine, like McCulloch, understood socialism in a
Christian and scientific framework that "the mighty powers of the State,
the city, and of the social organization" ought to use scientific and Christian revelation in order to "help the submerged tenth up into fuller life."[87]
Samuel "Golden Rule" Jones, the progressive mayor of Toledo, Ohio,
struck an early call for a radical form of charitable work in 1899 with the
aptly titled talk "Charity or Justice—Which?" In one of the most stri-
dent passages, Jones insisted that "the way to help the poor is to abandon
a social system that is making the men poor." Jones admonished his audience not to turn Jesus' words, "The poor ye have always with you"
into "an apology for the hideous wrongs of the present system."[88] Jones's
themes, that charity was no substitute for social justice and that at worst
it was a salve applied to the surface of a wound while missing the infec-
tion beneath, grew into a commonly expressed theme at the NCCC by
1910. Even Alexander Johnson conceded as much in the preface to the
1909 volume where he observed "that Justice is the Highest Charity and
that Justice means the equalizing of opportunity in the spirit of human
brotherhood."[89]

Jane Addams's 1909 election as the next year's conference president
confirmed its interest in social justice. In her presidential address, the
first woman to serve as conference president described the fusion of
charity workers' "pity for the poor" with the "hatred of injustice" that
characterized the radicals. She argued that the last decade revealed a convergence of interests between these two historically antagonistic groups.
The charity workers had come to accept the radicals' premise "that the

poverty and crime with which they constantly deal are often the result of untoward industrial conditions." The radicals, in turn, had grown to believe that an effective appeal to public opinion required the utilization of scientific data describing the conditions faced by the poor.[90]

The self-professed radicals were not so ready to toast their integration into the National Conference. In "A Criticism of Social Work and the Reform Program in the Light of the Complete Industrial Revolution by the Radicals," socialist Harold Varney announced to the 1918 conference that the social worker had discovered that the "feeble efforts of charity" in combating poverty were like "single rain drops in the parched dryness of a desert." They had no choice but to accept that poverty was "the inevitable corollary to existing modes of economic production."[91] Varney blasted middle-class reformers for abandoning the revolutionists and choosing instead to "cling resolutely to the framework of capitalism." In the discussion following the paper, Charles Sumner of the American Federation of Labor replied that the paper had "such an extreme presentation" as to warrant "very little sympathy" from organized labor, which sided instead with the progressive body of social workers.[92] Of course, the fact that the National Conference's organizers tolerated the paper's inclusion suggests that they had not in fact entirely abandoned the radicals.

Others argued that scientific social work was itself a radical proposition. University of Minnesota sociologist Arthur Todd recounted how a session that had been promoted as "something hot and radical, something that would probably prove highly offensive" to social workers, had failed to meet his expectations. Todd suggested that the only thing that might give offense was the claim that the revolutionary was a "man of feelings, emotion, temper," whereas the moderate social worker was a "man of ideas." Todd argued that if anything were true, it was the opposite: that the "real radicals" were the persons who would help rest social work on the foundations of science.[93]

Longtime scientific charity advocate and University of Missouri sociologist Charles Ellwood endorsed Todd's argument for coexistence between science and political radicalism. Science's ability to unearth the causes of social ills by use of the inductive method, and thereby command that the causes be reformed, made science an agent of radical change. Ellwood explained away the current state of tension between radicals and social workers as an artifact of social work's natural evolution. Once the transition was complete, there could be no possible room for tension between scientific social workers and radicals. Truly scientific social work would be radical but not revolutionary, because "it will also have the safety and sanity of science, in that it will proceed step by step by the experimental method." If social work failed to become "such a radically reconstructive program for society," it would be "discarded for revolutionary methods."[94]

Paine and Addams's turns as president of the NCCC indicate the conference's expansion to include more groups interested in more diverse issues from a greater range of ideological viewpoints with greater political influence in national politics. By the early twentieth century, the NCCC could "fittingly be called the mother of conferences in the field of social welfare."[95] As the conference's historian, Frank Bruno, described it, "The Conference, a forum for free discussion, where any competent person might state his opinion or tell his experience, was a nucleus about which clustered a large number of other national bodies, meeting at the same time to conserve the time and effort of several thousand men and women who came from all over the country, representing all sorts and forms of social work."

Not so much a single gathering but the central gravitational force in "a galaxy of conferences," the NCCC held its annual national meetings in association with other more narrowly focused groups. In its first years, that meant affiliation with the National Association for the Prevention of Insanity and the Protection of the Insane. But by the 1910s the list of groups meeting in association with the NCCC included "The National Probation Association, the Child Welfare League of America, the Family Welfare Association of America, the Young Men's Christian Association, the Salvation Army."[96]

Both the NCCC and individual COSs expanded their networks in the community of reformers and sought greater influence in both local and national politics in the early 1900s. Both at the NCCC and locally through the New York City Charity Organization Society, Paul Kellogg and Edward Devine spearheaded efforts to pair scientific charity organization with social investigation, in order to identify and ameliorate

causes of poverty external to the individual. The New York City COS
initiated two of the most significant studies. Tuberculosis, the dreaded
"white death," proved an obvious topic to bring within scientific charity
reformers' expanding range of vision. In addition to being the leading
cause of death in the nineteenth century and the "costliest" disease, con-
sumption shared much in common with pauperism.[97] It struck hardest
at impoverished, dirty urban centers, removed potential workers from
the economy and increased their risk of becoming public charges, dissipated their bodies, left their children more susceptible to the disease,
and prompted fears of "race suicide." As historian Georgina Feldberg
observes, "TB symbolized the imminent demise of the American Nation."[98] Those afflicted were obligated to work toward their own improvement. Proposed treatment included isolation in institutions, therapeutic work regimens, attention to cleanliness, systematic identification
and registration of all afflicted by the disease, and, not insignificantly, individual and social restoration projects based on the expert knowledge
held by middle-class professional reformers. "The public health movement," notes Sheila Rothman, "reflected an optimism that social engineering would be able to conquer deep-rooted problems; but it also assumed that unless coercive and exclusionary measures were adopted,
the physical well-being of the body politic would be endangered."[99] Few
lines of thought could so closely parallel each other as the public health
movement's approach to tuberculosis and scientific charity's approach
to pauperism and poverty.

That by 1900 tuberculosis had "become a disease of the poor," particularly immigrants, made it an especially inviting topic for the New York
City COS.[100] Following up the work studying the correlation between
poverty and tuberculosis documented by the New York State Tenement
House Commission Report of 1900, Devine and the Central Council
of the COS appointed a Committee on the Prevention of Tuberculosis.
The committee comprised "sixteen representative physicians and sixteen others," including Devine, charged with producing "an exhaustive
investigation of some of the social aspects of tuberculosis."[101] The result
of the examination, *A Handbook on the Prevention of Tuberculosis* (at over
400 pages, hardly a handbook), emphasized the need for cooperation
across private charities and public bureaus and defended the work as a

good financial investment, since it would be better "to cure tuberculosis in its incipient stages, rather than to allow almost the entire number ... to become a burden either upon their immediate family or upon the public at large."[102]

The cornerstone of the *Handbook*, Lilian Brandt's "The Social Aspects of Tuberculosis, Based on a Study of Statistics," stated, "Tuberculosis is a social disease not only in the sense that its prevalence and its persistence depend on social factors, but also because it is itself a factor of primary influence in other social problems.... [It] has no insignificant place among the causes of poverty."[103] Stuffed with detailed charts, graphs, and maps of incidences of tuberculosis among different segments of the population, Brandt's work resembled a more rigorous form of the tabulations conducted by COS and encouraged at the NCCC. Scientific charity advocates had long recognized illness as one of the most prominent causes of poverty; the *Handbook* was one of the first and most rigorous systematic efforts to document it with precision. City after city replicated New York City's cooperative venture between private charities and public boards of health. "The voluntary agencies," explains Feldberg, "offered the state several commodities in otherwise short supply: expertise, free and enthusiastic manpower, and a legitimate vehicle for achieving its goals when blunt state action might have appeared too intrusive."[104]

The *Handbook* represented the maturation of the COS's interest in social investigation, work which reached a zenith with the publication of the Pittsburgh Survey a few years later. Upon receiving a request from an officer from the Allegheny Juvenile Court, Paul Kellogg, editor of *Charities and the Commons*, the publication of the New York City COS, used COS Publications Committee money to initiate a comprehensive examination of industrial conditions in Pittsburgh, and he quickly secured $27,000 from the Russell Sage Foundation to support the project in its entirety, with an additional $20,000 for publishing expenses.[105] Kellogg supervised the survey, which was conducted by more than seventy investigators, including Devine, who had links to scientific charity. The survey was published incrementally in *Charities and the Commons* as well as in several other magazines before finally appearing in six complete volumes.

Contemporaries and historians alike have disputed both the influence and the scientific status of The Pittsburgh Survey. In favor of its
significance and scientific credentials, historians credit its "shocking
revelations of neglect or injustice suffered by the injured in the mills of
Pittsburgh" as the motivating force for the passage of workers' compensation legislation in thirty-four states and territories in the following
six years.[106] The Pittsburgh Survey quickly came to be regarded as "the
model of successful social action," a synthesis of social facts designed to
illicit more efficient and more democratic social action that "represented
the Progressive Era's lushest flowering of the belief that knowledge and
publicity were the first steps to reform."[107] It became "a model for future
sociological investigation," multiplying its influence as it spurred local
interest in conducting further surveys for the purpose of reform—more
than 2,500 in the following twenty years—such as the ones conducted
by the Indianapolis COS in the next chapter.[108] Such investigations allowed the COSs to become "incubators for new services in American
cities."[109] Finally and perhaps most consequentially, it represents the intersection of empirical investigation, large philanthropic interests, and
democratic government in efforts to identify and ameliorate the consequences of industrial capitalism. The term *survey*, borrowed from engineering, suggested that social scientific experts could identify and repair
structural weaknesses in American democracy.[110]

However, as has so often been the case concerning research that originated in scientific charity, sociologists and historians of social science
have been reluctant to characterize it as scientific, labeling it instead as
a form of "investigative journalism."[111] Particularly at the University of
Chicago, academic sociologists of the 1910s and 1920s differentiated their
work from amateurs and social reformers by disassociating descriptions
of what was from prescriptions of what ought to be. Overtly political
application of empirical social research to address the consequences of
an industrialized, capitalist economy did not prove to have a long-term
home in American social science.[112] Its lasting effect on Pittsburgh also is
doubtful, as the steel and iron corporations and Chamber of Commerce
painted it as the work of troublesome outsiders who did not understand
the city. Meaningful changes in the working conditions in the steel industry did not occur until the 1930s.[113]

The campaign against tuberculosis and The Pittsburgh Survey signified charity organization societies' expanding network of cooperation with public and private welfare organizations covering a broader range of social ills related to poverty and dependence, with a more ambitious effort to collect and analyze social data in pursuit of an explicitly partisan, reformist set of goals. With help once more provided by the Russell Sage Foundation, the NCCC used its position as the organizational hub for scientific charity reformers in general and charity organization societies in particular to influence politics at local levels. Mary Richmond, who rose from being the general secretary of the Baltimore COS to the director of the charity organization department of the Russell Sage Foundation, organized a session at the 1910 National Conference to discuss the relationship between national organizations and local charitable work, in hopes of better integrating local practices and national reform movements. She began by observing that "all but the least progressive of our charity organization societies has been made over by the national organizations" represented at the NCCC. Richmond suggested that local COS caseworkers should become "the point of intersection" with national reform movements in order to identify the proper sequence of reform projects needed in that particular city.[114] Reports followed from representatives of the Playground Association, National Housing Association, National Association for the Prevention of Tuberculosis, and National Child Labor Movement, in addition to papers on the use of social surveys, settlements, and commercial interests to advance reform.

Such pleas could not compel action, but the NCCC did function as a source of networking and intellectual exchange that often helped foster local developments. In the 1880s and 1890s, the effects might resemble McCulloch's work to establish a state board of charities and Butler's subsequent work to reduce and streamline outdoor relief expenditures. By the 1900s, the efforts took on a broader swath of social projects in a more clearly progressive manner. In Denver, for instance, reformist mayor Robert Speer appointed Gertrude Vaile the executive secretary to the city's Division of Charity and Correction. Vaile, a product of the Chicago School of Civics and Philanthropy, previously had worked with the Chicago United Charities. Like Butler had done in Indiana before her, Vaile sought to prove "that the methods found successful by charity or-

ganization in the private society could be applied to the public munici-
pal agency."[115] She explained to the 1915 National Conference, "As super-
visor of relief it is my task to grade the district visitors. . . . [A]lthough
ours is a public outdoor relief office we are trying to do a charity organization society sort of case work."[116] Vaile could not overcome the political objections to her vision of a strong program of public welfare, but
her views further indicate just how far scientific charity work had come
from its original policy goals of ending public outdoor relief. Addressing
the conference, Vaile said:

> The principle of poor relief by public authority is absolutely right. . . . The
> poor and suffering are so, not only by their own fault or peculiar misfortune,
> but also by the fault of us all. Government permits working and living condi-
> tions which create poverty and sickness—yea, even licenses some of them;
> and it is only just that organized society as a whole should struggle with the
> responsibility and pay the cost.[117]

The question was no longer whether or not aggressive government intervention on behalf of the poor was needed but how best to intervene.

This turn in favor of social insurance and other forms of public relief
and social legislation makes an appreciation of the ambivalence toward
proposals for providing pensions to widowed mothers all the more important. Some, like Mary Richmond, objected to them on the grounds
that they might become a source of graft and corruption; she and other
critics charged that the Civil War veterans' pension had become just
that. For Richmond and Devine, the key distinction was that a pension amounted to a handout that weakened individual resolve, whereas
health insurance provisions and other reform-minded legislation functioned to strengthen and reinforce an individual's will. Devine equated
pensions with any other form of outdoor relief in its "disastrous effect on
family life" by subverting a sense of responsibility.[118] Through the New
York City COS, he lobbied the city's mayor to veto a widows' pension bill
in 1897, and he continued to lobby against similar bills into the 1910s.[119]
Minimum wage laws, health insurance, workers' compensation, sanitation, and public health campaigns all fortified a poor person's initiative;
pensions did not.

As the National Conference expanded, so did its influence in progressive circles. After three years of work on the project, in 1912 the NCCC

issued the "Cleveland Statement," intended "to represent a wide-spread conviction that industry should be subjected to certain tests of social efficiency and should measure up to standards demanded by public health and safety."[120] The committee that drafted the statement, the Conference Committee on Standards of Living and Labor, included an all-star cast of progressive thinkers tied to the charity organization movement or scientific charity more broadly conceived, featuring Edward Devine, Lee Frankel, Florence Kelley, Alice Hamilton, Benjamin March, and Walter Rauschenbusch. The committee chair, Owen R. Lovejoy, was an "unsung hero of social work" whose sympathy for Eugene Debs's 1920 presidential campaign would later give him the distinction of being the only conference president to see a formal protest lodged against his election.[121] The report itself called for the establishment of a living wage, an eight-hour, six-day work week, workplace safety and health legislation, workers' compensation, the right to a home, the abolition of sweatshops and child labor, and compulsory unemployment and old age insurance. The committee urged that these standards be "promulgated before political parties, church conferences, women's clubs, federations of labor, associations of manufacturers, and other groups of citizens interested in public welfare."[122]

The Cleveland Platform soon found its audience in Theodore Roosevelt's presidential campaign. Leaving Cleveland as the annual meeting of the NCCC closed, some of the committee members next went to Chicago, where the Republican National Convention was in session. Although the GOP declined to adopt their platform, Roosevelt seemed interested. Paul Kellogg, the committee chair for the first year of the three-year project, met with Roosevelt later that summer, and much to Kellogg's amazement, "in less than two months" from its announcement, the platform had been "adopted bodily as the practical economic gospel of a new political party."[123] With a few notable exceptions like Edward Devine, who thought nonpartisanship to be the wiser approach, social workers and charity reformers enthusiastically supported Roosevelt's Progressive Party. Jane Addams thought its convention resembled a meeting of the NCCC, with all the same people in attendance.[124] Historian Allen Davis observes, "Many of the social workers who became Progressives in 1912 were employed by charity organization societies or the Consumers' League; more were residents of social settlements . . . and for years they had been talking and planning together at the National Conference of Charities and Correction."[125]

Scientific Charity as a Progressive Movement

The scientific charity movement enjoyed prolific expansion in the first two decades of the twentieth century as it drifted from its foundational principles, defying the narrative of decline found in most histories of the national movement. Frank Watson began his 1922 book on the history of the charity organization societies by trumpeting that the number of COSs had more than doubled since 1905.[126] Counting the number of friendly visitors, university classes and summer programs in philanthropic methods, number of people registered, investigated, and relieved, financial and institutional support from the Russell Sage Foundation, and the dollar value of the amounts given out, all indicators point to a dramatic improvement in the fortunes of the scientific charity elite and their charity organization societies.

By 1905, scientific charity's leading thinkers had removed the word *pauper* from their lexicon, had distanced themselves from the concept of worthiness, had accepted the necessity of material relief, and had begun efforts to calculate what constituted adequate relief. They had turned from a group committed to abolishing public charity to one demanding it, with some even arguing for compulsory universal health insurance or expressing support for protective labor and public health legislation as part of a larger environmental approach to fighting poverty. Finally, they moved to disassociate economic dependence from biological degeneracy. As they reconsidered the costs and benefits of material relief, their assessment of degeneracy and eugenics, scientific charity workers reframed poverty as a national social problem. The causes of poverty previously had been attributed to things like "hard times" or inebriation or occupational hazard or moral or biological weakness. But in the 1890s and early 1900s, facing a hostile public, powerful competitors in the field of charity, massive amounts of hardship, and their own discovery that alms had not demoralized the working poor, scientific charity leaders abolished pauperism.

6

THE POTENTIALLY NORMAL POOR:
PROFESSIONAL SOCIAL WORK,
PSYCHOLOGY, AND THE END
OF SCIENTIFIC CHARITY

In the late 1890s and early 1900s, influential leaders of the scientific charity movement repudiated their initial premise that most poverty originated in character defects and shied away from the more draconian approaches suggested from that premise. Reformulating scientific charity, they adopted a more lenient and environmental view of poverty that emphasized economic and social justice for the poor and elevated societal causes of poverty to a status equal to or above personal defects. The change of direction breathed new life into an embattled movement, as demonstrated in the establishment of so many new charity organization societies, changes in nomenclature and categorization, the liberalization of relief policies, and growth of political influence.

Among the rank and file of the movement, however, similar changes are more difficult to detect. In areas where the Indianapolis COS's work was not warped by the gravitational pull of McCulloch's personality—the system of friendly visiting and investigation, and the society members' work during the 1893 depression and 1907 panic—scientific charity did not bear much resemblance to the scientifically informed and potentially progressive project that McCulloch envisioned. While the 1890s brought some changes in nomenclature and relief decisions at the Indianapolis COS, the statements made by COS members, reports of the friendly visitors, and the COS's statistical data suggest volunteers deviated far less from the original intent of scientific charity: to control pauperism and instruct the poor. Lay members furthermore seem not to have shared the charity organization leaders' interest in a scientific analysis of poverty, either in the form of expression it took in the 1880s, where leaders emphasized repressive treatment of the paupers, or in the early 1900s, when the same scientific values informed their more liberal critique. If the introduction of training courses designed to provide friendly visitors with a scientific perspective toward poverty had any effect on attitudes or relief decisions, there is little evidence of it in the records of the friendly visitors and investigators.

The strains between national reform leaders and local volunteer friendly visitors concluded in the 1910s with the replacement of volunteer visitors who possessed uncertain levels of training in favor of professionally trained and salaried agents, the first social workers. As the movement professionalized, those leading the effort turned from sociology to psychology and psychiatry as the preferred sciences for reforming the poor.[1] Similar to what sociology had once offered scientific charity workers, psychology and psychiatry offered the first social workers new claims to expertise, greater professional recognition, and respectable moderation. Psychological analysis allowed them to reform the poor while placing responsibility for poverty in individuals' lack of psychological adjustment to their environment, thereby returning the onus for poverty back to the person and away from the society. The psychological turn further situated their profession in an enviable position where social workers could disavow eugenic solutions for their charges in one breath, while referring the more intractable cases to eugenics-friendly psychiatrists with the next.

From Poverty to Unemployment: The Panic of 1907

While the national scientific charity movement faced its greatest challenges with the depression of the mid-1890s, in Indianapolis the defining period arrived in November 1907 when a financial panic and weakened employment market led to rapid withdrawals from banks nationwide. The Indianapolis Dime Savings and Loan reported $11,000 in withdraw-

als in three months, while the COS registered a whopping 2,959 applications for relief from 1 December 1907 to 1 April 1908.[2] Their annual
report for 1908 added that they received 3,345 applicants for aid that
year, when a normal year averaged only about 800. Another estimation
declared, perhaps incongruously, that the COS had "received almost a
thousand applications for relief each week" in February 1908. The COS
described that winter's work as "the largest and in some respects the
most important done by the Society" in its history.[3] Later than most of
its brethren, the Indianapolis COS now declared its support for a more
generous policy on giving relief. A pamphlet released by the COS in 1908
recognized that the economic panic marked the beginning of a new era
in which it must prepare for a "much larger problem of relief" than its
original mission; their work now moved away from detecting the indo-
lent and the idle to concentrate instead on the problem of unemployment
and economic issues such as family budgeting.[4]

Belying the bold new pronouncements, the COS's relief projects stayed
fastened to the underlying presumption that relief ought to take the form
of temporary employment for those who would accept it, a position the
COS expressed with language steeped in class paternalism. Its publications claimed that in the panic, the COS gave "all able-bodied men . . .
relief through work." The society furthermore designed work assignments so as to "save the self-respect" of workers—not just hauling bricks
or splitting wood like the tramps had done for more than two decades
at the COS's Friendly Inn and Wood-yard, but civic improvement projects.[5] In a single day, 279 men came to work at the COS wage of fifteen
cents per hour along with supplies of food and coal, wages they might
use to buy groceries sold by the COS at wholesale prices "so that a man
by working two days could buy enough food to last a good-sized family a
week."[6] On days when weather forced the cancellation of work programs,
the COS still offered food and fuel rations on the good-faith expectation
that the men would work it off later.[7]

Lingering suspicions that the poor could not be trusted tempered this
incremental advance in generosity. Society members defended the modest wages on the grounds that they "might be used for things other than
food or fuel."[8] Indicative of their gendered understanding of labor and
continued suspicion of unemployed men, the COS maintained its policy

of not accepting applications from women or children in cases where members knew that a man or large boy in the family was available to make the request. As the COS described its efforts to combat indolence, men who wanted to "shift the responsibility" of supporting their families to the wife or children "were promptly made to see that that was not our plan, and were ordered to go to work without delay." The COS met women applicants with less suspicion but with the same gendered labor roles, assigning them work that could be done in the home, especially laundry. More often they gave relief without an expectation of work, since "in many cases the mothers were already overburdened."[9]

Persistent in their distrust, COS members invented new ways to monitor the activities of the poor. They enlisted "the better and stronger men and women among the unemployed" to supervise their peers. Those selected took part in the COS investigations and looked for "any serious cases of need" that the society might have missed, while at the same time scouting for "persons inclined to take advantage of the society." If the society's annual report is to be believed, the recruits appreciated the opportunity "so thoroughly" that "they would not permit a wrong to be perpetrated. Justice was soon meted out wherever it belonged." Any man unwilling to work was arrested and brought to court, where justice normally meant forcing the man to split wood at the wood-yard. It reported, "Several men were sent to the Workhouse for long terms because when work was offered them they would do nothing to support their families." Curious in light of these boasts, the number of beggars apprehended "was not large," and the streets held about the same number of beggars as normal.[10]

The COS also took a strict line with the city's immigrant population. A skeptical report noted that members had learned in mid-February of a number of "foreigners who were reported as being in a starving condition." The immigrants could not be put to work with the rest of the men due to the concern that "as soon as it was noised about that relief was to be secured, the entire foreign population would be in line for assistance." Their negative view of the immigrant population led the COS members to the ironic situation of giving immigrants relief without imposing any obligation that they work for the aid. The society furnished flour to the immigrant communities for about five weeks, then began providing bread while a cooperating organization dispensed soup, all without any work requirement.[11] The dim view of immigrants in the Indianapolis COS was rather out of step with the general position that charity organizations' national leaders took toward immigration. Although several individual COSs drew their initial motivation from anti-immigrant prejudices, and the staunch anti-immigrationist Charles Hoyt headed the NCCC's immigration committee for years, other COS and national leaders in scientific charity downplayed the need for more restrictive immigration laws and produced surveys and anecdotes that questioned the burden of the immigrant poor upon private and public relief. The conference "was inclined to be liberal" on immigration "on the ground that the country needed more rather than less workers." When the Supreme Court prohibited states from levying a tax on each arriving immigrant, the NCCC persuaded Congress to levy a fifty-cent tax per immigrant, in order to compensate states for the cost of providing the immigrants with charitable and medical care.[12]

As the economic crisis abated, Indianapolis's charity organization leaders interpreted the results of their labor as a victory for interclass solidarity. In addition to employing members of the out-of-work poor to assist in investigations, the COS had convened a daily council comprising regular charity workers, the "emergency workers" taken from the previously unemployed, and the still unemployed. There they discussed such questions as what goods to sell, prices to charge, and homes to visit. The COS enthused "that there never has been a time in the history of the city when all the people, from the poorest to the richest, were brought so closely together."[13] The scientific charity members seemingly survived the panic with their core principles intact. They still suppressed begging, insisted on work as the basis for relief, distrusted the poor, and emphasized the importance of men and older boys as the primary breadwinners.

But just as the changing terminology and classification schemes seen in the annual reports of the 1890s suggest a subtle shift within the Indianapolis COS toward a broader concept of relief and worthiness, the charitable and investigative projects initiated around the 1907 panic indicate similar changes. A special report of the COS noted that a working mother often must rely on public assistance and might have to choose

between sending her children to an orphanage or seeking out private relief, "either of which is liable to have a more disastrous effect upon the
family life." To mitigate the problem, the COS established the Mothers'
Aid Society to build three- and four-room cottages for such families, free
of rent until the children were old enough to help support the family.[14]
The Mothers' Aid Society soon found nearly five hundred members and
subscribers, virtually all of them women.[15]

Reflecting national trends, the Indianapolis COS also broadened the
scope of its investigative work to include not just employment circumstances among the poor but also their wages, expenditures, and family
composition. In conjunction with the foundation of the Mothers' Aid
Society, the COS investigated the conditions of poor working mothers.
The resulting study covered 234 people in 55 families, including 162 children, and examined the income and expenditures of a particular subset
of the working poor. All mothers selected for study were widows of men
who had been reliable family providers, as opposed to abandoned wives,
since an abandoned woman was presumed to already have learned to
fend for herself whereas the widow was left "more than helpless."[16] The
surveyors calculated the cumulative weekly income earned by the widows, by children above the age of fourteen, and by children between
the ages of six and fourteen. To figure the average income of these families, they simply added together these three sums and divided by 55. The
report thus concluded that the average family earned $5.35 a week, ig-
noring all differences in family composition. By the same method, the
surveyors calculated the average family's rent, $2 a week, its food expen-
ditures, $3.35, as well as life insurance and furniture bought by install-
ment or by mortgage.[17]

The analysis of the widowed mothers' circumstances included the
sorts of exhortations to promote self-reliance and preserve female domesticity that characterized the original ideology of scientific charity,
but also expressed greater sympathy and an interest in broader environmental conditions afflicting the mothers. The report lamented that
mothers could not devote more time to "building up ideals and principles" of home life due to their lack of energy, but this was less a criticism
of the mothers and more a criticism of social conditions that "forced"
widows to abandon domesticity from the exhaustion of "working and

grinding by day and by night" just to survive. A lack of domestic awareness "might teach that tendency to criminality and low ideals" to the
children and future generations, but the report did not dwell on this as an
immediate cause of poverty. Instead, it observed that the women could
afford to buy food and coal only in small quantities and thus at a greater
price rate than if they could buy in bulk. Likewise, wholesome food too
often had to be sacrificed for coffee and cakes that could be bought in
smaller quantities. The rent "for three or four miserable rooms" normally
had to be paid in advance and could account for up to half of a family's
income. Most women struggled with insurance policies meant to protect
their children if they ever became orphans, and they also faced monthly
or even weekly bills for their ramshackle furniture.[18] These truths should
inspire greater action by the community to support the mothers, the report concluded. Widowed working mothers had long represented the
worthiest of the worthy poor, but in a claim likely to have surprised an
earlier generation of scientific charity volunteers, the report's author presented the women as no different in kind than the readers. One widow
lamented, "We are just like other people. I wish I could be treated that
way."[19] In an emotional appeal concluding the report, readers were asked
to understand the terrible circumstances these women bravely faced and
how life's struggles could cause them to "drift into a feeling of hopelessness, a feeling that fate is against them."[20]

A decade after the reformers at the NCCC had started to address the
topic, the Indianapolis COS took an interest in unemployment; a survey
of the scope of unemployment in the city followed the survey of widows.
In the first months of the panic, COS investigators visited 119 factories
that had employed 20,484 men prior to the panic's onset. Their numbers
showed that only 4,387 men now worked full time, while 4,458 saw a reduction in their workload, and another 11,639 faced unemployment.[21]
With the change in focus toward unemployment came changes in remedies. Friendly visitors gained both the authority and the disposition to
give temporary relief, including money, much more freely and casually
to the poor. There are no records of friendly visitors distributing more
than shoes and clothes in the 1894–95 COS record volume. But one of
the next surviving volumes, a set of typed meeting minutes from 1911–
12, indicated that visitors gave relief quite freely. Even though David W.

"was able to work but was not working," a COS committee member mo-
tioned for temporary relief to his wife and child until the sick baby recovered.[22] A motion for the COS to aid a man able but unwilling to work
would have been implausible fifteen years earlier. Likewise, these meeting minutes abound with cases where visitors immediately handed out a
few dollars upon visiting the needy.

Most remarkable of all the Indianapolis COS's newfound interests
in social conditions, at least one case from 1911 expressed a concern for
racial injustice as a contributing factor in poverty. On 26 January, the
COS considered the case of Joseph and Dora P., recent black arrivals
from Mississippi with no friends in the city. Joseph worked for the Otis
Electric Company and had been in a fight with a white man that resulted
in Joseph being arrested and charged with assault and battery, with intent to kill. According to the COS records, a witness to the fight said the
white man was to blame, and Joseph's employers also took his side, but
the judge appeared to be siding with the white man, setting Mr. P.'s bail
bond at $100. By the time they took up the case, Joseph already had spent
three weeks in jail and had run out of money with three children to support. The meeting minutes indicate that the IBS sent the family groceries and suggest that they paid the family's rent of $8. The COS commit-
tee then approved the sending of a petition to the judge asking that he
free Mr. P. and declared it would investigate his side of the story and appoint a committee to visit him in jail.[23] There is not enough evidence to
build a definitive understanding of how Indianapolis charity organization volunteers viewed the intersection of race, poverty, and worthiness,
but Joseph P.'s case suggests that the COS members were not entirely
oblivious to the relationship between racial injustice and poverty.[24] Indeed, as early as 1894, Stephen Humphreys Gurteen had said that the
"one thing more than another that has led to pauperism and all its attendant evils ... is the existence of denominational exclusiveness and racial
prejudice. The antidote to all this is charity organization."[25]

The depictions of struggling families suggested in the unemployment
survey, the widowed mothers' survey, and the case of Joseph P. are a far
cry from those of the Tribe of Ishmael or Big Moll. The projects supported by the COS and its affiliates show halting but noticeable movement toward a more generous policy on the distribution of relief, a more

flexible classification system, even an awareness of racial injustice as a cause of poverty. The presumed guilt and otherness of the poor waned, while interest in the poor's struggles with greater economic and social forces brought some in the COS to treat the poor as similar to their better-off peers. In these respects, the experiences of Indianapolis's lay volunteers recapitulated those of national leaders described in chapter 4 and mirrored to at least some degree McCulloch's own transformation in chapter 5.

In more important ways, however, the history of Indianapolis's COS beyond McCulloch shows more differences than commonalities. While the lay volunteers who ran the COS in Indianapolis and elsewhere moved to support a more liberal relief policy, rejected or at least softened the pauper/poor dichotomy, and deemphasized moral and especially biological failings as factors in poverty in favor of unemployment, they also continued to express more doubt about the poor's desire to work and their ability to transcend a debased environment. Relief continued to amount to connecting individuals to modest employment as laborers and punishing those who would not accept the opportunity. COS members showed no interest in translating their concern for individual instances of unemployment into a broader social criticism, and they did not locate the source of poverty in the economic and social organization of America. Their examination of unemployment and food budgets rarely if ever extended to address the labor question, health insurance, or social justice. Instead, charity organization in Indianapolis remained an effort to promote interclass harmony by teaching the poor to realize their middle-class potential.

What accounts for the growing divergence between the daily, local practitioners of scientific charity and the leading intellectuals who sought to define and direct proper investigation and relief practices? In addition to the host of factors involved in the leaders' changes in outlook discussed in chapters 3 through 5, the ugliest characteristics of poverty visible from close proximity may have softened, the further up the ranks of scientific charity and thus away from the poor a person moved. While the reports of friendly visitors and local COS committee heads remained relatively constant in their paternalist concern for the poor's dirtiness and idleness, persons who moved up through the ranks from conducting charity investigations to attaining positions of national prominence like Oscar McCulloch and Josephine Shaw Lowell grew more sympathetic and less draconian as their experiences as charity investigators receded further into the past.

The average charity organization volunteer also likely ranked the importance of adopting a scientific perspective far lower on her list of priorities than did the national leaders. Almost all national leaders in scientific charity came to the movement already possessing some sort of scientific background and an interest in identifying general laws of pauperism and poverty. Local volunteers likely came to scientific charity for more practical and personal reasons, such as a desire for civic engagement and for doing good works or to start a career, but perhaps not to identify root causes of poverty. Judging by the persistent criticism expressed by national leaders toward the friendly visitors' training and the gradual replacement of volunteer friendly visitors with paid agents, the training courses in scientific charity look more like an imposition from leaders frustrated that the visitors did not share their scientific outlook than a response to an upwelling demand for scientific training from the visitors. Indeed, the history of charity organization in Indianapolis concluded with professionally trained social workers replacing the friendly visitors, while a series of different charitable groups carved up the areas of work formerly belonging to the COS. In this respect, the local history of scientific charity's demise resembles the national history.

From Worthiness to Normalcy:
The Psychological Basis of Social Work

Historians of social work identify the profession's origin in the scientific charity movement of the 1910s. Increasingly skeptical of friendly visitors' efficacy, scientific charity's elite identified a lack of proper scientific credentials as their greatest obstacle to gaining professional recognition. In a telling shift from scientific charity's origins in amateur social science, the presence or absence of professional recognition became tantamount to a judgment of charitable and social work's scientific credentials. As Charles Weller, the chairman of Washington's COS explained in 1902, "Charity work may be expected to become scientific . . . by the development of professional skill, professional schools, and authoritative standards of entrance and excellence in the profession."[26] The training program for friendly visitors instituted by the New York COS with help from Columbia University developed from a single summer course in 1894 to become in 1919 the New York School of Social Work. Harvard, Chicago, and other universities quickly followed Columbia's lead in establishing social work programs.[27] Years after its members had started referring to themselves as social workers, in 1917 the National Conference of Charities and Correction was renamed the National Conference of Social Work.

The gatekeepers to professional recognition looked skeptically upon social workers' claims of professionalism. Self-styled expert on professionalism and noted education reformer Abraham Flexner dismissed their claims for professional recognition in a much-discussed presentation to the 1915 National Conference. Flexner defined professions as lines of work that "involve essentially intellectual operations with large individual responsibility; they derive their raw material from science and learning; this material they work up to a practical and definite end; they possess an educationally communicable technique; they tend to self-organization; they are becoming increasingly altruistic in motivation."[28] Flexner thought that social workers did not rise above the professional bar in three areas: they did not hold final responsibility for their subjects' well-being, but served more as mediators; they lacked an extensive body of scholarly literature to communicate their techniques; and their work lacked a "practical and definite end." Flexner conceded social work's learned and scientific intellectual foundation, but with only a perfunctory acknowledgment that their material "comes obviously from science."[29]

In their effort to buoy their professional credentials, the leaders of scientific charity, now social work, once more stressed their use of scientific concepts to analyze the conditions of the poor. First biological degeneration, then sociology and economics, now they incorporated a psychological analysis of poverty that stressed the "whole man," an individual's degree of adjustment to his surroundings. Psychologists and psychiatrists, for their part, eagerly peddled their expertise to the renamed NCSW, insisting that "the one science that has the most to contribute, now or ultimately, to social case work is unquestionably the

science of the mind."[30] The concept of individual psychological adjustment promoted by the first social workers has had profound implications in the history of twentieth- and twenty-first-century American attitudes toward poverty. It returned more of the onus for poverty back to
the poor than at any time since the 1893 depression, while social workers distanced themselves from the increasingly radical demands for
social change voiced by some of their associates at the National Conference. Similar to how the threat of social disorganization and labor
violence in the 1870s and again in the 1890s motivated scientific charity
work, in the 1910s social workers also framed their work as a way to de-
fuse revolutionary complaints. Social workers needed to keep at arm's
length the radicals comingling with the scientific charity movement if
they hoped to win professional respectability—a matter complicated
by former NCCC president Jane Addams's unpopular denunciation of
World War I—and the staid language of individual psychological adjustment threw a rhetorical wet blanket on the fiery radical contingent at the
NCSW. At the same time, however, social workers continued to deny the
inherent depravity, hopelessness, and otherness of the poor, as well as a
hereditary disposition toward pauperism. Their analysis suggested that
almost all of the poor suffered the same problems as anyone else, only in
larger degrees, and therefore were "potentially normal."

No one provided such essential guidance in charting this course as
Mary Richmond. From the general secretary of Baltimore's COS, Richmond emerged as the linchpin figure advising friendly visitors and social caseworkers on professional methods. Her *Friendly Visiting amongst
the Poor,* first published in 1899 as an extension of the lectures she gave to
Baltimore COS friendly visitors in an evening training course, defined
the parameters of individual casework with the poor. In 1917 as the director of the Russell Sage Foundation's Charity Organization Department, she authored *Social Diagnosis,* which attempted to define the very
field and intellectual foundations of professional social work.[31] Her biographer described Richmond's approach as one seeking to synthesize
the Victorian concern for the moral health of the family, the Christian
exhortation to befriend the poor, and social scientific, bureaucratic, and
medical models for organizing charity into an analysis that would "forge
a middle ground between the stark individualism of laissez-faire capi-

talism and the impersonal bureaucracy of state socialism."[32] She similarly endeavored to balance the need for greater training among friendly visitors with the dangers she identified in handing their work over to university-educated professional social workers, who would not be able to renew interclass social bonds the way a volunteer visitor could. Richmond envisioned *Friendly Visiting* and *Social Diagnosis* as correctives to the overdeveloped concern for social and economic factors of poverty at the expense of recognizing individual responsibility and as foundational training manuals that would set social work on an empirical, data-driven foundation, confer to it professional recognition, and yet preserve the importance of the volunteer visitor.

In *Friendly Visiting* Richmond also rebuked the environmental analysis of scientific charity preferred by movement leaders from the late 1890s. She observed that charity and social workers "often exaggerate the causes of poverty that are external to the individual. Bad industrial conditions and defective legislation seem to them the causes of nearly all the distress around them." Settlement workers in particular were liable to absolve the poor from any responsibility for their condition. Richmond cautioned friendly visitors to avoid being "swept away by enthusiastic advocates of social reform" and to remain instead in the "safe middle ground which recognizes that character is at the very centre of this complicated problem."[33] Strengthening the family's character must rest at the center of the visitor's work. She recommended that visitors distribute relief only through the head of the household, so as to keep pauper men from winning relief through their wives or children, and to emphasize cleanliness and domestic skills for the mother and thrift for everyone. While Richmond claimed to use a balanced approach that included economic and social factors in her advice to visitors, her references to parasitism when describing the pauper poor suggested a more circumscribed view of poverty's social causes.[34]

Social Diagnosis further stressed the importance of a balanced approach, tilting neither too far in favor of those current figures who looked at the poor as helpless victims of social forces, nor toward the penurious COS investigators of the 1880s who had looked at the poor as a completely rational and free "economic man." They "looked to the repression of unnecessary demands upon public bounty," she explained, "rather

than to the release of energy, the regenerating of character, or the mul-
tiplication of health opportunities, opportunities for training, and the
like."[35] By attending to the medical, biological, psychological, and moral
condition of the individual as she advocated in *Social Diagnosis,* Richmond claimed that a social worker would be treating the "whole man"
without stumbling toward unnecessary radicalism.

Her critics, however, argued that *Social Diagnosis* was a misnomer; a
more proper title would have been *Individual Diagnosis,* since she made
no pretense to identifying the ills of society, just the ills of the psyche.[36]
To Richmond, "social" referred to the broad idea that "wherever there
are two individuals instead of one, human association or society begins."[37] The methodology and format of *Social Diagnosis* similarly indicated Richmond's focus on the individual. Richmond compiled letters,
questionnaires, and case records sent in from social caseworkers and
friendly visitors across America that she believed represented the best
and most instructive examples of investigation into the ailments of the
poor. With grand aspirations she hoped that caseworkers would come to
accept social diagnosis and make it the basis of their work, thereby adding to the professional literature that practitioners shared in common
and that Flexner had claimed social work lacked. Yet Richmond cautioned against any leaps of induction from the examples given, warning, "For the most part the subject of social diagnosis defies statistical
treatment."[38] The rejection of statistics is a striking demonstration of
just how far the understanding of science had moved from the first days
of scientific charity, when science essentially meant counting individuals in hopes of finding patterns that might be designated laws of society.
By the 1890s, however, the work of Karl Pearson in England had steadily
driven statistical analysis in a direction that ultimately would "remove
serious statistical discussion from the hands of the 'dilettanti' and . . .
place it in the hands of the trained mathematical statistician."[39] *Social
Diagnosis* instead taught social caseworkers the art of how to conduct
interviews and weigh different sorts of evidence in order to make a diagnosis that reflected the unique circumstances of an individual person or
family.

Using Richmond's work as a primer, social workers returned in the
1910s to an analysis of poverty that gave greater priority to individual re-

sponsibility than to social and economic causes. They did so not by revisiting arguments over degeneration and moral failure but by incorporating a psychological and psychiatric analysis of character. In one vivid example of the new union of psychology and the ethos of personal responsibility, Porter Lee of the New York School of Philanthropy spoke to the NCSW on the psychological component of dependence. Lee stressed the importance of how the poor responded when faced with the painful self-awareness of their own limitations and failures. Whether a man recovered or sank into a life of dependence, suggested Lee, depended on his psychological response.[40]

In making the poor's failure to adjust to their environment the chief cause of poverty, social workers distinguished between the poor and "normal" society while granting an almost unbounded opportunity for the poor to return to the flock. The poor were abnormal yet also potentially normal. In her paper to the 1918 NCSW, Angie Kellogg of Bryn Mawr College observed that social workers had grown skeptical of the concept of a "normal family," which smacked of a "dogmatic, mechanical interpretation and treatment" of poverty.[41] Yet in spite of the concept's flaws, Kellogg felt compelled to continue treating poor families in reference to the ideal of normalcy. Since social work aimed to be a diagnostic science with normative standards, and since social workers admittedly came upon a case only because of some implicit recognition of the person's abnormal conditions, the concept of normalcy still had use. The social worker dealt with the "educable, or potentially normal" family exclusively, said Kellogg, but she defined normalcy so that it cut the broadest possible swath through humanity. A "typical situation" that a social worker might find, explained Kellogg, was "a family of good stock in which, however, exist poverty and contentious domestic relations, physical deformity, adolescent instability, truancy and delinquency, defective speech and school room dullness in the children, inebriety in the father, shiftlessness, querulousness, and ill health in the mother, a tangle of unorganized and disorganized instinctive, habitual, and emotional behaviors."

The first standard, good stock, might suggest a biological distinction between two types of poor people, but Kellogg meant the term as a more general reference to any person who did not exhibit mental deficiency. The other criteria show how much more inclusive the category of the normal poor had become. A generation earlier, physical deformity, speech defects, poor academic achievement, alcoholism, shiftlessness, and querulousness all had been signs of or euphemisms for pauperism.

For Kellogg and the new social workers, shiftlessness and the other pathologies once associated with pauperism became mere temporary ailments. "If the family is potentially normal," she said, "the tangle can be smoothed out." Just as physical flaws that caused impairment could be corrected—like removing adenoids and swollen tonsils that caused the speech defect or straightening out the deformed leg—so too could psychological defects like intemperance, delinquency, and dependence be fixed. She insisted the task was a "comparatively simple" matter of teaching new habits to the poor.

> [T]he father must dissociate the experiences he has had which have become identified for him with a desire for drink—such as the hunger he feels because of an unbalanced diet, the discontent he feels because of the querulousness of his wife and children, the shiftlessness and emptiness of his home, his lack of recreation, the community and school complaints against the truancy, the dullness, and the delinquencies of his children. His wife must unlearn the irritabilities and shiftlessness she has acquired through worry and deprivation. The children must unlearn their animosities and fighting which have developed because they have been ridiculed for their defects and deformities and because they have been scolded and blamed by their teachers for inattention and dullness attendant inevitably upon their physical defects. New habits . . . must be learned; the old stimuli and emotions . . . must be attached to new objects.

Psychology could inculcate those new habits. It offered "scientific simplicity and power to control" one's environment."[42] Even better, Kellogg hoped it would give social workers the same professional status that physicians enjoyed.

A Residuum? Social Work, Psychiatry, and Eugenics

Defining their area of concern as the rehabilitation of the potentially normal let social workers put professional distance between their work and that of the eugenicists, while shrewdly conceding that there also existed hopelessly abnormal persons whom they could not pull out of poverty. Their indigence could be explained as a secondary effect of feeblemindedness, insanity, or criminality, areas requiring an exper-

tise outside of social work's purview. The founders of professional social work have been described as "accepting the inevitability of urban,
industrial society and the fragmentation of social roles that it produced"
and, therefore, unlike an earlier generation, "they no longer felt the need
to preserve Victorian values by punishing those who seemed to deviate
most from them."[43] This put the first professional social workers in the
enviable position of offering an optimistic vision of human improvement that required their specialized knowledge and practice, without
challenging the eugenic assumptions found in the social sciences. It also
allowed scientific charity members to explain away their failure to end
chronic poverty in spite of having first implemented their highly restrictive relief policies, then later their far more liberal approach. Perhaps neither approach could end the poverty of a certified "moron," but the moron was not their primary concern.

No matter how broadly they defined the potentially normal, the social workers did not doubt that a residuum of hopelessly abnormal persons remained in their midst, people who could never be brought from
poverty to self-sufficiency. The fact that social workers continued treating some portion of the poor as beyond rehabilitation might seem to suggest that they simply relabeled the hereditary pauper and continued to
treat the poor as two different sorts, with the permanently abnormally
poor perhaps still being subject to eugenic solutions as the pauper once
had been. For instance, some argued that large numbers of the poor were
abnormal due to psychiatric illness, feeblemindedness, or insanity. Mary
Jarrett, associate director of the Smith College Training School for Social Work, claimed that half of all cases cited by Richmond in *Social Diagnosis* indicated a psychopathic condition, and she thought that ratio
held more or less true for the applicants visiting the Boston-area charities. Jarrett did not, however, use these statistics as a platform for issuing
moral condemnations and warnings of hereditary catastrophe. Psychiatry instead gave the social worker a greater respect for "the high spots in
even the most unsuccessful individual" while supposedly claiming scientific charity's holy grail: methodical and scientific investigation that
did not ossify into impersonal or mechanical treatment.[44]

Just as useful if less explicitly stated, a psychological analysis of the
poor and their distance from normalcy also let social workers admit
that some poor suffered from problems beyond their reach. Responsi-

bility for treating the hardened group of feebleminded poor belonged exclusively to the psychiatrists who, with their mental tests, would identify the feebleminded and take appropriate eugenic action.[45] With this division of labor, social workers could present a program for correcting most social ills without recourse to eugenics but also without challenging the authority of psychiatrists and without sounding like the political radicals associated with the National Conference. Dr. E. E. Southard, director of the Psychopathic Department of Boston State Hospital, graphically illustrated poverty's place within a eugenic world. Southard constructed an organizational chart of social problems covered by eugenics, those under the domain of "euthenics," or the arts and sciences that sought social improvement through the environment, and "demotherapy," or preventative medicine. Charities and unemployment both fell exclusively under the euthenic category, while the feebleminded and insane belonged to demotherapy and eugenics.[46]

Eugenicists themselves noted with annoyance the social workers' resistance to eugenics. Maurice Parmelee, a professor of sociology at Kansas State University, complained to the NCSW that charity or social workers stuck with theories of heredity that were "now very generally discredited by most biologists," referring to Lamarckian theories of the inheritance of acquired characteristics. The thought that a parent might transmit to its offspring attributes that the parent acquired in response to a changed environment gave them a false hope of solving social problems quickly and with relative ease, Parmelee complained. It made alleviating hereditary vices as simple as improving the surrounding environment.[47] Although he overstated the divergence between charity workers' thinking and that of biologists, Parmelee's remarks point to a growing estrangement.

The sharpest indication of that divergence was found in the committee on sex hygiene, which the National Conference added in 1912; it featured addresses from prominent eugenicists Robert Yerkes and Charles Davenport and several reports on intelligence testing. While this committee strongly favored eugenic solutions for the feebleminded and other psychiatrically suspect groups, the participants in the committee and the topics discussed did not resemble the composition or discourse of the larger conference. The best illustration of their isolation within the

conference came from the wildly inaccurate description of the principles
of scientific charity offered by Davenport. The head of the Cold Spring
Harbor Center for Experimental Evolution, the institutional center of
American eugenics research, Davenport made several ill-informed claims
about scientific charity's study of the pauper, which he claimed to have
learned through the work of a COS of "a great city," presumably New
York City. Davenport claimed that scientific charity based its work on
the fact "that the poor are of two sorts which are unlike to start with and
are without the same capacity for achieving equality—these sorts are
the undeserving poor and the deserving poor. The first class cannot be
made good social units by the gift of money; the second class, it is hoped,
may." He further advised, "Only experts can distinguish between the
classes, so give your alms to the experts and then they will be of use to
bring about the desirability [sic] equality." At the end of his comments,
Proceedings editor Alexander Johnson added an asterisk, unique in the
publication's history. Fifteen years earlier, Johnson had given the pro-
eugenic presidential address "Mother-State and Her Weaker Children."
He now noted that Davenport's comments were "probably the furthest
from an accurate statement of the position of organized charity that has
ever appeared in the *Proceedings* of the National Conference."[48]

Johnson and Davenport's comments illuminate one of the perils faced
by the first social workers in their quest for professionalization. The adoption of a psychological interpretation of poverty that concentrated on individual psychological restoration frustrated the radicals who demanded
sweeping social reform and befuddled the eugenicists who espoused a
biological analysis of deviance. Ironically, the psychological, individualized approach that so annoyed the radicals and the eugenicists also
failed to satisfy critics who thought the new casework departed too far
from the traditional bonds of charity and had instead devolved into bu-
reaucratized relief. Perhaps no single concern carried through from the
founding of scientific charity into the transition to social work as the
fear that organized charity could not simultaneously rationalize charitable relief while restoring traditional bonds of obligation and compassion between social classes. Warnings of mechanized charity abounded
throughout the history of scientific charity, and critics of social work argued that in spite of social workers' best efforts, they had failed to keep

sight of the individual. The Reverend Francis Gavisk of Indianapolis, an old veteran of the scientific charity movement, warned in his presidential address to the 1916 conference that recent trends threatened to make social work a "passionless intellectuality" and a "frigid officialism." He warned, "To lose human sympathy, which is the very essence of charity, "would be to quench the vital spark of a heavenly flame."[49]

Once the movement's greatest source of pride, a quantitative approach to poverty now became one of the greatest threats to individualized treatment. Richmond's skepticism toward quantification was more significant, but one of the most unusual protests against the statistical method came from a woman with one of the most unusual names, Viola Paradise. By the time she addressed the NCSW in 1923, volunteer scientific charity had been dispersed almost entirely into professional social work, settlement house work, and federal programs like the Children's Bureau. Paradise, formerly of the bureau, spoke to the conference about child labor and the effect of statistics on the public. She began by citing census data on child labor, such as the 1,060,858 working children between ages ten and fifteen. Since it was impossible to truly know or comprehend the aggregate, Paradise explained that smaller investigations were made of groups like coal miners, beet-field laborers, and oyster shuckers. By contriving an artificial picture of the hard life of an oyster shucker from the lives of maybe 500 or 5,000 shuckers investigated, such studies ought to be enough to rouse the nation to collective action. But sadly this was not so; Paradise accused the national imagination of being "too callous" and "blind-hearted" for action. People no longer could see "the people behind the statistics," and they learned more from large figures than from individuals.[50] To illustrate this point, Paradise read a poem composed by a fellow government agent, Helen Wilson:

> Little black figures in rows,
> Little crooked black figures,
> Numberless columns
> To add,
> To distribute into little square spaces.
> Strutting black insects,
> Imposters,
> Who juggle our tragedies.
> "Vital statistics"

Marriages,
Babies dead,
Broken lives,
Men gone mad,
Labor and crime,
All treated in bulk, with the tears wiped off.
Numbered.

Paradise hoped to shake Americans out of their ennui, to make the fact
of child labor a matter for sensational newspaper headlines, not an acceptable part of life. Numbers could not do the task; they turned human
misery into an abstraction.[51] The "bludgeon" of numbers might be accumulated to inspire action, but in reality statistics only "stupefy" the
public.

Scientific Charity's Legacy

Scientific charity began as an ambitious, sweeping program conducted
by private voluntary groups for investigating, identifying, explaining,
and eliminating poverty and pauperism, uniting all charitable and public
relief in a coordinated program transcending old ethnic and denominational lines, and rebuilding personal bonds across social classes. A posi-
tivist faith in the progress of science and its application to all facets of social life held these ambitions together in a seemingly coherent agenda, so
long as one did not inquire too deeply into the potential contradictions.
Paradise's remarks exemplified the simultaneous disintegration of that
faith in science and the splintering of scientific charity reformers into
compartmentalized subgroups. As scientific charity at once fractured
and professionalized, social radicals, moderate reformers, government
agencies, and social workers each co-opted some element of the movement's methods and agenda in their diverse approaches to poverty. The
U.S. Census and academic sociology departments took over the charity
organization societies' work in social surveying. Social workers inherited the mission of the friendly visitors. Radicals pursued systematic social transformation. Eugenicists took up the business of explaining dependence through biology.

　While assessing the institutional and professional legacies of the scientific charity movement is a relatively straightforward affair, coming
to terms with its social and intellectual impact is complicated by the

constantly evolving attitudes of the leaders. Introduced to the United States in 1877, the movement's leadership endured the changing intellectual, social, cultural, and economic landscapes with enough dexterity to claim great influence in both the Gilded Age and the Progressive Era. In a sense the movement lived long enough for its leaders to reject most of their initial premises and in some cases even long enough to return to them once more.

In the Gilded Age, scientific charity's leaders sought organizational and intellectual coherence for one of the largest and most geographically diffuse nominally secular movements Americans had yet seen. The broad appeal of the movement came from several sources. The movement's leaders expressed the postbellum American optimism of the intelligentsia that they could soon discover simple, scientific laws governing the causes and remediation of deviance and suffering, transforming fallen individuals and the nation. This enthusiasm was readily applied to issues of public trepidation and discontent: the perceived menace of the paupers and roving tramps, representative of larger fears of violent class-based social conflict, and inefficient, often corrupt public outdoor relief and private charity. Finally, the social gospel movement produced talented, young, progressive Protestant ministers like Oscar McCulloch who were dedicated to addressing matters of social reform, while the state boards of charity and U.S. Sanitary Commission provided experienced administrators. Scientific charity reformers of the Gilded Age certainly worked to identify and suppress pauperism through investigation, supervision, and promotion of restrictive relief policies. However, due to the discordant trends that informed scientific charity, the movement never quite matched in practice the dogmatic, repressive uniformity articulated in its leaders' official pronouncements.

The scientific charity leaders' evolving views on the worthiness of the poor, their rejection of the pauper category, and support of public relief near the turn of the century cannot be explained exclusively by reference to their scientific predilections, but neither can those developments be understood without them. Their commitment to a scientifically informed investigation into the nature of poverty outlasted nearly every other stated principle, save the insistence that assisting the poor must be mediated through personal connections and individualized treatment. The devil lay in the details of determining what was properly scientific. From 1877 to about 1895, science amounted to an enthusiasm for counting, classification, Darwinism, and degeneration. The poor might neatly be divided into the worthy and unworthy based on an objective scrutinizing of their circumstances that illuminated the want of the modest widow, who did not call attention to her suffering, while seeing through the lies of the huckstering beggar. Laziness, alcoholism, dirtiness, any nonconformist sexual or economic habits—all indicated degenerate pauperism, a condition that could be traced by genealogical studies inspired by the work of Francis Galton. Giving causal explanations of poverty was a relatively simple endeavor of drawing a straight line from a single cause of misfortune or misbehavior to its effect.

By 1898 at the latest, many of these same advocates of scientific charity organization such as McCulloch and Lowell, reinforced by new leaders like Devine, reconsidered the reality of pauperism and the tenability of restrictive relief policies based on distinguishing between the moral and biological fitness of different relief applicants. They came to reject an analysis of poverty and pauperism based solely or even primarily on idiosyncratic instances of bad character or bad luck, in favor of viewing pauperism as a causally more complex problem of biological and environmental conditions informed not just by biology and statistical case-counting, but also by public health, economics, and sociology. These changes in scientific charity reformers' views of pauperism and poverty were motivated by the data compiled by individual COSs investigating and relieving the poor and sent in to the NCCC for commentary, which then motivated changes in local practices of relief. Into the NCCC went Oscar McCulloch's Tribe of Ishmael, surveys on the charitable practices of dozens of COSs, volumes of investigative data from the COSs, especially those from Boston, New York, and Baltimore, as well as results from surveys of poorhouses, asylums, and hospitals. From the NCCC back to the COSs went recommended statistical blanks by which to evaluate causes of poverty, templates for training courses by which to improve friendly visiting and investigation, knowledge of broader trends in the liberalization or restriction of relief giving, and endorsement from sociologists, economists, statisticians, biologists, and psychologists that their work was part of a larger process by which scientific knowledge would usher in social improvement.

In an ironic consequence of scientific charity members' enthusiasm for science, through their investigations the leaders came to reject the optimistic predictions that their work would unearth universal laws governing the creation and eradication of pauperism and poverty. Their work instead raised several unsettling questions for the leaders about the foundational assumptions of their movement. If pauperism was a biological failing instead of a moral one, in what sense could the paupers be held accountable for their state? What good could come of befriend-ing the poor and teaching them the virtue of thrift when poverty origi-nated in the economic and social organization of American life? Was good advice and private charitable assistance enough to lift people out of poverty? Even if scientific laws of poverty were found, the hope that they would usher in sweeping social reforms as they had once hoped grew equally dim. Events of the early twentieth century left the movement a long way from the first pronouncements that scientific charity should rest on local knowledge of the poor and a sense of personal obligations connecting the giver and recipient of charity. Similarly, it is reasonable to imagine that the figures with the greatest faith in science's ability to produce systemic social laws and therefore act as an engine to social re-form likely would have been dismayed to see social workers abandon the pursuit of generalized laws of dependence.

While charity and social workers' adoption of psychology as the dis-cipline of choice in the 1910s promised a return to individualized treat-ment and supposedly sympathetic understanding of poor people, it also returned almost complete culpability to the poor for their circumstances and treated poverty, once again, as an atomistic collection of unique cases that defied much broader generalization or statistical analysis. Al-though they no longer categorized individuals as belonging to the ranks of either the worthy poor or the unworthy pauper, social workers used "maladjustment" for the similar purpose of evaluating the extent of indi-viduals' responsibility for their state. Social workers took what once had been labeled poverty due to hereditary pauperism and repackaged it as poverty due to psychiatric conditions. Each winnowed out a subpopulation of the poor as beyond the normal, acceptable range of social behavior and explained away the behavior as due to unique biological or medical circumstances that did not threaten normal persons. In so doing, poverty once more became primarily a matter of individual reformation, a problem that was almost but not quite worthy of coordinated social reform.

EPILOGUE

When asked what my historical study of scientific charity organizers and their struggle to end poverty can teach us about the problem of poverty today, I prefer to demur. My reluctance to connect the dots between past and present tends to disappoint those undergraduate students who begin each semester by eagerly telling me that the value of studying history is that it teaches us lessons to help us avoid the mistakes of the past. Almost as frequently, they tell me that history shows us the stepping-stones to the present, generally with the unstated assumptions that everything was a stepping-stone and that the present is a very good thing. But when I think about how proponents of scientific charity organization pursued the incredibly difficult challenges of understanding and ending poverty and chronic dependence, I find myself wondering if we learned any lessons from their mistakes—or even what the lessons were that we ought to have learned. While I see places where scientific charity helped to pave the way to our current thinking about poverty, I am more impressed by the number of dead ends and doubtful that the stepping-stones did in fact lead anywhere good.

The more idealistic of the scientific charity organization enthusiasts, who so confidently predicted the discovery of iron laws governing dependence and the right methods for ending want, seem not just naïve but alien. I struggle to fathom their confidence and optimism. Instead, I am more impressed by observations I regularly heard from my dissertation advisor, Victor Hilts: that the social sciences have been more notable for their scientific failures than successes, that the most notable theories have been as much a reflection of personal philosophy as of scientific content, and that purportedly scientific laws governing human behavior, therefore, tend to have a much shorter shelf life than other scientific laws. The history of scientific charity reformers' efforts to solve the poverty problem, I think, validates this skepticism. The poor are still with us; the scientific charity organizers are not. No doubt the last forty years of scientific investigation have yielded far more objective, useful, sophisticated knowledge of the complex weave of factors that cause and perpetuate poverty, keeping even the most worthy and best-intentioned of souls in abject want. We similarly better understand what sorts of policies are more or less effective in helping people out of poverty and keeping them out. Historians of social welfare have documented a seemingly endless series of well-intentioned mistakes made in the past that, if my earnestly hopeful students are correct, ought to help us in the present. But as a depressingly steady stream of events suggest—Hurricane Katrina, the Great Recession, childhood poverty rates approaching 25 percent—we have failed to translate much improved knowledge of poverty, its causes and relief, into much improved results. Wedding knowledge to action and getting the desired results has turned out to be a more difficult task than the Oscar McCullochs of the world imagined.

I, therefore, am reluctant to judge the scientific charity enthusiasts too harshly. It turns out that effectively studying and relieving poverty in a compassionate manner that respects the dignity of the relieved and the democratic institutions of American society is difficult work. Of course, I feel moral revulsion at their authoritarian, eugenic worldview that saw a certain type of poor people as subhuman parasites: instead of seeing parasites, I am inclined to see anyone who is suffering as worthy of relief. As a matter of both moral philosophy and good policy, I am unimpressed by their opposition to pensions and just about every other form of what we now refer to as welfare. Yet in spite of my sharp personal disagreements and disappointments with key elements of their ideology, my analysis of scientific charity presented in *Almost Worthy* is among the more charitable interpretations of the movement.

This is especially true of my view of the Reverend Oscar McCulloch. The most personally compelling, intellectually demanding, and longest running challenge in my study of scientific charity has been making sense of McCulloch. The Tribe of Ishmael is a nasty document. It expresses a view of poverty and dependence that advocates of eugenic sterilization of the "unfit" saw as validation for their work. In ways McCulloch never could have appreciated, we can now appreciate the horrific similarities between his rhetoric about armies of parasites and the eliminationist rhetoric characteristic of genocide. But I cannot judge the man or his historical legacy with reference only to this one statement. Instead of indicting McCulloch for publishing bad research in 1888 that echoed the logic behind the first sterilization laws in 1907, I would rather understand how, in the course of three years, one man could write both some of the vilest statements I have ever read about humanity and some of the most uplifting. Other than its presentation to the 1888 NCCC, there is scant evidence to suggest that McCulloch spent much time thinking about the Tribe of Ishmael after 1881. In the mid-1880s he was more inclined to defend socialists, anarchists, and (alleged) terrorists, absolving them of their acts because of their poverty, than to convict people for their poverty. It is difficult not to read his final remarks on poverty in *The Open Door* and "The True Spirit of Charity Organization" as deathbed recantations of the Tribe of Ishmael. They contain passages concerning our obligations for each other's well-being that can move me to tears. McCulloch went from seeing "armies of vice" amid the poor to declaring that no such army existed. How could this be? When I look at McCulloch, I do not see an intellectual godfather to eugenic sterilizations. I see a thoughtful man who spent his adult life struggling to reconcile his personal prejudices toward a subsection of the poor with his idealized notion of what the humanity could be and his earnest conviction that Christian theology and scientific principles could be synthesized and ought to be applied to individual and social uplift. We should not be surprised that a complex man tackling a complex problem was subject to relatively sudden and dramatic changes in his thinking about the poverty problem. The same might be said of scientific charity reformers as a collective.

If some readers feel that I have been overly sympathetic to McCulloch, others are liable to view *Almost Worthy* as too uniformly sympathetic to the poor who found themselves caught up in the scientific charity investigations. Big Moll, the reportedly foul-mouthed, hot-headed, simple-minded, syphilitic woman who may also have been responsible for the death of one of her children, probably was an unpleasant woman, the sort who easily could serve as the disturbing face of a failing system of social welfare. For all the examples of middle-class prejudice and ignorance of the structural causes of poverty, the investigative records of the Indianapolis Charity Organization Society similarly document cases of poverty that clearly were due to the moral failings of the individual, not the society. Yet whatever their shortcomings, I am more inclined to empathize with them than to blame them for their circumstances. Moll seems to have received a raw deal. We struggle today to imagine the conditions of her existence in institutions like the Marion County Poorhouse. She was utterly forgotten by society, with no one aware of the abuse and degradation that she suffered or what she may also have inflicted on others, until her miserable life was presented to the public as a spectacle. I am left wondering about Moll's fate after the trial. In the moments when I doubted my capacity to see *Almost Worthy* through to completion, my need to bring her life back to the public's attention compelled me to keep writing.

My original project was to study changes in American views of pauperism by examining McCulloch's life, the interplay of ideas between local charity societies and national institutions and spokespersons for reform, and the consequences visited upon the poor. While I always appreciated the importance of the friendly visitors in this nexus, understanding their experiences has been more elusive. Did these charitable volunteers see themselves as taking part in some larger project to study and eradicate pauperism? Did they spend their days fretting over precise observations, the interplay of heredity and environment, and the construction of social scientific laws of dependence and relief? Somehow I doubt it. At least before the 1900s, the average visitor's experience with scientific charity organization is even more difficult to flesh out than the experience of the average charity applicant. But once more my inclination is to view her sympathetically. The clues suggest a woman who meant well, genuinely wished to befriend and aid the worthy poor, earnestly thought that she could offer the necessary moral uplift, and was hopelessly unprepared for the moment when she encountered the grim reality of poverty. For her efforts she often was repaid with resentment from the poor and scorn from charity organization executives. I wish I could follow her experience as closely as I have McCulloch's or Moll's.

But again, I have skirted the opportunity to suggest what a decade of studying Oscar McCulloch, Big Moll, the friendly visitors, or the arc of scientific charity in general might tell us about our relationship with poverty today, beyond the trite reminder that life is complex and therefore we should be slow to judge another's actions too harshly. Walking further out on the limb, I am struck by how the impulse to judge the poor primarily by standards of moral worth—and typically, to judge them harshly—endures, while interest in placing individuals within broader patterns in dependence, let alone identifying structural causes of poverty, wanes. In reality television shows that often feature lower-income participants, such as *Big Brother, Extreme Home Makeover, Undercover Boss,* and *American Idol,* we continue to prefer narratives that would appeal to scientific charity advocates. Such shows and countless human-interest news segments demonstrate our desire to see the triumphs of humble and self-effacing people who are unassuming about the hardships they have faced. We especially prefer that their hardships be of the medical, childhood trauma, and natural disaster varieties. Recent bills proposed in state legislatures that applicants for food stamps first pass drug tests, Republican presidential candidate Newt Gingrich's suggestion that poor children learn the value of hard work by serving as assistant custodians in their schools, the controversy around health insurance reform, and the Tea Party movement similarly grew at least in part out of beliefs characteristic of the scientific charity movement: that financial assistance to those in need must be predicated first on a determination of individual worth, and that government assistance tends as often as not to go to the unworthy.

Finally, I wonder if the demise of the scientific charity movement might address a far larger issue concerning the cultural authority of science in America. Scientific charity organizers' rush to claim the authority of science as the preferred means of accomplishing moral, social, and political reform also seems alien to us today. Contemporary public skepticism toward matters that scientists considered settled long ago, ranging from evolution to global warming to the safety and efficacy of vaccines, suggests that Americans have only a piecemeal, limited interest in accepting and adopting a scientific worldview. Too often, those who are more enthusiastic about such a worldview, myself included, rush to criticize the scientific illiteracy or indifference of others. We might, instead, seek to understand the idiosyncratic ways in which Americans filter and apply popular scientific findings to their lives. The history of scientific charity ably demonstrates this phenomenon. For all their rhetoric and actual application of science, I envision scientific charity enthusiasts as having reviewed a broad menu of scientific, religious, ethical, and political beliefs, from which they selected à la carte options they intuitively suspected might complement each other and be amenable to their unique palettes. If this crude analogy resembles the process by which people integrate science into their lives, we might be less surprised at its limited influence and uneasy cohabitation with prescientific and ascientific attitudes, whether toward evolution or medicine or poverty.

APPENDIX 1.

Course Syllabus, Alexander Johnson: Study Class in Social Science in the Department of Charity

LESSON I NOVEMBER 3, 1890 • THEORIES AND DEFINITIONS

- Is there a Social Science, or Sociology? (*Cf. Spencer, "The Study of Sociology," especially Chapter 2.*) Can we hope for a department of "*Philanthropics*"? (*Cf. Warner, "Charities."*) (*Johns Hopkins Series of Studies, pp. 1, 2.*)
- Science and Common Knowledge. (*Cf. Spencer, "First Principles," sections 5 and 37.*)
- The Scientific Method—Induction—Deduction—Verification. (*Cf. Huxley, "Introductory Science Primer," section 11.*)
- Scientific Terminology—Progress of a science as indicated by the copiousness and accuracy of its terms—Inexactness of terms of Sociology.
- Theory of Definitions—Difficulty of Definitions of Social Science.
- Definitions of Charity. (*Cf. 1 Cor. XIII; Acts of 43rd Elizabeth, Chap. 4; List of Sections of National Conference of Charities; Publications of London C.O.S. [Poor Law v. Charity] Modern Usage.*)
- Charity as a Generic Term—Definition for use of present Study.

LESSON II NOVEMBER 17, 1890 • ETHICS AND ECONOMICS

- The Economists v. the Philanthropists—Their Conflict in England—Poor Law and Factory Legislation—Self-Interest v. Self-Sacrifice—Laissez-Faire. (*Cf. Carlyle, "Past and Present"; also Adam Smith and other English Economists.*)
- Charity and the Evolution Philosophy—Progress of the Race by the Survival of the Fittest.

- The Ethical Basis of Charity—Development of the Emotions—Altruism. (*Cf. Spencer, "The Data of Ethics," Chaps. XIII and XIV.*)
- The Higher Economics—Is Life Worth Living?

LESSON III DECEMBER 1, 1890 • POVERTY AND PAUPERISM

- Poverty Relative and Absolute—Savage, Barbarian, and Civilized Life— Relative Poverty a Condition of Progress.
- Causes of Poverty. (*Cf. Warner, "Charities," also "Notes on Statistical Determination of the Causes of Poverty," published by Am. Stat. Asso., Boston, 1889.*)
- Poverty and Pauperism. (*Cf. Hale, in Lend a Hand no. 1; Reports on Pauperism in Proceedings of National Conference.*)
- Causes of Pauperism—Heredity. (*Cf. Dugdale, "The Jukes"; McCulloch, "The Tribe of Ishmael."*) Habits—Conditions—Unwise Philanthropy. (*Cf. Bunce, "A Millionaire's Millions."*) Law of Direction of Motion. (*Cf. Spencer, "First Principles," Chapter IX, especially Section 10.*)
- The Law of the Individual—A Deduction.

LESSON IV DECEMBER 15, 1890 • SUBJECTS, AGENTS, MOTIVES, ENDS

- Division of Charity as to its Subjects—Classification of Dependents— Permanent, Temporary, Casual.
- Division of Charity as to its Agents—Public (The State, the County, the Municipality); Quasi-Public (Voluntary Associations and Institutions, Churches); Private (Individual Benevolence).
- Division of Charity as to its Motives—Mutual Assurance Against Destitution—Protection of Society—Sympathy with Suffering—Social Distinction, or Worldliness—Reward in a Future State, or Other Worldliness—Mixed Motives.
- Division of Charity as to its Ends—Prevention, mainly Educative. (*Cf. Reports of Children's Aid Societies, New York and others; The Waif, June, 1889. Reports of Kindergarten Societies, especially those of San Francisco and Indianapolis, etc.*) Relief, Reformatories, Protection, Betterment of Life.
- The Fourth Step in Charity, is it the Last?

LESSON V JANUARY 12, 1891 • PUBLIC CHARITY NO. 1—THE STATE

- Public Servants v. Politicians—State Institutions as Business Enterprises.
- Care of the Insane—Hospitals or Asylums?—State Hospitals in Indiana— The Wisconsin system.

- Care of the Defective Classes—(Blind, Deaf-Mute, Feeble-Minded). Education or Charity?
- Reform Schools—Penal, Charitable, or Educational?
- State Homes for Dependent Children—Home Life v. Institution Life. (This subject will be more fully treated in Lesson 7 on County Orphans' Homes.)
- Preparatory to Lesson V, the class will visit the Central Hospital for the Insane on Saturday, Jan 3. Particulars of the trip will be announced. Students are requested to visit the other State Institutions in Indianapolis.

LESSON VI JANUARY 26, 1891 • PUBLIC CHARITY NO. 2—THE COUNTY

- Historical Development of Legal Poor-Relief—The English Poor Laws— In-Door Relief and Out-Door Relief—The "House Test."
- County Poor Asylums. (*Cf. "County Poor Asylums," appendix to Report of Board of State Charities of Indiana.*)
- Out-Door Relief—the Overseers of the Poor—the Brooklyn Experiment— Center Township, Marion county, 1876—The English Poor Law Commission of 1832.
- The Labor Test—Relief by Employment—How it Works in France.
- Preparatory to this lesson the class will visit the Marion County Poor Asylum. Particulars will be announced.

LESSON VII FEBRUARY 9, 1891 • PUBLIC CHARITY NO. 3—THE COUNTY (CONTINUED)

- Dependent Children—Home Life v. Institution Life—The Placing Out Plan—"Homes in the West." (*Cf. N.Y. Children's Aid Society Reports, etc.; also Letchworth, "Seventeen Propositions on Child Saving," in The Council for October, 1888*)
- County Orphans' Homes of Indiana. (*Cf. Appendix to Board of State Charities Report.*)
- Partnerships between Public and Voluntary Agencies in care of Dependent Children—Results in New York and California.
- Preparatory to this lesson the class will visit the Indianapolis Orphan Asylum, the German Protestant Orphan Asylum, and the Home for Friendless Colored Children, or as many of them as practicable. Particulars will be announced.

LESSON VIII FEBRUARY 23, 1891 • QUASI-PUBLIC AND PRIVATE CHARITY

- Benevolent Associations and Institutions—Some Effects of Large Relief Societies—Foundlings' Homes and Baby Farms.

- Charities of a Vast City—The "Bitter Cry of Outcast London."
- Effects of Endowment. (Cf. Hobhouse, "The Dead Hand.")
- Private Charities—My Brother's Keeper—Evils of Promiscuous Alms-Giving—Officialism v. Individualism.
- Justice or Charity.
- Preparatory to this lesson, members of the class will visit the City Hospital, the Free Kindergarten, and the rooms of the Indianapolis Benevolent Society and the Flower Mission. Particulars will be announced.

LESSON IX MARCH 9, 1891 • THE CHURCH IN CHARITY

- Value of the Individual—The Classic View and the Christian View.
- The Law and the Gospel—Poor Relief in the Old Testament and the New.
- Early Christian Communism—The First Deacons.
- Medieval Alms—The Convent Gate.
- The Parish System—Dr. Chalmers in Glasgow.
- Charity and XIXth Century Christianity—Our Modern Parish Lines.
- Religious Emotion—Emotion with and without Resultant Action.
- Missions in Large Cities—The "Mission" of To-Day—Possible Mission Stations among City Heathen.

LESSON X MARCH 23, 1891 • ASSOCIATED CHARITIES

- Rise of the Charity Organization Movement. (*Cf. Crooker, "Origin of Scientific Charity" in Lend a Hand for January and February, 1889; "The Elberfeld System," in the Council for June, 1888; Gurteen, "Handbook of Charity Organization."*)
- C.O.S. in the United States. (*Cf. Smith, Charity Organization in the United States," in the Council for September, 1888.*)
- Place of the C.O.S. in the Circle of Charities. (*Cf. "The Year Book of Charities," Indianapolis, 1890.*)
- Business Methods in Charity—The Charity "Clearing House" and "Mercantile Agency."
- Relations of the Churches to C.O.S.
- Personal Charity and the C.O.S. (*Cf. McCulloch, "The Personal Element in Charity," in Proceedings of 12th National Conference, also in pamphlet form; Putnam, "Friendly Visiting," in the Council for March, 1888.*)
- The Charity of the Future.

APPENDIX 2.

Course Syllabus, Mrs. S. E. Tenney:
The Class for Study of the Friendly Visitor's Work

- Session 1: Charity,—definitions, outlines, terminology.
- Session 2: What should I do for one who must have food or fuel or clothing and cannot earn them?
- Session 3: What should I do for a case of sickness?
- Session 4: What should I do for one who is in the distress of poverty, and is able and willing to work? What should I do for one who is in the distress of poverty, and is able, but not willing to work?
- Session 5: What are the objects which I should most endeavor to realize through industrial education and relief in work?
- Session 6: The friendly visitor's special opportunity.
- Session 7 and 8: How can I help to improve the home and home influences?
- Session 9: How can I best apply direct effort to aid the right structure of character?
- Session 10: How can workers in the service of charity best aid each other?
- Session 11: How, and how far, should I discriminate between the worthy and the unworthy?
- Session 12: The recognition of success.

NOTES

1. INTRODUCTION

1. "The County Asylum," *Indianapolis Journal*, 9 June 1881.
2. "Grinding Away," *Indianapolis News*, 8 July 1881.
3. "Dr. Culbertson," *Indianapolis Journal*, 9 July 1881.
4. "The Investigation," *Indianapolis Sentinel*, 14 June 1881.
5. "The Poor Farm," *Indianapolis Sentinel*, 13 July 1881; "Grinding Away," *Indianapolis News*, 8 July 1881; "The Poor Farm Inquiry," *Indianapolis News*, 6 July 1881.
6. David Rothman, *The Discovery of the Asylum: Social Order and Disorder in the New Republic* (Boston: Little, Brown, 1971), 188.
7. Alice Shaffer, Mary Wysor Keefer, and Sophonisba P. Breckinridge, *The Indiana Poor Law: Its Development and Administration with Special Reference to the Provision of State Care for the Sick Poor* (Chicago: University of Chicago Press, 1936), 34.
8. "Grinding Away," *Indianapolis Sentinel*, 15 June 1881; "The Investigation," *Indianapolis Journal*, 15 June 1881.
9. "The Poor Farm," *Indianapolis Sentinel*, 13 July 1881.
10. "Poor Farm," *Indianapolis Sentinel*, 9 July 1881.
11. "Dr. Culbertson," *Indianapolis Journal*, 9 July 1881.
12. "Big Moll," *Indianapolis News*, 9 July 1881.
13. "The Poor Farm," *Indianapolis Sentinel*, 13 July 1881; "The Case Closed," *Indianapolis News*, 13 July 1881.
14. "The Poor Farm Inquiry" *Indianapolis News*, 6 July 1881; "Poor Farm," *Indianapolis News*, 7 July 1881; "Poor Farm," *Indianapolis Sentinel*, 9 and 13 July 1881; "The Investigation" *Indianapolis Sentinel*, 14 June 1881; "The Poor Farm," *Indianapolis Journal*, 6 July 1881; "The Other Side," *Indianapolis Journal*, 25 June 1881.
15. Richard Dugdale, *The Jukes: A Study in Crime, Pauperism, Disease, and Heredity*, 3rd ed. (New York: G. P. Putnam, 1877).
16. "The Poor Farm," *Indianapolis News*, 12 July 1881.
17. "A Decision," *Indianapolis Sentinel*, 14 July 1881. The article Mr. Norton quoted from is Octave Thanet [Alice French], "The Indoor Pauper: A Study," *Atlantic Monthly* 47 (June 1881): 749–61. See also Karen Tracey, "Stories of the Poorhouse," in *Our Sisters' Keepers: Nineteenth-Century Benevolence Literature by American Women*, ed. Jill Bergman and Debra Bernardi (Tuscaloosa: University of Alabama Press, 2005), 23–48.

18. "A Decision"; "The Case Closed," *Indianapolis News*, 13 July 1881.

19. See, e.g., Blanche D. Coll, "The Baltimore Society for the Prevention of Pauperism, 1820–1822," *American Historical Review* 61, no. 1 (October 1955): 77–87; Carroll Smith Rosenberg, *Religion and the Rise of the American City: The New York City Mission Movement, 1812–1870* (Ithaca: Cornell University Press, 1971); Suzanne Lebsock, *The Free Women of Petersburg: Status and Culture in a Southern Town, 1784–1860* (New York: W. W. Norton, 1984), 195–236; Kenneth L. Kusmer, "The Origins of Homelessness in Early America," in *Down & Out, on the Road: The Homeless in American History* (Oxford: Oxford University Press, 2002), 13–34; Paul Boyer, *Urban Masses and Moral Order in America, 1820–1920* (Cambridge: Harvard University Press, 1978); James Leiby, *A History of Social Welfare and Social Work in the United States* (New York: Columbia University Press, 1978).

20. David Ward, *Poverty, Ethnicity, and the American City, 1840–1925: Conceptions of the Slum and the Ghetto* (Cambridge: Cambridge University Press, 1989), 27; John Webb Pratt, *Religion, Politics, and Diversity: The Church-State Theme in New York History* (Ithaca: Cornell University Press, 1967), 206–207; Dorothy M. Brown and Elizabeth McKeown, *The Poor Belong to Us: Catholic Charities and American Welfare* (Cambridge: Harvard University Press, 1997), 15–17.

21. Robert H. Bremner, *The Public Good: Philanthropy and Welfare in the Civil War Era* (New York: Alfred A. Knopf, 1980), 144.

22. Kusmer, *Down & Out*, 7–8; Paul T. Ringenbach, *Tramps and Reformers, 1873–1916: The Discovery of Unemployment in New York* (London: Greenwood Press, 1973), 4.

23. Robert Wiebe, *The Search for Order, 1877–1920* (New York: Hill and Wang, 1967), 12, 44.

24. Ward, *Poverty, Ethnicity, and the American City*, 43.

25. Burton J. Bledstein, *The Culture of Professionalism: The Middle Class and the Development of Higher Education in America* (New York: W. W. Norton, 1976), 7; Heather Cox Richardson, *West from Appomattox: The Reconstruction of America after the Civil War* (New Haven: Yale University Press, 2007), 2–3; Jackson Lears, *Rebirth of a Nation: The Making of Modern America, 1877–1920* (New York: HarperCollins, 2009).

26. The idea of applying rational, scientific organizational techniques to charity went by a variety of names, of which scientific charity was most common. Other names included charity organization, the associated charities movement, and scientific philanthropy. The last term, however, generally refers to the rational management of large trusts by a few paid experts, like that of the Laura Spellman Rockefeller Memorial Fund. Members of the scientific charity movement sometimes referred to themselves as scientific philanthropists, but for the sake of simplicity, terms like "scientific charity volunteers" and "charity organizers" have been employed in lieu of "scientific philanthropists."

27. James Leiby, "Charity Organization Reconsidered," *Social Service Review* 58, no. 4 (1984): 525–27.

28. Bledstein, *The Culture of Professionalism*, 39, 87; John Recchiuti, *Civic Engagement: Social Science and Progressive-Era Reform in New York City* (Philadelphia: University of Pennsylvania Press, 2007), 12.

29. L. L. Bernard and Jessie Bernard, *Origins of American Sociology: The Social Science Movement in the United States* (New York: Russell & Russell, 1965), 584–85; Franklin Sanborn, "The Work of Social Science in the United States," *Journal of Social Science* 7 (July 1874): 36.

30. Genevieve Weeks, *Oscar Carleton McCulloch, 1843–1891: Preacher and Practitioner of Applied Christianity* (Indianapolis: Indiana Historical Society, 1976), 199; Oscar McCulloch, "Associated Charities," in *Proceedings of the Seventh Annual Conference of Charities, Held at Cleveland, June and July 1880*, ed. F. B. Sanborn (Boston: A. Williams, 1880), 122–35. Also published as *Organized Charity in Cities: A Paper Read before the National Conference of Charities, held at Cleveland, Ohio* (Indianapolis, 1880).

31. McCulloch, "Associated Charities," 123.

32. Ibid., 127.

33. See Joel Schwartz, *Fighting Poverty with Virtue: Moral Reform and America's Urban Poor, 1825–2000* (Bloomington: Indiana University Press, 2000), 161–62.

34. Rosenberg, "New York Association for Improving the Condition of the Poor," in *Religion and the Rise of the American City*, 245–73.

35. *The Encyclopedia of Social Reforms: Including Political Economy, Political Science, Sociology, and Statistics, Covering Anarchism, Charities, Civil Service, Currency, Land and Legislation Reform, Penology, Socialism, Social Purity, Trade Unions, Woman Suffrage, Etc.*, 3rd ed. (New York: Funk and Wagnalls, 1897), 530. See also W. Walter Edwards, "The Poor-Law Experiment at Elberfeld," *Contemporary Review* 52 (July 1878): 675–93.

36. *Encyclopedia of Social Reforms*, 531.

37. Rosenberg, *Religion and the Rise of the American City*, 260.

38. Charles Loch Mowat, *The Charity Organization Society, 1869–1913: Its Ideas and Work* (London: Methuen, 1961), 10. Also see Ward, *Poverty, Ethnicity, and the American City*, 22; Rosenberg, *Religion and the Rise of the American City*, 260–61; Nathan Irvin Huggins, *Protestants against Poverty: Boston's Charities, 1870–1900* (Westport, Conn.: Greenwood, 1971), 17–19, 23.

39. Gareth Stedman Jones, *Outcast London: A Study in the Relationship between Classes in Victorian Society* (Oxford: Clarendon Press, 1971), 5, 16, 247.

40. On the Poor Laws and the founding of the London COS, see Michael J. D. Roberts, "Charity Disestablished? The Origins of the Charity Organization Society Revisited, 1868–1871," *Journal of Ecclesiastical History* 54, no. 1 (January 2003): 40–61; Alan Kidd, *State, Society, and the Poor in Nineteenth-Century England* (New York: St. Martin's Press, 1999); Seth Koven, *Slumming: Sexual and Social Politics in Victorian London* (Princeton: Princeton University Press, 2004); Koven, *Culture and Poverty: The London Settlement House Movement, 1870–1914* (New York: Routledge, 2009); Mowat, *The Charity Organization Society*.

41. A. S. Wohl, "Octavia Hill and the Homes of the London Poor," *Journal of British Studies* 10, no. 2 (May 1971): 105–31.

42. Octavia Hill, "The Importance of Aiding the Poor without Almsgiving," in *Transactions of the National Association for the Promotion of Social Science: Bristol Meeting, 1869*, ed. Edwin Pears (London, 1870), 591–92.

43. Jane Lewis, *Women and Social Action in Victorian and Edwardian England* (Stanford: Stanford University Press, 1991), 24, 44.

44. Hill, "The Importance of Aiding the Poor without Almsgiving," 593.

45. *COS 5th Annual Report* (1875), 5–6. Found in Mowat, *The Charity Organization Society*, 25–26.

46. Daniel Rodgers, *Atlantic Crossings: Social Politics in a Progressive Age* (Cambridge: Belknap Press, 1998); Walter Nugent, *Crossings: The Great Transatlantic Migrations, 1870–1914* (Bloomington: Indiana University Press, 1992); Axel R. Schäfer, *American Progres-*

sives and German Social Reform, 1875–1920: Social Ethics, Moral Control, and the Regulatory State in a Transatlantic Context (Stuttgart: Franz Steiner, 2000).

47. McCulloch, "Associated Charities," 126.

48. Alexander Johnson, "Report of Committee on Charity Organization," in *Proceedings of the National Conference of Charities and Correction, at the Twelfth Annual Session Held in Washington, D.C., June 4–10, 1885*, ed. Isabel C. Barrows (Boston: Press of Geo. H. Ellis, 1885), 316. Even that loose criterion may have underestimated the extent of the movement, as the survey did not count attempts made to organize charity in rural areas, even though sporadic reports of such efforts filtered in to the NCCC with some frequency. See Alexander Johnson, "Organization of Charity—Report of the Committee," in *Proceedings of the National Conference of Charities and Correction, at the Thirteenth Annual Session Held in St. Paul, Minn., July 15–22, 1886*, ed. Isabel C. Barrows (Boston: Press of Geo. H. Ellis, 1886), 168–69; Amos Warner, Stuart Queen, and Ernest Harper, *American Charities and Social Work*, 4th ed. (New York: Thomas Y. Crowell, 1930), 205; Charles D. Kellogg, "Charity Organization in the United States—Report of the Committee on History of Charity Organization," in *Proceedings of the National Conference of Charities and Correction at the Twentieth Annual Session Held in Chicago, Ill., June 8–11, 1893*, ed. Isabel C. Barrows (Boston: Press of Geo. H. Ellis, 1893), 52–89, and appendixes A and B; Hon. Charles S. Fairchild, "Objects of Charity Organization," in *Proceedings of the National Conference of Charities and Correction, at the Eleventh Annual Session, Held at St. Louis, October 13–17, 1884*, ed. Isabel C. Barrows (Boston: Press of Geo. H. Ellis, 1884), 65–68.

49. Charles D Kellogg, "Report of the Committee on the Organization of Charities," in *Proceedings of the National Conference of Charities and Correction, at the Fourteenth Annual Session Held in Omaha, Neb., August 25–31, 1887*, ed. Isabel C. Barrows (Boston: Press of Geo. H. Ellis, 1887), 128.

50. Nathaniel S. Rosenau, "Report of the Committee on Charity Organization," in *Proceedings of the National Conference of Charities and Correction at the Seventeenth Annual Session Held in Baltimore, Md., May 14–21, 1890*, ed. Isabel C. Barrows (Boston: Press of Geo. H. Ellis, 1890), 25–26.

51. Kellogg, "Charity Organization in the United States," 62, 81.

52. Recchiuti, *Civic Engagement*, 6; Dawn Greeley, "Beyond Benevolence: Gender, Class, and the Development of Scientific Charity in New York City, 1882–1935" (PhD diss., New York State University–Stony Brook, May 1995).

53. George Frederickson, *The Inner Civil War: Northern Intellectuals and the Crisis of the Union* (New York: Harper & Row, 1965), 107, 111–12.

54. Frank Bruno, *Trends in Social Work, 1874–1956: A History Based on the Proceedings of the National Conference of Social Work* (New York: Columbia University Press, 1948), 41.

55. Ibid., 3, 31–34.

56. Thomas Haskell, *The Emergence of Professional Social Science: The American Social Science Association and the Nineteenth-Century Crisis of Authority* (Urbana: University of Illinois Press, 1977), 95.

57. Mary O. Furner, *Advocacy & Objectivity: A Crisis in the Professionalization of American Social Science, 1865–1905* (Lexington: Published for the Organization of American Historians by the University Press of Kentucky, 1975), 13–14.

58. Dorothy Ross, *The Origins of American Social Science* (Cambridge: Cambridge University Press, 1991); Furner, *Advocacy and Objectivity*; Haskell, *The Emergence of Professional Social Science*.

59. Bruno, *Trends in Social Work,* 6.

60. Ibid., 354–56.

61. Ibid., 10–11.

62. Ibid., 16.

63. Ibid., 145; Anthony Oberschall, "The Institutionalization of American Sociology," in *The Establishment of Empirical Sociology: Studies in Continuity, Discontinuity, and Institutionalization,* ed. Oberschall (New York: Harper and Row, 1972), 207.

64. Bruno, *Trends in Social Work,* 359.

65. Ringenbach, *Tramps and Reformers,* 25; Huggins, *Protestants against Poverty,* 125–27.

66. Frank Sanborn, "The Year's Work in Administration and Legislation," in *Proceedings of the Sixth Annual Conference of Charities, Held at Chicago, June 1879,* ed. F. B. Sanborn (Boston: A. Williams, 1879), 32.

67. William P. Letchworth, "President's Address," *Proceedings of the National Conference of Charities and Correction at the Eleventh Annual Session, Held at St. Louis, October 13–17, 1884,* ed. Isabel C. Barrows (Boston: Press of Geo. H. Ellis, 1885), 10.

68. Bruno, *Trends in Social Work,* 7, 30.

69. Frances Fox Piven and Richard A. Cloward, *Regulating the Poor: The Functions of Public Welfare* (New York: Pantheon Books, 1971), 3.

70. For instance, Walter Trattner, *From Poor Law to Welfare State: A History of Social Welfare in America* (New York: Free Press, 1974), 75–95, 159–60; Roy Lubove, *The Professional Altruist: The Emergence of Social Work as a Career, 1880–1930* (Cambridge: Harvard University Press, 1965), 7; Paul Boyer, "Building Character among the Urban Poor: The Charity Organization Movement," in *Urban Masses,* 142–62; Michael Katz, *In the Shadow of the Poorhouse: A Social History of Welfare in America* (New York: Basic Books, 1986), 83–86, 113; Katz, *Poverty and Policy in American History: Studies in Social Discontinuity* (New York: Academic Press, 1983), 90–92; Huggins, *Protestants against Poverty,* 10–12, 199; Marvin E. Gettleman, "Philanthropy as Social Control in Late Nineteenth-Century America: Some Hypotheses and Data on the Rise of Social Work," *Societas* 5, no. 1(1975): 49–59; Emily K. Abel, "Medicine and Morality: The Health Care Program of the New York Charity Organization Society," *Social Service Review* 71, no. 4 (1997): 634–51; Fredrickson, *The Inner Civil War,* 98.

71. For instance, see Furner, *Advocacy and Objectivity;* Haskell, *The Emergence of Professional Social Science;* Martin Bulmer, *The Chicago School of Sociology: Institutionalization, Diversity, and the Rise of Sociological Research* (Chicago: University of Chicago Press, 1984); Ross, *Origins of American Social Science;* Ellen Fitzpatrick, "Social Welfare," in *The Cambridge History of Science, Volume 7: The Modern Social Sciences,* ed. Theodore M. Porter and Dorothy Ross (Cambridge: Cambridge University Press, 2002), 608–20.

72. Mary Jo Deegan, *Jane Addams and the Men of the Chicago School, 1892–1918* (New Brunswick: Transaction Books, 1988); Deegan, ed., *Women in Sociology: A Bio-bibliographical Sourcebook* (New York: Greenwood Press, 1991); Deegan, *Race, Hull-House, and the University of Chicago: A New Conscious against Ancient Evils* (Westport, Conn.: Praeger, 2002); Deegan, "The Second Sex and the Chicago School: Women's Accounts, Knowledge, and Work, 1945–1960," in *A Second Chicago School? The Development of a Postwar American Sociology,* ed. Gary Alan Fine (Chicago: University of Chicago Press, 1995), 322–35; Ellen Fitzpatrick, *Endless Crusade: Women Social Scientists and Progressive Reform* (New York: Oxford University Press, 1990); Robyn Muncy, *Creating a Female Dominion in American Reform, 1890–1935* (New York: Oxford University Press, 1991); Helene Silverberg, ed., *Gender and American Social Science: The Formative*

Years (Princeton: Princeton University Press, 1998). On Du Bois, see Martin Bulmer, "W. E. B. Du Bois as a Social Investigator: *The Philadelphia Negro, 1899,*" in *The Social Survey in Historical Perspective, 1880–1940,* ed. Martin Bulmer, Kevin Bales, and Kathryn Kish Sklar (Cambridge: Cambridge University Press, 1991), 170–88; Michael Katz and Thomas Sugrue, eds., *W. E. B. Du Bois, Race, and the City: The Philadelphia Negro and Its Legacy* (Philadelphia: University of Pennsylvania Press, 1998), 4–17.

73. Joan Waugh, *Unsentimental Reformer: The Life of Josephine Shaw Lowell* (Cambridge: Harvard University Press, 1997) 93; Waugh, "'Give This Man Work.' Josephine Shaw Lowell, the Charity Organization Society of the City of New York, and the Depression of 1893," *Social Science History* 25, no. 2 (Summer 2000): 217–46; Elizabeth N. Agnew, *From Charity to Social Work: Mary E. Richmond and the Creation of an American Profession* (Urbana: University of Illinois Press, 2004). Other historians who have recognized the role of science in scientific charity include Greeley, "Beyond Benevolence"; Ruth Crocker, *Mrs. Russell Sage: Women's Activism and Philanthropy in Gilded Age and Progressive Era America* (Bloomington: Indiana University Press, 2006); Recchiuti, *Civic Engagement.* In 1956, Robert Bremner first identified the potentially radical implication of scientific charity that poverty was a social problem that could be controlled and eliminated through science. Robert H. Bremner, *From the Depths: The Discovery of Poverty in the United States* (New York: New York University Press, 1956), 55–56.

74. Ward, *Poverty, Ethnicity, and the American City,* 127; David C. Hammack and Stanton Wheeler, *Social Science in the Making: Essays on the Russell Sage Foundation, 1907–1972* (New York: Russell Sage Foundation, 1994), 12. More generally see Crocker, *Mrs. Russell Sage;* John M. Glenn, Lilian Brandt, and F. Emerson Andrews, *Russell Sage Foundation, 1907–1946,* vol. 1 (New York: Russell Sage Foundation, 1947).

75. Hammack and Stanton, *Social Science in the Making,* 14.

76. Ringenbach, *Tramps and Reformers,* 18–20.

77. Daniel Kevles, *In The Name of Eugenics: Genetics and the Uses of Human Heredity* (Cambridge: Harvard University Press, 1995), 120.

78. These works include Mark Largent, *Breeding Contempt: The History of Coerced Sterilization in the United States* (New Brunswick: Rutgers University Press, 2008); Ian Robert Dowbiggin, *Keeping America Sane: Psychiatry and Eugenics in the United States and Canada* (Ithaca: Cornell University Press, 1997); Lois A. Cuddy and Claire M. Roch, eds., *Evolution and Eugenics in American Literature and Culture, 1880–1940: Essays on Ideological Conflict and Complicity* (London: Associated University Presses, 2003); Nicole Hahn Rafter, *Creating Born Criminals* (Urbana: University of Illinois Press, 1997); Nicole Hahn Rafter, ed., *White Trash: The Eugenic Family Studies, 1877–1919* (Boston: Northeastern University Press, 1988); Wendy Kline, *Building a Better Race: Gender, Sexuality, and Eugenics from the Turn of the Century to the Baby Boom* (Berkeley: University of California Press, 2001); Barbara Kimmelman, "The American Breeders' Association: Genetics and Eugenics in an Agricultural Context, 1903–1913," *Social Studies of Science* 13 (1983): 163–204; Edward Larson, *Sex, Race, and Science: Eugenics in the Deep South* (Baltimore: Johns Hopkins University Press, 1995); Diane Paul, *Controlling Human Heredity: 1865 to the Present* (Atlantic Highlands, N.J.: Humanities Press, 1995); Christine Rosen, *Preaching Eugenics: Religious Leaders and the American Eugenics Movement* (Oxford: Oxford University Press, 2004); Alexandra Minna Stern, *Eugenic Nation: Faults and Frontiers of Better Breeding in Modern America* (Berkeley: University of California Press, 2005).

79. Alice O'Connor, *Poverty Knowledge: Social Science, Social Policy, and the Poor in Twentieth-Century U.S. History* (Princeton: Princeton University Press, 2001), 15.

2. "ARMIES OF VICE"

1. Katz, *In the Shadow of the Poorhouse*, 85.

2. For instance, in 1899 the influential leader of the New York City COS, Edward Devine, declared that no discussion of organized charity was "more complete, more convincing, more inspiring" than McCulloch's "Associated Charities" paper from 1880. Devine, "Organization of Charity," in *Proceedings of the National Conference of Charities and Correction at the Twenty-sixth Annual Session Held in the City of Cincinnati, Ohio, May 17–23, 1899*, ed. Isabel C. Barrows (Boston: George H. Ellis, 1900), 274.

3. Frederick Doyle Kershner Jr., "A Social and Cultural History of Indianapolis, 1860–1914" (PhD diss., University of Wisconsin–Madison, 1950), 1–10.

4. See, e.g., Don Harrison Doyle, *The Social Order of a Frontier Community: Jacksonville, Illinois, 1825–70* (Urbana: University of Illinois Press, 1978); Stephan Thernstrom, *Poverty and Progress: Social Mobility in a Nineteenth-Century City* (Cambridge: Harvard University Press, 1964); Peter R. Knights, *Yankee Destinies: The Lives of Ordinary Nineteenth-Century Bostonians* (Chapel Hill: University of North Carolina Press, 1991).

5. Kershner, "A Social and Cultural History of Indianapolis," 19–20.

6. U.S. Bureau of the Census, *Fifteenth Census of the United States, 1930: Population* (Washington, D.C., 1931), 18–19, in Kershner, "A Social and Cultural History of Indianapolis," 54, 95.

7. Gregory Rose, "Upland Southerners: The County Origins of Southern Migrants to Indiana by 1850," *Indiana Magazine of History* 82, no. 3 (September 1986): 242–63; Rose, Hoosier Origins: The Nativity of Indiana's United States–Born Population in 1850," *Indiana Magazine of History* 81, no. 3 (September 1985): 201–32; Andrew Cayton, *Frontier Indiana* (Bloomington: Indiana University Press, 1996), 272; James J. Divita, "Demography and Ethnicity," in *The Encyclopedia of Indianapolis*, ed. David J. Bodenhamer and Robert G. Barrows (Bloomington: Indiana University Press, 1994), 53.

8. Emma Lou Thornbrough, *Indiana in the Civil War Era, 1850–1880* (Indianapolis: Indiana Historical Bureau and Indiana Historical Society, 1965), 275–76.

9. Kershner, "A Social and Cultural History of Indianapolis," 74.

10. William Doherty, "John Caven," in *The Encyclopedia of Indianapolis*, 392; Nathaniel Deutsch, *Inventing America's "Worst" Family: Eugenics, Islam, and the Fall and Rise of the Tribe of Ishmael* (Berkeley: University of California Press, 2009), 21.

11. Kershner, "A Social and Cultural History of Indianapolis," 19, 39.

12. John Butler, "The New Charity," *Year Book of Charities 1886* (Indianapolis, 1886), 7–9, 14–15, box 5, folder 3, Family Service Association of Indianapolis Records, 1879–1971, Collection M0102, Indiana Historical Society, Indianapolis [hereafter FSA]; Kershner, "A Social and Cultural History of Indianapolis," 38.

13. U.S. Bureau of the Census, *Tenth Census of the United States, 1880: Wages* (Washington, D.C., 1886), 42, 62, 76, 142, 385–86, 414–15, 442, 465; Thornbrough, *Indiana in the Civil War Era*, 277–78, 559; Clifton J. Phillips, *Indiana in Transition: The Emergence of an Industrial Commonwealth, 1880–1920* (Indianapolis: Indiana Historical Society, 1968), 469–70; Weeks, *McCulloch*, 57–58. James H. Madison notes that while the city experienced great population growth, its residents were much more likely than other city-dwellers to settle permanently. Madison, *The Indiana Way: A State History* (Bloomington: Indiana University Press, 1986), 177–78.

14. As economic history, see Stephen Thomas Ziliak, "Essays on Self-Reliance: The United States in the Era of 'Scientific Charity'" (PhD diss., University of Iowa, 1996);

Ziliak, "Self-Reliance before the Welfare State: Evidence from the Charity Organization Movement in the United States," *Journal of Economic History* 64, no. 2 (June
2004): 433–61. Works linking McCulloch to the eugenics movement include Alexandra
Minna Stern, "'We Cannot Make a Silk Purse Out of a Sow's Ear': Eugenics in the Hoosier Heartland," *Indiana Magazine of History* 103 (March 2007): 3–38; Elof Axel Carlson, "The Jukes and the Tribe of Ishmael," in *The Unfit: A History of a Bad Idea* (Cold
Spring Harbor: Cold Spring Harbor Laboratory Press, 2001), 161–82; Stephen Ray Hall,
"Oscar McCulloch and Indiana Eugenics" (PhD diss., Virginia Commonwealth University, 1993); Elsa Kramer, "Recasting the Tribe of Ishmael: The Role of Indianapolis's
Nineteenth-Century Poor in Twentieth-Century Eugenics," *Indiana Magazine of History*
104 (March 2008): 36–64; Rafter, *White Trash.* Hugo Leaming, commonly credited for
rediscovering the Tribe of Ishmael in the 1970s, claimed they originated in the American Revolutionary War, were tri-racial, and may have been the first Muslims in America.
Hugo P. Leaming, "The Ben Ishmael Tribe: A Fugitive 'Nation' of the Old Northwest,"
in *The Ethnic Frontier: Essays in the History of Group Survival in Chicago and the Midwest,*
ed. Melvin G. Holli and Peter d'A. Jones (Grand Rapids William B. Eerdmans, 1977),
98–141. Nathaniel Deutsch dismisses this interpretation while recasting the Ishmael
family as symbolic of the larger American discourse on Orientalism, poverty, and race.
Deutsch, *Inventing America's "Worst" Family.* McCulloch's biographer situates him in a
religious context. Weeks, *McCulloch;* Weeks, "Religion and Social Work as Exemplified
in the Life of Oscar C. McCulloch," *Social Service Review* 39 (March 1965): 38–52.

15. Weeks, *McCulloch,* 8, 88.

16. Weeks, *McCulloch,* 13. See also Weeks, "Oscar C. McCulloch: Leader in Organized Charity," *Social Service Review* 39 (June 1965): 209–21.

17. McCulloch diary, 17 November 1879, box 2, Oscar McCulloch Collection
(OMC), Indiana State Library, Indianapolis; Weeks, *McCulloch,* 60.

18. Weeks, *McCulloch,* 159.

19. McCulloch diary, 7 June 1877, box 2, OMC. For the larger history of the religious
tradition in scientific charity, see Leiby, "Charity Organization Reconsidered," 523–38.

20. Weeks, *McCulloch,* 24–33, esp. 25, 42–43.

21. Henry F. May, *Protestant Churches and Industrial America* (New York: Harper,
1949), 91; Weeks, *McCulloch,* 87.

22. Weeks, *McCulloch,* 24, 52.

23. "The Lake Shore Disaster," *New York Times,* 31 December 1876.

24. McCulloch diary, 7 January 1877, box 2, OMC.

25. McCulloch diary, 16–17 May 1877, box 2, OMC.

26. Weeks, *McCulloch,* 32.

27. McCulloch diary, 7 June 1877, box 2, OMC.

28. Weeks, *McCulloch,* 50; McCulloch diary, 3 June 1877, box 2, OMC.

29. Deutsch, *Inventing America's "Worst" Family,* 25.

30. McCulloch diary, 18 January 1878, box 2, OMC.

31. Deutsch, *Inventing America's "Worst" Family,* 29–30.

32. McCulloch diary, 20 January 1878, box 2, OMC.

33. Bruno, *Trends in Social Work,* 57–60; Bruce Bellingham, "Waifs and Strays: Child
Abandonment, Foster Care, and Families in Mid-Nineteenth-Century New York," in
The Uses of Charity: The Poor on Relief in the Nineteenth-Century Metropolis, ed. Peter
Mandler (Philadelphia: University of Pennsylvania Press, 1990), 123–60.

34. "Condensed Reports of the COS, the IBS, and the Children's Board of Guard-ians, 1889–1890" (Indianapolis, 1890), in *Indianapolis Benevolent Society Minute Book, 1879–1918,* BV1178, FSA; *Year Book of Charities, 1890–1891* (Indianapolis, 1892), back cover, box 5, folder 4, FSA.

35. Bruce Aldridge, "The Tribe of Ishmael Came and Multiplied," *Indianapolis Magazine* (July 1972): 37; Deutsch, *Inventing America's "Worst" Family,* 49.

36. Deutsch, *Inventing America's "Worst" Family,* 58–59, 98–99; Hall, "McCulloch and Indiana Eugenics," 109–14.

37. Rafter, *White Trash.*

38. Weeks, *McCulloch,* 173.

39. McCulloch diary, 16 January 1879, box 2, OMC; Weeks, *McCulloch,* 174.

40. McCulloch diary, 9 January 1879, box 2, OMC.

41. Ruth Hutchinson Crocker, "Making Charity Modern: Business and the Reform of Charities in Indianapolis, 1879–1930," *Business and Economic History,* 2nd ser., 12 (1984): 161; Phillips, *Indiana in Transition,* 481–5.

42. *Indianapolis Sentinel,* 14 November 1885.

43. Oscar McCulloch, "Annual Public Meeting of the Indianapolis Benevolent So-ciety," 30 November 1879, in *Indianapolis Benevolent Society Minute Book, 1879–1918,* BV 1178, FSA.

44. Ibid.

45. "Charity Organization Society," *Indianapolis Journal* 16 April 1880.

46. "Charity Organization Society: Three Months Work," *Indianapolis News,* 1 May 1880.

47. Deutsch, *Inventing America's "Worst" Family,* 77; Charity Organization Society Case Book, 1880, FSA.

48. Hall, "McCulloch and Indiana Eugenics," 112.

49. "Charity Organization," *Indianapolis Journal,* 4 December 1879; Weeks, *McCul-loch,* 184–85, 173.

50. Verl S. Lewis, "Stephen Humphreys Gurteen and the American Origins of Charity Organization," *Social Service Review* 40, no. 2 (1966): 190–201; Erik Schneider-han, "Jane Addams and Charity Organization in Chicago," *Journal of the Illinois Histori-cal Society* 100, no. 4 (Winter 2007–2008): 302. For more on Gurteen, see Boyer, *Urban Masses,* 145; Agnew, *From Charity to Social Work,* 67–68; Ziliak, "Self-Reliance before the Welfare State," 433–61.

51. S. Humphreys Gurteen, *What Is Charity Organization?* (Buffalo, 1880), 4.

52. Ibid., 5.

53. S. Humphreys Gurteen, *A Handbook of Charity Organization* (Buffalo, 1882), 197.

54. Ibid., 198, and Gurteen, "Address," *Proceedings at the Fourth Annual Meeting of the Charity Organization Society of Buffalo: Embracing the Address of the Rev. S. Humphreys Gurteen, the Report of the Council, the Reports of Co-operative Societies, etc.* (1882), 14.

55. For more on Spencerian philosophy and analogical reasoning, see Victor Hilts, "Towards the Social Organism: Herbert Spencer and William B. Carpenter on the Ana-logical Method," in *The Natural and the Social Sciences, Some Critical and Historical Per-spectives,* ed. I. B. Cohen. (Boston: Kluwer Academic, 1994), 275–303.

56. Arthur Mitchell, *The Past in the Present: What Is Civilisation?* (Edinburgh, 1880), 169–70.

57. Gurteen, *A Handbook of Charity Organization,* 201–202.

58. Ibid., 202.

59. Ziliak, "Essays on Self-Reliance," 100.

60. Gurteen, *A Handbook of Charity Organization*, 110, 112.

61. James W. Trent Jr., *Inventing the Feeble Mind: A History of Mental Retardation in the United States* (Berkeley: University of California Press, 1994); Rafter, *Creating Born Criminals*; Bruno, *Trends in Social Work*, 52–53.

62. Richard Dugdale, "Hereditary Pauperism," in *Proceedings of the Conference of Charities Held in Connection with the General Meeting of the American Social Science Association at Saratoga, September, 1877* (Boston: A. Williams, 1877), 81–95; Bruno, *Trends in Social Work*, 50.

63. Dugdale, "Hereditary Pauperism," 82.

64. Bruno, *Trends in Social Work*, 50.

65. Dugdale, "Hereditary Pauperism," 91–92.

66. Dr. Diller Luther, "Causes and Prevention of Pauperism," in *Proceedings of the Seventh Annual Conference of Charities and Correction, Held at Cleveland, June and July, 1880*, ed. F. B. Sanborn (Boston: A. Williams, 1880), 242, 243–44, 246.

67. Mrs. Louise Rockwood Wardner, "Girls in Reformatories," in *Proceedings of the Sixth Annual Conference of Charities, Held at Chicago, June, 1879*, ed. F. B. Sanborn (Boston: A. Williams, 1879), 178–79, 188.

68. Josephine Shaw Lowell, "One Means of Preventing Pauperism," in *Proceedings of the Sixth Annual Conference of Charities, Held at Chicago, June, 1879* ed. F. B. Sanborn (Boston: A. Williams, 1879), 189, 193, 195.

69. McCulloch, "Associated Charities," 123.

70. Recchiuti, *Civic Engagement*, 177–79.

71. Deutsch, *Inventing America's "Worst" Family*, 5.

72. Ibid., 37, 64; Matthew Frye Jacobson, *Barbarian Virtues: The United States Encounters Foreign Peoples at Home and Abroad, 1876–1917* (New York: Hill and Wang, 2000).

73. Stern, "We Cannot Make a Silk Purse Out of a Sow's Ear," 20.

74. Oscar McCulloch, "The Tribe of Ishmael: diagram, accompanying paper read before the National Conference of Charities at Buffalo, July 5–11, 1888" (Indianapolis, 1891); "The Tribe of Ishmael: A Study of Social Degradation," in *Proceedings of the National Conference of Charities and Correction at the Fifteenth Annual Session Held in Buffalo, N.Y. July 5–11, 1888*, ed. Isabel C. Barrows (Boston: Press of Geo. H. Ellis, 1888), 154–59.

75. Deutsch, *Inventing America's "Worst" Family*, 39–40, 78.

76. Brent Ruswick, "Just Poor Enough: Gilded Age Charity Applicants Respond to Charity Investigators," *Journal of the Gilded Age and Progressive Era* 10, no. 3 (July 2011): 265–87.

77. McCulloch, "Associated Charities," 124–25. See Victor Hilts, "Obeying the Laws of Hereditary Descent: Phrenological Views on Inheritance and Eugenics," *Journal of the History of the Behavioral Sciences* 18 (January 1982): 62–77.

78. McCulloch, "Associated Charities," 125.

79. George W. Stocking Jr., "Lamarckianism in American Social Science: 1890–1915," *Journal of the History of Ideas* 23, no. 2 (April–June 1962): 246–47.

80. McCulloch, "The Tribe of Ishmael," 159.

81. Jacob Riis, *How the Other Half Lives: Studies among the Tenements of New York* (New York: Scribner, 1890), 244.

82. Charles Richmond Henderson, *An Introduction to the Study of the Dependent, Defective, and Delinquent Classes* (Boston, 1893), 5.

83. "Charity Organization," *Indianapolis News*, 8 November 1890.

84. David Starr Jordan, *The Days of a Man: Being Memories of a Naturalist, Teacher, and Minor Prophet of Democracy*, vol. 1 (New York: World Book, 1922), 132–33. Also see Carlson, *The Unfit*, 174, 185.

85. David Starr Jordan, "Report of the Committee on Eugenics," in *American Breeders' Association: Report of the Meeting Held at Washington, D.C., January 28–30, 1908* (Baltimore: Kohn & Pollock, Inc., 1908): 201. Also see Jordan, *The Blood of a Nation: A Study of the Decay of Races through the Survival of the Unfit* (Boston: American Unitarian Association, 1902).

86. "Charities and Corrections," *Indianapolis Times*, 15 June 1885; McCulloch diary, 30 September 1883, box 3, OMC; McCulloch diary, 6 October 1889, box 5, OMC.

87. "Social Solidarity," *Indianapolis Journal*, 12 April 1886.

88. C. S. Watkins, "Pauperism and Its Prevention," in *Proceedings of the Ninth Annual National Conference of Charities and Corrections Held at Madison, Wis., Aug. 7–12, 1882*, ed. A. O. Wright (Madison, Wis.: Midland, 1883), 95.

89. Letchworth, "President's Address," 16–17.

90. Ibid., 16.

91. Josephine Shaw Lowell, "How to Adapt 'Charity Organization' Methods to Small Communities," in *Proceedings of the National Conference of Charities and Correction at the Fourteenth Annual Session Held in Omaha, Neb., August 25–31, 1887*, ed. Isabel C. Barrows (Boston: Press of Geo. H. Ellis, 1887), 139.

92. See, e.g., Charles S. Hoyt, "Presidential Address," in *Proceedings of the National Conference of Charities and Correction at the Fifteenth Annual Session Held in Buffalo, N.Y., July 5–11, 1888*, ed. Isabel C. Barrows (Boston: Press of Geo. H. Ellis, 1888), 8–23; Homer Folks, "The Removal of Children from Almshouses," in *Proceedings of the National Conference of Charities and Correction at the Twenty-first Annual Session Held in Nashville, Tenn., May 23–29, 1894*, ed. Isabel C. Barrows (Boston: Press of Geo. H. Ellis, 1894), 119–23.

3. FRIENDLY VISITORS OR SCIENTIFIC INVESTIGATORS?

1. Frank Dekker Watson, *The Charity Organization Movement in the United States: A Study in American Philanthropy* (New York: Macmillan, 1922), 148.

2. Oscar McCulloch, "Associated Charities," 129.

3. Alexander Johnson, "Charity Organization: Report of the Committee on Charity Organization," in *Proceedings of the National Conference of Charities and Correction, at the Twelfth Annual Session Held in Washington, D.C., June 4–10, 1885*, ed. Isabel C. Barrows (Boston: Press of Geo. H. Ellis, 1885), 316. See also Amos Warner, *American Charities: A Study in Philanthropy and Economics* (New York: Thomas Y. Crowell, 1894), 27; Charles Kellogg, *Hand-Book for Friendly Visitors among the Poor: Compiled and Arranged by the Charity Organization Society of the City of New York* (New York: Putnam, 1883), 9.

4. Alexander Johnson, *Adventures in Social Welfare: Being Reminiscences of Things, Thoughts and Folks during Forty Years of Social Work* (Fort Wayne, Ind.: privately published, 1923), 130.

5. Sheila Rothman, *Living in the Shadow of Death: Tuberculosis and the Social Experience of Illness in American History* (New York: Basic Books, 1994), 180.

6. Mrs. James T. Fields, "Upon the Constitution and Duties of a District Conference," in *Proceedings of the Eighth Annual Conference of Charities and Correction, Held at
Boston, July 25–30, 1881*, ed. F. B. Sanborn (Boston: A. Williams, 1881), 130.

7. *Annual Reports of the Indianapolis Benevolent Society and Charity Organization Society, 1883–1884* (Indianapolis, 1884), box 4, folder 7, Family Service Association (FSA) of
Indianapolis Records, 1879–1971, Collection M0102, Indiana Historical Society, Indianapolis, 26–27.

8. See, e.g., Lebsock, *The Free Women of Petersburg*, 202–204; David C. Hammack,
Power and Society: Greater New York at the Turn of the Century (New York: Russell Sage
Foundation, 1982), 79; Rosenberg, *Religion and the Rise of the American City*, 79; Theda
Skocpol, *Protecting Soldiers and Mothers: The Political Origins of Social Policy in the United
States* (Cambridge: Belknap Press, 1992), 52–57.

9. John T. Cumbler, "The Politics of Charity: Gender and Class in Late Nineteenth-
Century Charity Policy," *Journal of Social History* 14, no. 1 (Fall 1980): 99–112. Also see
Agnew, *From Charity to Social Work*, 79; Kellogg, "Charity Organization in the United
States," 67 and insert, appendix F.

10. Louise Wolcott, "Treatment of Widows with Dependent Children," in *Proceedings of the National Conference of Charities and Correction at the Fifteenth Annual Session
Held in Buffalo, N.Y., July 5–11, 1888*, ed. Isabel C. Barrows (Boston: Press of Geo. H. Ellis,
1888), 137.

11. Mrs. Jacobs, "Minutes and Discussions," in *Proceedings of the National Conference
of Charities and Correction at the Seventeenth Annual Session Held in Baltimore, Md., May
14–21, 1890*, ed. Isabel C. Barrows (Boston: Press of Geo. H. Ellis, 1890), 376.

12. Harriet Noble, *The Indianapolis Friendly Visitor: Friendly Visiting* (Indianapolis:
Indianapolis Society of Friendly Visitors Committee, 1903), 2, 10–12, 19.

13. Ibid., 6.

14. Ibid., 6–7. On the gendered nature of visiting, see Sherri Broder, *Tramps, Unfit
Mothers, and Neglected Children: Negotiating the Family in Nineteenth-Century Philadelphia* (Philadelphia: University of Pennsylvania Press, 2002); Agnew, *From Charity to Social Work.*

15. Noble, *The Indianapolis Friendly Visitor*, 7, 9.

16. Gurteen, *Handbook of Charity Organization*, 186

17. See also Linda Gordon, "Social Insurance and Public Assistance: The Influence
of Gender in Welfare Thought in the United States, 1890–1935," *American Historical Re-
view* 97, no. 1 (February 1992): 19–54; Ruth Crocker, "'I Only Ask You Kindly to Divide
Some of Your Fortune with Me': Begging Letters and the Transformation of Charity in
Late Nineteenth-Century America," *Social Politics* 6, no. 2 (1999): 131–60; Gettleman,
"Philanthropy as Social Control"; Watson, *Charity Organization*, 181; Stephen Ziliak,
"Self-Reliance before the Welfare State: Evidence from the Charity Organization Move-
ment in the United States," *Journal of Economic History* 64, no. 2 (June 2004): 433–61.

18. Crocker, "Making Charity Modern," 162.

19. "COS Application for Aid," June 1881, box 3, Oscar McCulloch Collection
(OMC), Indiana State Library, Indianapolis.

20. *Year Book of Charities Indianapolis, 1892–1893* (Indianapolis: 1894), 27, box 5,
folder 4, FSA.

21. Bruno, *Trends in Social Work*, 103.

22. John Butler, "Scientific Charity, and Organized Effort to Effect It: An Address
Delivered at the Annual Meeting of the Charity Societies, Sunday Evening, Dec 2d,

1883," 1–2, 1884 diary, box 4, OMC. Also *Annual Reports of the Indianapolis Benevolent Society and Charity Organization Society, 1883–1884,* 21.

23. Case Record no. 62, Charity Organization Casebook, 1880, FSA. Last names of individuals who requested or received relief from the COS have been abbreviated at the request of the Family Service Center of Central Indiana. Portions of this chapter also appear in Ruswick, "Just Poor Enough: Gilded Age Charity Applicants Respond to Charity Investigators."

24. Case Record no. 63, Charity Organization Society Casebook, 1880, FSA.

25. Case Record no. 132, Charity Organization Casebook, 1880, FSA. On the history of begging letters, see Crocker, "'I Only Ask You Kindly to Divide Some of Your Fortune with Me.'"

26. Case Record no. 132, Charity Organization Casebook, 1880, FSA.

27. *Annual Reports of the Indianapolis Benevolent Society and Charity Organization Society, 1883–1884,* 24.

28. Ibid., 25–26.

29. Ibid., 25.

30. Ibid., 24–26.

31. *Year Book of Charities, 1889–1890. Addresses Given on Phases of Charity at the Fifty-fourth Anniversary of the Indianapolis Benevolent Society* (Indianapolis: 1891), 8, box 5, folder 4, FSA.

32. Warner et al., *American Charities and Social Work,* 45. Cited in Linda Gordon, *Pitied but Not Entitled: Single Mothers and the History of Welfare, 1890–1935* (New York: Free Press, 1994), 176.

33. *Annual Reports of the Indianapolis Benevolent Society and Charity Organization Society, 1883–1884,* 24–25; *Year Book of Charities, 1889–1890,* 9–10.

34. *Annual Reports of the Indianapolis Benevolent Society and Charity Organization Society, 1883–1884,* 24; *Indianapolis Benevolent Society, Forty-ninth Annual Report* (Indianapolis, 1885), 21, box 4, folder 7, FSA; *Year Book of Charities Indianapolis, 1892–1893* (Indianapolis, 1894), 29, box 5, folder 4, FSA.

35. Case Record no. 80, Charity Organization Society Casebook, 1880, FSA.

36. For instance, see Case Record nos. 95, 113, 123, and 193, Charity Organization Society Casebook, 1880, FSA.

37. Case Record no. 80, Charity Organization Society Casebook, 1880, FSA.

38. Ibid.

39. Luther, "Causes and Prevention of Pauperism," 244.

40. Dr. Charles E. Cadwalader, "Organization of Charities in Cities—Report of the Standing Committee," in *Proceedings of the Eighth Annual Conference of Charities and Correction, Held at Boston, July 25–30, 1881,* ed. F. B. Sanborn (Boston: A. Williams, 1881), 115–16. Portland presumably referred to Maine and not Oregon.

41. Frank Sanborn, "The Prevention of Pauperism: Report of the Standing Committee," in *Proceedings of the National Conference of Charities and Correction, Twelfth Annual Session Held in Washington, D.C., June 4–10, 1885,* ed. Isabel C. Barrows (Boston: Press of Geo. H. Ellis, 1885), 403.

42. W. L. Bull, "Trampery: Its Causes, Present Aspects, and Some Suggested Remedies," in *Proceedings of the National Conference of Charities and Correction, at the Thirteenth Annual Session Held in St. Paul, Minn., July 15–22, 1886,* ed. Isabel C. Barrows (Boston: Press of Geo. H. Ellis, 1886), 195.

43. Fred H. Wines, "Report of Committee on Causes of Pauperism and Crime," in

Proceedings of the National Conference of Charities and Correction, at the Thirteenth Annual Session Held in St. Paul, Minn., July 15–22, 1886, ed. Isabel C. Barrows (Boston: Press of Geo. H. Ellis, 1886), 207, 211–13.

44. Bull, "Trampery," 195.

45. Bruno, *Trends in Social Work,* 27–28.

46. Ringenbach, *Tramps and Reformers,* 27.

47. Warner, *American Charities,* 31.

48. Ibid., 31–34 and insert.

49. Ibid., 60–61.

50. Victor Hilts, "Causes and Correlations: The Reception of Mathematical Statistics by American Social Scientists circa 1900," History of Science Society Annual Meeting, 1982. Referenced in Charles Camic and Yu Xie, "The Statistical Turn in American Social Science: Columbia University, 1890–1915," *American Sociological Review* 59, no. 5 (October 1994): 783; Hilts, *Statist and Statistician* (New York: Arno Press, 1982), 504.

51. Fred Wines, "Ninth Session," in *Proceedings of the National Conference of Charities and Correction at the Sixteenth Annual Session Held in San Francisco, Cal., September 11–18, 1889,* ed. Isabel C. Barrows (Boston: Press of Geo. H. Ellis, 1889), 264.

52. Bruno, *Trends in Social Work,* 134.

53. Camic and Xie, "The Statistical Turn," 776, 778.

54. Ibid., 782; Gordon, "Social Insurance and Public Assistance," 38.

55. Camic and Xie, "The Statistical Turn," 791.

56. See Trattner, *From Poor Law to Welfare State,* 92.

57. Weeks, *McCulloch,* 120; McCulloch diary, 2 May 1886, box 4, OMC.

58. Oscar C. McCulloch, *The Open Door: Sermons and Prayers* (Indianapolis: Wm. B. Burford, 1892), 8; Weeks, *McCulloch,* 103–106, 127–29.

59. Weeks, *McCulloch,* 113–14.

60. "Study Class in Social Science in the Dept. of Charity," *Indianapolis Yearbook of Charities: 1889–1890* (Indianapolis: 1891), 34–35, box 5, folder 4, FSA. Also in "Plymouth Institute Autumn Leaflet, Announcements of Classes, Lectures, Etc., 1890–1891," Misc. Plymouth Church Papers, 1889–91, box 1, OMC.

61. Johnson, *Adventures in Social Welfare,* 81. See also Trent, *Inventing the Feeble Mind,* 174–78.

62. "Study Class in Social Science in the Dept. of Charity," 34–39.

63. "Sociological Lectures," *Annual Report of the Charity Organization Society, 1904–1905* (Indianapolis: Baker-Randolph Litho and Eng Co., 1905) 12, box 4, folder 8, FSA.

64. Kershner, "A Social and Cultural History of Indianapolis," 289; "Sociological Discussions," flier, box 1, folder 1, FSA; "Sociological Lectures."

65. Case Record no. 70, Charity Organization Society Casebook, 1880, FSA.

66. Margaretta S. Elder, "On the Care of Neglected Girls," *Year Book of Charities 1889–1890,* 17.

67. *Year Book of Charities, 1892–1893,* inside cover.

68. Mrs. S. E. Tenney, "The Class for Study of the Friendly Visitor's Work: An Experiment," in *Proceedings of the National Conference of Charities and Correction at the Nineteenth Annual Session Held in Denver, Col., June 23–29, 1892,* ed. Isabel C. Barrows (Boston: Press of Geo. H. Ellis, 1892), 452.

69. Trattner, *From Poor Law to Welfare State,* 199; Ringenbach, *Tramps and Reformers,* 59.

70. Mary Richmond, "The Need of a Training School in Applied Philanthropy," in *Proceedings of the National Conference of Charities and Correction at the Twenty-fourth Annual Session Held in Toronto, Ontario, July 7–14, 1897*, ed. Isabel C. Barrows (Boston: Geo. H. Ellis, 1897), 182, 184; See also Agnew, *From Charity to Social Work*, 134–37.

71. Bruno, *Trends in Social Work*, 141.

72. Lilian Brandt, *The Charity Organization Society of the City of New York: 1882–1907.* (New York: B. H. Tyrrell, 1907), 44–45, 51–52.

73. Trattner, *From Poor Law to Welfare State*, 200; Bruno, *Trends in Social Work*, 142.

74. "Johns Hopkins University: President Gilman's Course on Social Science," *Lend a Hand* 4, no. 3 (March 1889): 234–38.

75. Daniel Fulcomer, "Instruction in Sociology in Institutions of Learning," in *Proceedings of the National Conference of Charities and Correction at the Twenty-first Annual Session Held in Nashville, Tenn., May 23–29, 1894*, ed. Isabel C. Barrows (Boston: Press of Geo. H. Ellis, 1894), 67–68.

76. Greeley, "Beyond Benevolence," 454–55.

77. Johnson, *Adventures in Social Welfare*, 310.

78. Seth Low, "The Problem of Pauperism in the Cities of Brooklyn and New York," in *Proceedings of the Sixth Annual Conference of Charities, Held at Chicago, June 1879*, ed. F. B. Sanborn (Boston: A. Williams, 1879), 200–210.

79. Camic and Xie, "The Statistical Turn," 781; Roger Geiger, *To Advance Knowledge: The Growth of American Research Universities, 1900–1940* (Oxford: Oxford University Press, 1986), 11.

80. Recchiuti, *Civic Engagement*, 4.

81. Oberschall, "Institutionalization," 189.

82. Hamilton Cravens, *The Triumph of Evolution: The Heredity-Environment Controversy, 1900–1941* (Philadelphia: University of Pennsylvania Press, 1978), 126.

83. Edwin Sutherland, "Social Pathology," *American Journal of Sociology* 50, no. 4 (May 1945): 429. Found in Oberschall, "Institutionalization," 204, 206, 221.

84. Oberschall, "Institutionalization," 198–203; Cravens, *Triumph*, 140.

4. OPPOSITION, DEPRESSION, AND THE REJECTION OF PAUPERISM

1. Brown and McKeown, *The Poor Belong to Us*, 24–25; Pratt, *Religion, Politics, and Diversity*, 222; Ringenbach, *Tramps and Reformers*, 101.

2. Hammack, *Power and Society*, 77–78.

3. *Charities Review*, 9, no. 1 (March 1899): 5; no. 3 (July 1899): 103; Edward Devine, "The Reform of the Subsidy System: New York's Appropriations to Private Charities under Investigation," *Charities Review* 9, no. 8 (October 1899): 338–51.

4. Bruno, *Trends in Social Work*, 193.

5. Ibid., 203–204.

6. Greeley, "Beyond Benevolence," 241–42. For an example, see Konrad Bercovici, *Crimes of Charity* (New York: Alfred A. Knopf, 1917).

7. Greeley, "Beyond Benevolence," 122.

8. Ibid., 324. See also Kusmer, *Down & Out*, 81–82; Charles O. Burgess, "The Newspaper as Charity Worker: Poor Relief in New York City, 1893–1894," *New York History* 43 (July 1962): 249–68.

9. *New York World*, 25 August 1893. Quoted in Greeley, "Beyond Benevolence," 325.

10. Greeley, "Beyond Benevolence," 326; *Fifteenth Annual Report of the New York*

Charity Organization Society (1897), 19. For additional incidents, see Marvin E. Gettleman, "Charity and Social Classes in the United States, 1874–1900, II," *American Journal
of Economics and Sociology* 22, no 3 (July 1963): 417–26.

11. On the antagonism between labor movements and COS, see Broder, *Tramps,
Unfit Mothers, and Neglected Children*. On the settlement movement's relationship with
scientific charity, see Allen F. Davis, *Spearheads for Reform: The Social Settlements and the
Progressive Movement, 1890–1914* (New York: Oxford University Press, 1967); Trattner,
From Poor Law to Welfare State, 136–59; Agnew, *From Charity to Social Work*, 78–88.

12. *Charities Review* 9, no. 1 (March 1899): 31–32; no. 2 (April 1899): 66.

13. Greeley, "Beyond Benevolence," 66; Skocpol, *Protecting Soldiers and Mothers*, 95;
Recchiuti, *Civic Engagement*, 51–52; *Charities Review* 9, no. 3 (April 1899): 124; *Charities:
A Weekly Review of Local and General Philanthropy* 8, no. 3 (18 January 1902): 70.

14. Karen Sawislak, *Smoldering City: Chicago and the Great Fire, 1871–1874* (Chicago:
Chicago University Press, 1995).

15. Kusmer, *Down & Out*, 81, 88–89.

16. Hammack and Wheeler, *Social Science in the Making*, 10.

17. Bremner, *From the Depths*, 52; also Bremner, ""Scientific Philanthropy" 1873–93,"
Social Service Review 30 (June 1956): 168–73; Trattner, *From Poor Law to Welfare State*, 86.

18. "Discussions of Benevolence," *Indianapolis News*, 26 January 1880.

19. *Indianapolis People*, 8 March 1879, from Weeks, *McCulloch*, 175; "To the Editor,"
Indianapolis Journal, 15 November 1884, from Weeks, "Oscar C. McCulloch: Leader in
Organized Charity," 215.

20. "The Benevolent Society," *Indianapolis News*, 27 January 1880.

21. "The Ministers and Charity," *Indianapolis Journal*, 2 March 1886.

22. "Public Charities," *Indianapolis News*, 12 April 1886.

23. Ibid.

24. "Methods of Charity Work," *Indianapolis Journal*, 13 April 1886.

25. "Public Charities."

26. "Methods of Charity Work."

27. Ibid.

28. "The Methodist Ministers," *Indianapolis News*, 26 February 1886.

29. "The Public Poor," *Indianapolis News*, 25 January 1886.

30. Charles Hoffman, "The Depression of the Nineties," *Journal of Economic History*
16, no. 2 (June 1956): 137–64, esp. 138; Hoffman, *The Depression of the Nineties* (Westport,
Conn.: Greenwood, 1970).

31. Benjamin Harrison, "Phases of Charity," *Year Book of Charities Indianapolis,
1892–1893* (Indianapolis: 1894), 12, box 5, folder 4, Family Service Association Records
Mo102, series 1, Indiana Historical Society (hereafter FSA).

32. Kershner, "A Social and Cultural History of Indianapolis," 283–86, and Ruth
Hutchinson Crocker, *Social Work and Social Order: The Settlement Movement in Two Industrial Cities, 1889–1930* (Chicago: University of Illinois Press, 1992), 15.

33. Commercial Club Relief Committee, *Relief for the Unemployed in Indianapolis:
Report of the Commercial Club Relief Committee and Its Auxiliary, the Citizen's Finance
Committee, 1893–1894* (Indianapolis: Carlon & Hollenbeck, 1894), 5. Cited in Edward T.
Devine, *The Principles of Relief* (New York: Macmillan, 1904), 420; Watson, *Charity Or-
ganization*, 259.

34. *Annual Report of the Charity Organization Society of Indianapolis, 1908–1909* (In-

dianapolis: Charity Organization Society, 1909), 9–11, box 5, folder 1, FSA; Crocker, "Making Charity Modern," 164; *A Partial Report of Four Months' Work of the Unemployed by the Charity Organization Society of Indianapolis* (Indianapolis: Hollenbeck Press, 1908), 10, box 5, folder 12, FSA; Kershner, "A Social and Cultural History of Indianapolis," 82–83, 85; Amos Warner, *American Charities*, rev. ed. (New York: Thomas Y. Crowell, 1908), 258.

35. *Year Book of Charities, 1892–1893* (Indianapolis: 1894), 56–58, box 5, folder 4, FSA.

36. *The Charity Organization Society of Indianapolis: A Brief Report, 1896–97* (Indianapolis, 1897), 11–13, box 4, folder 8, FSA.

37. *Year Book of Charities, 1892–1893*, 14.

38. *The Charity Organization Society of Indianapolis: A Brief Report 1896–97*, 6.

39. Ibid., 4.

40. Watson, *Charity Organization*, 258.

41. Watson, *Charity Organization*, 262 and Devine, *Principles of Relief*, 420.

42. *Charities of Indianapolis, 1893–1894* (Indianapolis: 1894), back cover, box 4, folder 7, FSA.

43. Charity Organization Society Case Book, 1893–1896, 34–35, 40, 43, 107, 123. BV1174, FSA.

44. Ibid., 34, 82.

45. Ibid., 81–82.

46. Charity Organization Society Casebook, 1880, BV 1198, FSA, Case Record no. 89.

47. Ibid., Case Record no. 99.

48. Ibid., Case Record no. 127.

49. "The Public's Poor," *Indianapolis News*, 25 January 1886.

50. *The Charity Organization Society of Indianapolis: A Brief Report, 1896–1897* (Indianapolis, 1897), 7, box 4, folder 8, FSA.

51. Crocker, "Practical Philanthropy along the Color Line: Flanner House, 1898–1930," in *Social Work and Social Order*, 68–93. See also Linda Gordon, "Black and White Visions of Welfare: Women's Welfare Activism, 1890–1945," *Journal of American History* 78, no. 2 (September 1991): 559–90; Alvin B. Kogut, "The Negro and the Charity Organization Society in the Progressive Era," *Social Service Review* 44, no. 1 (1970): 11–21.

52. Martin Gilens argues that the tendency for white Americans to cast more doubt on a poor black's worthiness for relief than they did toward poor whites fully developed only as recently as the mid-twentieth century. The stances of the scientific charity elite seem to corroborate this conclusion. Gilens, *Why Americans Hate Welfare: Race, Media, and the Politics of Antipoverty Policy* (Chicago: University of Chicago Press, 1999). This also is consistent with Edward Larson's observation that in southern states eugenicists were more concerned with the lower class of whites than with African Americans. *Sex, Race, and Science: Eugenics in the Deep South* (Baltimore: Johns Hopkins University Press, 1995).

53. Bruno, *Trends in Social Work*, 76.

54. Mina Carson, *Settlement Folk: Social Thought and the American Settlement Movement, 1885–1930* (Chicago: University of Chicago Press, 1990), 66.

55. On the scientific background of settlement workers, see Deegan, "The Second Sex and the Chicago School," 322–64; Deegan, *Jane Addams and the Men of the Chicago School*; Silverberg, *Gender and American Social Science*; Bulmer, Bales, and Sklar, *The Social Survey in Historical Perspective*; Fitzpatrick, *Endless Crusade*.

56. Carson, *Settlement Folk*, 66–67.

57. Boyer, *Urban Masses*, 155–56.

58. Julia Lathrop, "Hull House as a Laboratory of Sociological Investigation," in *Proceedings of the National Conference of Charities and Correction at the Twenty-first Annual Session Held in Nashville, Tenn. May 23–29, 1894*, ed. Isabel C. Barrows (Boston: Press of Geo. H. Ellis, 1894), 313–19.

59. Julia Lathrop, "What the Settlement Work Stands For," in *Proceedings of the National Conference of Charities and Correction at the Twenty-third Annual Session Held in Grand Rapids, Mich. June 4–10, 1896*, ed. Isabel C. Barrows (Boston: Geo. H. Ellis, 1896), 107.

60. Mary E. McDowell, "The Settlement and Organized Charity," in *Proceedings of the National Conference of Charities and Correction at the Twenty-third Annual Session Held in Grand Rapids, Mich. June 4–10, 1896*, ed. Isabel C. Barrows (Boston: Geo. H. Ellis, 1896), 124.

61. Ibid., 125.

62. Ringenbach, *Tramps and Reformers*, 101.

63. Boyer, *Urban Masses*, 156.

64. Davis, *Spearheads for Reform*, 22, 25.

65. Bruno, *Trends in Social Work*, 7, 42.

66. Waugh, *Unsentimental Reformer*, 11; Waugh, "'Give This Man Work!'"

67. Recchiuti, *Civic Engagement*, 53; Hammack, *Power and Society*, 77, 143.

68. Josephine Shaw Lowell, "Poverty and Its Relief: The Methods Possible in the City of New York," in *Proceedings of the National Conference of Charities and Correction at the Twenty-second Annual Session Held in New Haven, Conn., May 24–30, 1895*, ed. Isabel C. Barrows (Boston: Geo. H. Ellis, 1895), 44.

69. Ibid., 44.

70. Ibid., 45.

71. Ibid., 47.

72. Ibid., 49.

73. Watson, *Charity Organization*, 332.

74. Edward T. Devine, "The Value and the Dangers of Investigation," in *Proceedings of the National Conference of Charities and Correction at the Twenty-fourth Annual Session Held in Toronto, Ontario, July 7–14, 1897*, ed. Isabel C. Barrows (Boston: Geo. H. Ellis, 1897), 194–95; See also Devine, *The Practice of Charity: Individual, Associated, and Organized* (New York: Lentilhon, 1901), 45.

75. Devine, *Practice of Charity*, 52.

76. Lawrence Veiller to Josephine Shaw Lowell, 3 May 1898, Community Service Society of New York Papers, Columbia University, taken from Hammack and Wheeler, *Social Science in the Making*, 10.

77. Gettleman, "Charity and Social Classes," 418.

78. Kate Holladay Claghorn, "The Use and Misuse of Statistics in Social Work," in *Proceedings of the National Conference of Charities and Correction at the Thirty-fifth Annual Session held in the City of Richmond, Va., May 6th to 13th 1909*, ed. Alexander Johnson (Fort Wayne: Fort Wayne Printing Co., 1908), 234–51; Claghorn, "Some New Developments in Social Statistics," in *Proceedings of the National Conference of Charities and Correction at the Thirty-seventh Annual Session Held in the City of St. Louis, Mo., May 19th to 26th, 1910*, ed. Alexander Johnson (Fort Wayne: Archer Printing, 1910), 507–14; Louise

Bolard More, *Wage Earners' Budgets: A Study of Standards and Cost of Living in New York City* (New York: Henry Holt, 1907); Royal Meeker, "What Is the American Standard of Living?" 164–72; Elizabeth F. Moloney, "The Family Budget and the Adequacy of Relief," 299–302; F. Stuart Chapin, "Relations of Sociology and Social Case Work," 358–62, all from *Proceedings of the National Conference of Social Work at the Forty-sixth Annual Session Held in Atlantic City, New Jersey, June 1–8,1919* (Chicago: Rogers & Hall, 1920).

79. Charles M. Hubbard, "Relation of Charity-Organization Societies to Relief Societies and Relief-Giving," *American Journal of Sociology* 6, no. 6. (May 1901): 783–89; Cumbler, "The Politics of Charity"; Watson, *Charity Organization,* 323–24.

80. Peter Mandler, "Poverty and Charity in the Nineteenth-Century Metropolis: An Introduction," in *The Uses of Charity: The Poor on Relief in the Nineteenth-Century Metropolis* (Philadelphia: University of Pennsylvania Press, 1900), 25; Lubove, *Professional Altruist,* 7–11.

81. Homer Folks, "Disease and Dependence," in *Proceedings of the National Conference of Charities and Correction at the Thirtieth Annual Session Held in the City of Atlanta, May 6–12, 1903,* ed. Isabel C. Barrows (Columbus, Ohio: Fred J. Heer, 1903), 335, 337.

82. Lee K. Frankel, "Needy Families in Their Homes: Report of the Committee," in *Proceedings of the National Conference of Charities and Correction at the Thirty-third Annual Session Held in the City of Philadelphia, Penna., May 9–16, 1906,* ed. Alexander Johnson (Columbus, Ohio: Fred J. Heer, 1906), 325–26.

83. Ibid., 326, 330.

84. Edward Devine, "The Dominant Note of the Modern Philanthropy," *Proceedings of the National Conference of Charities and Correction at the Thirty-third Annual Session Held in the City of Philadelphia, Penna., May 9–16, 1906,* ed. Alexander Johnson (Columbus, Ohio: Fred J. Heer, 1906), 9.

85. Ward, *Poverty, Ethnicity, and the American City,* 98.

86. Kusmer, *Down & Out,* 58.

87. Alexander Keyssar, *Out of Work: The First Century of Unemployment in Massachusetts* (Cambridge: Cambridge University Press, 1986), 251–52; Ringenbach, "The Recognition of Unemployment in New York," in *Tramps and Reformers,* 161–83.

88. Mary Birtwell, "The Causes of Poverty—Discussion," in *Proceedings of the National Conference of Charities and Correction at the Twenty-sixth Annual Session Held in the City of Cincinnati, Ohio, May 17–23, 1899,* ed. Isabel C. Barrows (Boston: George H. Ellis, 1900), 374.

89. Samuel McCune Lindsay, "The Causes of Poverty—Discussion," in *Proceedings of the National Conference of Charities and Correction at the Twenty-sixth Annual Session Held in the City of Cincinnati, Ohio, May 17–23, 1899,* ed. Isabel C. Barrows (Boston: George H. Ellis, 1900), 369–75.

90. Warner et al., *American Charities and Social Work,* 48.

91. Lindsay, "The Causes of Poverty," 372.

92. Camic and Xie, "The Statistical Turn," 792–93.

93. Recchiuti, *Civic Engagement,* 53, 58.

94. Lindsay, "The Causes of Poverty," 372–73.

95. Oberschall, "Institutionalization," 226.

96. Lindsay, "The Causes of Poverty," 371.

97. Ibid., 371–72.

5. "I SEE NO TERRIBLE ARMY"

1. Oscar McCulloch, "The True Spirit of Charity Organization," 18 May 1891, box 1, folder 1, Family Service Association of Indianapolis Records (FSA), 1879–1971, Collection M0102, Indiana Historical Society. Also appears in "The Charity Organization Society of Indianapolis: A Brief Report, 1896–1897," 3, box 4, folder 8. Portions of this chapter first appeared in "The Measure of Worthiness: The Rev. Oscar McCulloch and the Pauper Problem, 1877–1891," *Indiana Magazine of History* 104 (March 2008): 3–35.

2. Deutsch, *Inventing America's "Worst" Family*, 35.

3. Charles Rosenberg, "The Bitter Fruit: Heredity, Disease, and Social Thought," in *No Other Gods: On Science and American Social Thought* (Baltimore: Johns Hopkins University Press, 1976), 35–36; Stocking, "Lamarckianism"; Bruno, *Trends in Social Work*, 50–51.

4. Ronald Numbers, *Almost Persuaded: American Physicians and Compulsory Health Insurance, 1912–1920* (Baltimore: Johns Hopkins University Press, 1978), 59. See Isaac M. Rubinow, "20,000 Miles over the Land: A Survey of the Spreading Health Insurance Movement," *Survey* 37 (1917): 631–35.

5. Hammack and Wheeler, *Social Science in the Making*, 7–8, 10–12; M. Glenn et al., *Russell Sage Foundation* 1:6, 32.

6. See, e.g., Charles A. Ellwood, "Social Facts and Scientific Social Work," in *Proceedings of the National Conference of Social Work at the Forty-fifth Annual Session Held in Kansas City, Missouri, May 15–22, 1918* (Chicago: Rogers & Hall, 1918), 686–91.

7. McCulloch diary, 20 January 1878, box 2, Oscar McCulloch Collection (OMC), Indiana State Library, Indianapolis.

8. McCulloch, "The Tribe of Ishmael," 154–59, and *The Tribe of Ishmael: A Study in Social Degradation* (Indianapolis, 1889)

9. Linda Gordon, *The Great Arizona Orphan Abduction* (Cambridge: Harvard University Press, 1999); Bellingham, "Waifs and Strays."

10. "Pulpit Utterances," *Indianapolis Journal*, 15 December 1879.

11. McCulloch's closest ministerial friend and ally in scientific charity, the Reverend Myron Reed, shared this analysis of the division of modern industrial labor and its impact on poverty. James A. Denton, *Rocky Mountain Radical: Myron W. Reed, Christian Socialist* (Albuquerque: University of New Mexico Press, 1997), 108–13

12. "Pulpit Utterances."

13. *Indianapolis Saturday Herald*, 30 March 1878, 4. Found in Weeks, "Religion and Social Work," 42.

14. "The Public's Poor," *Indianapolis News*, 25 January 1886.

15. *Indianapolis Journal*, 10 April 1886, 4, col 2.

16. "Mr. George's Idea," *Indianapolis News*, 9 April 1885; "Land Tax Only," *Indianapolis News*, 11 April 1885.

17. W. S. Wandby to McCulloch, 11 July 1885, box 1, folder 1, OMC.

18. "Mr. McCulloch's Conversion," *Indianapolis Journal*, 27 October 1885. Also McCulloch diary, 20 July and 27 October 1885, box 4, OMC.

19. Hall, "McCulloch and Indiana Eugenics," 223–25.

20. Recchiuti, *Civic Engagement*, 53–54.

21. "Pastor McCulloch Serenaded," *Indianapolis Journal*, 3 January 1886; "Serenaded

by Socialists," unidentified newspaper clipping, 3 January 1886, in McCulloch diary, 3 January 1886, box 3, OMC.

22. "The Industrial Situation," *Indianapolis News,* 22 March 1886; "Pulpit Themes Yesterday—The Industrial Situation," *Indianapolis Journal,* 22 March 1886; "Voice of the People, O. C. M'Culloch for Congress," *Labor Signal,* found in McCulloch diary, 13 March 1886, box 3, OMC.

23. Weeks, *McCulloch,* 34.

24. "Labor's Day of Display," *Indianapolis Journal,* 20 September 1886.

25. "The Labor Demonstration," *Indianapolis News,* 20 September 1886.

26. Gaines M. Foster, "Conservative Social Christianity, the Law, and Personal Morality: Wilbur F. Crafts in Washington," *Church History* 71, no. 4 (December 2002): 803–804.

27. "Yesterday's Pulpit," *Indianapolis News,* 27 September 1886; "How to Spend Sunday," *Indianapolis Sentinel,* 27 September 1886.

28. "How to Spend Sunday." Again, McCulloch's stance is mirrored by that of his friend Reed, who defended a similar Knights of Labor parade in Denver in 1884. Denton, *Rocky Mountain Radical,* 101–102.

29. "How to Spend Sunday." Also see the note of thanks issued by the Central Trade Union, McCulloch diary, 1 October 1886, box 4, OMC.

30. McCulloch diary, 7 May 1886, box 4, OMC.

31. Weeks, *McCulloch,* 30.

32. McCulloch had expressed his dislike of the death penalty as early as 1879. "Sunday Discourses. The Ref. O. C. McCulloch on the Proper Treatment of Criminals," *Indianapolis Daily Sentinel,* 3 February 1879; Weeks, "Religion and Social Work," 50.

33. "Mr. M'Culloch and the Anarchists," *Indianapolis Journal,* 30 November 1886. While McCulloch rarely addressed matters of race in his diary and even less frequently in public, during this time he considered the plight of African Americans and immigrants, with similar conclusions. In a tantalizingly brief diary entry, he wondered of African Americans, "What is the future? Peace on earth! Yes but first a sword. First Discerning of rights, dissension, strife, fighting for right or their justice which is *peace.*" Hall, "McCulloch and Indiana Eugenics," 228, McCulloch diary, 24 December 1885, box 4, OMC.

34. "Mr. M'Culloch and the Anarchists."

35. McCulloch diary, 6 December 1886, box 4, OMC; Weeks, *McCulloch,* 144–45.

36. Indianapolis Charity Organization Society, "Dime Savings and Loan Society," in McCulloch diary, 25 March 1887, box 4, OMC.

37. "Charity Organization," *Indianapolis News,* 8 November 1890.

38. "The Charity Organization Society of Indianapolis: A Brief Report, 1896–1897" (Indianapolis, 1897), 6, box 4, folder 8, FSA.

39. "The Charity Organization Society of Indianapolis, 1897–1898" (Indianapolis, 1898), 12, box 4, folder 8, FSA.

40. "The Charity Organization Society of Indianapolis: A Brief Report, 1896–1897," 6.

41. Indianapolis Charity Organization Society, "Dime Savings and Loan Society," 1887, box 4, OMC.

42. "Condensed Report of the COS, IBS and Children's Board of Guardians" (Indianapolis, 1889 or 1890), iv, BV 1178, FSA.

43. Ringenbach, *Tramps and Reformers,* 27.

44. Rev. Oscar C. McCulloch, "Report of the Standing Committee," in *Proceedings of the National Conference of Charities and Correction at the Sixteenth Annual Session Held in San Francisco, Cal., September 11–18, 1889,* ed. Isabel C. Barrows (Boston: Press of Geo. H. Ellis, 1889), 12.

45. "How the Other Half Lives," *Indianapolis News,* 24 December 1890.

46. "The Poor Farm," *Indianapolis Sentinel,* 13 July 1881; A. G. Byers, "The Ohio System of Care for Dependent Children," in *Proceedings of the Seventh Annual Conference of Charities and Correction, Held at Cleveland, June and July 1880,* ed. F. B. Sanborn (Boston: A. Williams, 1880), 177–86.

47. Weeks, *McCulloch,* 207.

48. Ibid.

49. Shaffer et al., *Indiana Poor Law,* 46.

50. Weeks, *McCulloch,* 210; McCulloch diary, 8 March 1889, box 5, OMC; Milton Gaither, "The Rise and Fall of a Pedagogical Empire: The Board of State Charities and the Indiana Philosophy of Giving," *Indiana Magazine of History* 96 (December 2000): 336–46; "Charity Organization Society Call for a Meeting," 23 February 1889, box 5, folder 2, OMC, and box 1, folder 1, FSA.

51. Bruno, *Trends in Social Work,* 207.

52. Amos W. Butler, "Discussion on Charity," in *Proceedings of the National Conference of Charities and Correction at the Thirtieth Annual Session Held in the City of Atlanta, May 6–12, 1903,* ed. Isabel C. Barrows (Press of Fred J. Heer, 1903), 549.

53. Amos W. Butler, *Indiana, a Century of Progress: A Study of the Development of Public Charities and Correction, 1790–1915* (Indianapolis: Indiana Reformatory Printing Trade School, 1916), 2, 146; Shaffer et al., *Indiana Poor Law,* 48–49; Bruno, *Trends in Social Work,* 207.

54. Butler, "*Indiana,* 148; Butler, "Discussion on Charity," 550; Shaffer et al., *Indiana Poor Law,* 53–54.

55. McCulloch diary, 17 May 1881, box 3, OMC; Schaffer et al., *Indiana Poor Law,* 50–51.

56. Butler, *Indiana,* 43–51.

57. McCulloch, *The Open Door,* 9.

58. Ibid., 157–58.

59. Ibid., 38, 58, 143.

60. Ibid., 237–38.

61. Ibid., 239–40.

62. Ibid., 242. See also Thomas Huxley, "The Struggle for Existence: A Programme," *Nineteenth Century* 23 (February 1888): 161–80; Petr Kropotkin, "The Coming Reign of Plenty," *Nineteenth Century* 23 (June 1888): 817–37; Kropotkin, "Mutual Aid among Animals," *Nineteenth Century* 28 (September 1890): 337–54; and Kropotkin, *Mutual Aid: A Factor in Evolution* (London, 1902).

63. "Co-Operation," *Indianapolis Sentinel,* 14 November 1881; "Advice to the Toiler," *Indianapolis Times,* 3 May 1886.

64. John Wesley Powell, "Competition as a Factor in Human Evolution," *American Anthropologist* 1, no. 4 (October 1888): 297–324; Stocking, "Lamarckianism," 243.

65. Edward C. Rafferty, *Apostle of Human Progress: Lester Frank Ward and American Political Thought, 1841–1913* (London: Rowman and Littlefield, 2003), 128.

66. *Wisconsin State Journal*, 19, 22, 23, 24 April 1901; Richard Ely to Jane Addams, 10 April 1901, Richard Ely Papers, box 18, folder 1, Wisconsin State Historical Society, Madison.

67. McCulloch, *The Open Door*, 242.

68. Oscar McCulloch, "President's Address: State and National Registration of the Dependent, The Defective, and the Delinquent Classes," in *Proceedings of the National Conference of Charities and Correction at the Eighteenth Annual Session Held in Indianapolis, Ind., May 13–20, 1891*, ed. Isabel C. Barrows (Boston: Press of Geo. H. Ellis, 1891), 10–19.

69. Deutsch, *Inventing America's "Worst" Family*, 3, 76.

70. Rosenberg, "The Bitter Fruit," 33–37, 47.

71. Albert O. Wright, "The New Philanthropy," in *Proceedings of the National Conference of Charities and Correction at the Twenty-third Annual Session Held in Grand Rapids, Mich., June 4–10, 1896*, ed. Isabel C. Barrows (Boston: Geo. H. Ellis, 1896), 4, 5, 7.

72. Ibid., 5–6.

73. Alexander Johnson, "President's Address: The Mother-State and Her Weaker Children," in *Proceedings of the National Conference of Charities and Correction at the Twenty-fourth Annual Session Held in Toronto, Ontario, July 7–14, 1897*, ed. Isabel C. Barrows (Boston: Geo. H. Ellis, 1898), 5.

74. Agnes Maule Machar, "Outdoor Relief in Canada," in *Proceedings of the National Conference of Charities and Correction at the Twenty-fourth Annual Session Held in Toronto, Ontario, July 7–14, 1897*, ed. Isabel C. Barrows (Boston: Geo. H. Ellis, 1898), 241.

75. Based on a reading of all results obtained from a proximity search of the roots *heredit** and *pauper** at the online archive of the *Proceedings*, http://www.hti.umich.edu/n/ncosw/.

76. F. M. Powell, "Growth and Arrested Development," in *Proceedings of the National Conference of Charities and Correction at the Twenty-sixth Annual Session Held in the City of Cincinnati, Ohio, May 17–23, 1899*, ed. Isabel C. Barrows (Boston: George H. Ellis, 1900), 259–73.

77. Charles Henderson, "President's Address: The Relation of Philanthropy to Social Order and Progress," in *Proceedings of the National Conference of Charities and Correction at the Twenty-sixth Annual Session Held in the City of Cincinnati, Ohio, May 17–23, 1899*, ed. Isabel C. Barrows (Boston: George H. Ellis, 1900), 14–15.

78. Riis, *How the Other Half Lives*, 244.

79. Jacob A. Riis, "A Blast of Cheer," in *Proceedings of the National Conference of Charities and Correction at the Twenty-eighth Annual Session Held in the City of Washington, D.C., May 9–15, 1901*, ed. Isabel C. Barrows (Boston: George H. Ellis, 1901), 21. See also James B. Lane, "Jacob A. Riis and Scientific Philanthropy during the Progressive Era," *Social Service Review* 47, no. 1 (March 1973): 32–48

80. Rev. S. G. Smith, "Opening Address: The Heart of the Problem," in *Proceedings of the National Conference of Charities and Correction at the Twenty-eighth Annual Session Held in the City of Washington, D.C., May 9–15, 1901*, ed. Isabel C. Barrows (Boston: George H. Ellis, 1901), 14.

81. Alexander Johnson, "The Segregation of Defectives: Report of Committee on Colonies for Segregation of Defectives," in *Proceedings of the National Conference of Charities and Correction at the Thirtieth Annual Session Held in the City of Atlanta, May 6–12, 1903*, ed. Isabel C. Barrows (Boston: Press of Fred J. Heer, 1903), 246, 249.

82. Ibid., 246.

83. Mary E. Perry, "Minority Report," in *Proceedings of the National Conference of Charities and Correction at the Thirtieth Annual Session Held in the City of Atlanta, May 6–12, 1903*, ed. Isabel C. Barrows (Boston: Press of Fred J. Heer, 1903), 253–54.

84. Edward Devine, *The Family and Social Work* (New York: Association Press, 1912), 21. Also see Devine, *The Practice of Charity*, 12.

85. Devine, *The Family and Social Work*, 24.

86. Ibid., 43, 45, 46, 117.

87. Robert Treat Paine, "President's Address," in *Proceedings of the National Conference of Charities and Correction at the Twenty-second Annual Session Held in New Haven, Conn., May 24–30, 1895*, ed. Isabel C. Barrows (Boston: Press of Geo. H. Ellis, 1895), 9–10.

88. Hon. S. M. Jones, "Charity or Justice—Which?" in *Proceedings of the National Conference of Charities and Correction at the Twenty-sixth Annual Session Held in the City of Cincinnati, Ohio, May 17–23, 1899*, ed. Isabel C. Barrows (Boston: George H. Ellis, 1899), 136–37.

89. Alexander Johnson, "Preface," in *Proceedings of the National Conference of Charities and Correction at the Thirty-sixth Annual Session held in the City of Buffalo, N. Y., June 9th to 16th 1909*, ed. Alexander Johnson (Fort Wayne: Fort Wayne Printing, 1909), iv.

90. Jane Addams, "Presidential Address: Charity and Social Justice," in *Proceedings of the National Conference of Charities and Correction at the Thirty-seventh Annual Session held in the City of St. Louis, Mo., May 19th to 26th, 1910*, ed. Alexander Johnson (Fort Wayne: Archer Printing, 1910), 1.

91. Harold Varney, "A Criticism of Social Work and the Reform Program in the Light of the Complete Industrial Revolution Demanded by the Radicals," in *Proceedings of the National Conference of Social Work at the Forty-fifth Annual Session Held in Kansas City, Missouri, May 15–22, 1918* (Chicago: Rogers & Hall, 1918), 401.

92. Charles Sumner, "Informal Discussion," in *Proceedings of the National Conference of Social Work at the Forty-fifth Annual Session Held in Kansas City, Missouri, May 15–22, 1918* (Chicago: Rogers & Hall, 1918), 407.

93. Arthur J. Todd, "Social Problems of the War and Reconstruction," in *Proceedings of the National Conference of Social Work at the Forty-fifth Annual Session Held in Kansas City, Missouri, May 15–22, 1918* (Chicago: Rogers & Hall, 1918), 683.

94. Charles Ellwood, "Social Facts and Scientific Social Work," in *Proceedings of the National Conference of Social Work at the Forty-fifth Annual Session Held in Kansas City, Missouri, May 15–22, 1918* (Chicago: Rogers & Hall, 1918), 687, 689.

96. Bruno, *Trends in Social Work*, 361.

96. Ibid., 151.

97. Georgina D. Feldberg, *Disease and Class: Tuberculosis and the Shaping of Modern North American Society* (New Brunswick, N.J.: Rutgers University Press, 1995), 13, 2; Trattner, *From Poor Law to Welfare State*, 123. See also Barbara Bates, *Bargaining for Life: A Social History of Tuberculosis, 1876–1938* (Philadelphia: University of Pennsylvania Press, 1992); Judith Walzer Leavitt, *The Healthiest City: Milwaukee and the Politics of Health Reform* (Princeton: Princeton University Press, 1982); Rothman, *Living in the Shadow of Death*.

98. Feldberg, *Disease and Class*, 105.

99. Ibid., 36, 82; Rothman *Living in the Shadow of Death*, 22–23, 183.

100. Rothman, *Living in the Shadow of Death*, 183–84.

101. *A Handbook on the Prevention of Tuberculosis: Being the First Annual Report of the Committee on the Prevention of Tuberculosis of the Charity Organization Society of the City of New York* (New York City: Charity Organization Society, 1903), 3–4; Bruno, *Trends in Social Work*, 250.

102. Ibid., 5.

103. Lilian Brandt, "The Social Aspects of Tuberculosis, Based on a Study of Statistics," in *A Handbook on the Prevention of Tuberculosis*, 107–108.

104. Feldberg, *Disease and Class*, 110.

105. Paul Stuart, "Linking Clients and Policy: Social Work's Distinctive Contribution," *Social Work* 44 (July 1999): 337; Recchiuti, *Civic Engagement*, 62; [104]Maurine W. Greenwald and Margo Anderson, eds., *Pittsburgh Surveyed: Social Science and Social Reform in the Early Twentieth Century* (Pittsburgh: University of Pittsburgh Press, 1996), 7; Martin Bulmer, "The Survey Movement and Sociological Methodology" in *Pittsburgh Surveyed*, ed. Greenwald and Anderson, 17.

106. Bruno, *Trends in Social Work*, 224; Glenn et al., *Russell Sage Foundation*, 1:212.

107. Stuart, "Linking Clients and Policy," 337, 339; Carson, *Settlement Folk*, 125.

108. Recchiuti, *Civic Engagement*, 62; Bulmer, "The Survey Movement and Sociological Methodology," 16.

109. Stuart, "Linking Clients and Policy," 337.

110. Anderson and Greenwald, eds., *Pittsburgh Surveyed*, 3; Stephen Turner, "The Pittsburgh Survey and the Survey Movement," in ibid., 37, 43–44.

111. Bulmer, Bales, and Sklar, *The Social Survey in Historical Perspective*, 30.

112. Steven R. Cohen, "The Pittsburgh Survey and the Social Survey Movement," in *The Social Survey in Historical Perspective*, ed. Bulmer et al., 247; Bulmer, "The Survey Movement and Sociological Methodology," 28–30.

113. Anderson and Greenwald, eds., *Pittsburgh Surveyed*, 8–9.

114. Mary Richmond, "Families and Neighborhoods: Report of the Committee," in *Proceedings of the National Conference of Charities and Correction at the Thirty-seventh Annual Session held in the City of St. Louis, Mo., May 19th to 26th 1910*, ed. Alexander Johnson (Fort Wayne: Archer Printing, 1910), 214, 218; Stuart, "Linking Clients and Policy," 337.

115. Bruno, *Trends in Social Work*, 212.

116. Gertrude Vaile, "An Experiment in Trying to Grade District Visitors," in *Proceedings of the National Conference of Charities and Correction at the Forty-second Annual Session Held in Baltimore, Maryland, May 12–19, 1915* (Chicago: Hildmann Printing Co., 1915), 88.

117. Gertrude Vaile, "Principles and Methods of Outdoor Relief," in *Proceedings of the National Conference of Charities and Correction at the Forty-second Annual Session Held in Baltimore, Maryland, May 12–19, 1915* (Chicago: Hildmann Printing, 1915), 479.

118. Skocpol, *Protecting Soldiers and Mothers*, 426; Agnew, *From Charity to Social Work*, 109, 127; Devine, *The Family and Social Work*, 72. On the limitations of pensions, see Skocpol, *Protecting Soldiers and Mothers*, 476; Judith Sealander, *Private Wealth and Public Life: Foundation Philanthropy and the Reshaping of American Social Policy from the Progressive Era to the New Deal* (Baltimore: Johns Hopkins University Press, 1997), 113–16; Recchiuti, *Civic Engagement*, 143.

119. Greeley, "Beyond Benevolence," 380–81, 406–19.

120. Owen R. Lovejoy, "Standards of Living and Labor," in *Proceedings of the National Conference of Charities and Correction at the Thirty-ninth Annual Session Held in Cleveland, Ohio, June 12–19, 1912*, ed. Alexander Johnson (Fort Wayne: Fort Wayne Printing, 1912), 376.

121. Bruno, *Trends in Social Work*, 161.

122. Lovejoy, "Standards of Living and Labor," 376.

123. Paul U. Kellogg, "The Industrial Platform of the New Party," *Survey* 28 (24 August 1912), 668; Bruno, *Trends in Social Work*, 221–23; Allen F. Davis, "The Social Workers and the Progressive Party, 1912–1916," *American Historical Review* 69, no. 3 (April 1964): 675.

124. Jane Addams, *The Second Twenty Years at Hull-House* (New York: Macmillan, 1930), 28; Stuart, "Linking Clients and Policy," 340; Davis, "The Social Workers and the Progressive Party," 675; Davis, *Spearheads for Reform*, 204.

125. Davis, "The Social Workers and the Progressive Party," 672.

126. Watson, *Charity Organization*, 5. Also Glenn et al., *Russell Sage Foundation*, 32.

6. THE POTENTIALLY NORMAL POOR

1. Bruno, *Trends in Social Work*, 135, 187.

2. *Annual Report of the Charity Organization Society of Indianapolis, 1908–1909* (Indianapolis: Indianapolis COS, 1909), 12, box 5, folder 1, and *A Partial Report of Four Months' Work of the Unemployed by the Charity Organization Society of Indianapolis* (Indianapolis: Hollenbeck Press, 1908), 1, box 5, folder 12, Family Service Association of Indianapolis Records, 1879–1971, Collection M0102, Indiana Historical Society (hereafter FSA).

3. *Annual Report*, 9, 17, 19.

4. *A Partial Report*, 1.

5. Ibid., 3.

6. Ibid., 5.

7. *Annual Report*, 16.

8. *A Partial Report*, 5.

9. Ibid., 3.

10. *Annual Report*, 19–20.

11. Ibid., 24.

12. Bruno, *Trends in Social Work*, 121–23. See, e.g., Philip Garrett, "Immigration to the United States: Report of the Committee on Immigration," in *Proceedings of the National Conference of Charities and Correction at the Fifteenth Annual Session Held in Buffalo, N.Y., July 5–11, 1888*, ed. Isabel C. Barrows (Boston: Geo. H. Ellis, 1888), 185–92; Albert O. Wright, "Discussion of Immigration," in *Proceedings of the National Conference of Charities and Correction at the Eighteenth Annual Session Held in Indianapolis, Ind., May 13–20, 1891*, ed. Isabel C. Barrows (Boston: Geo. H. Ellis, 1891), 386–87; Richard Guenther, "Report of Committee on Immigration and Interstate Migration," in *Proceedings of the National Conference of Charities and Correction at the Twenty-fifth Annual Session Held in the City of New York, May 18–25, 1898*, ed. Isabel C. Barrows (Boston: Geo H. Ellis, 1898), 262–68; George H. Mead, "The Adjustment of Our Industry to Surplus and Unskilled Labor," in *Proceedings of the National Conference of Charities and Correction at the Thirty-sixth Annual Session Held in the City of Buffalo, N.Y., June 9th to 16th, 1909*, ed.

Alexander Johnson (Fort Wayne: Fort Wayne Printing, 1909), 222–27; Don S. Kirschner, "The Ambiguous Legacy: Social Justice and Social Control in the Progressive Era," *Historical Reflections* 2 (Summer 1975): 69–88.

13. *A Partial Report*, 15, 17. Similar efforts to combat unemployment during the panic could be found elsewhere in Indiana. See Joan E. Marshall, "The Charity Organization Society and Poor Relief for the Able-Bodied Unemployed: Lafayette, Indiana, 1905–1910," *Indiana Magazine of History* 93, no. 3 (September 1997): 217–43.

14. *A Partial Report*, 3, 5.

15. *Annual Report*, 29. Also see Bishop John H. Vincent, "Mothers' Aid Society," *Addresses of Bishop John H. Vincent and Rev. James D. Stanley at a Public Meeting of the Mothers' Aid Society* (Indianapolis: Charity Organization Society of Indianapolis, 1909).

16. *Mothers Aid and Convalescent Work: An Investigation of Fifty-five Mothers Who Support Families by Their Own Labor* (Indianapolis: Charity Organization Society, 1907), 9, box 5, folder 11, FSA.

17. Ibid., 2.

18. Ibid., 2, 4-7.

19. Ibid., 8.

20. Ibid., 9.

21. *A Partial Report*, 16.

22. COS Meeting Minutes, 16 January 1911, box 1, folder 3, FSA.

23. COS Meeting Minutes, 23 January 1911, box 1, folder 3, FSA.

24. Also see Gordon, "Black and White Visions of Welfare"; Kogut, "The Negro and the Charity Organization Society in the Progressive Era."

25. S. Humphreys Gurteen, "Beginning of Charity Organization in America," *Lend a Hand* 15, no. 5 (November 1894): 366.

26. Charles Frederick Weller, "How Charity May Become a Science," in *Proceedings of the National Conference of Charities and Correction at the Twenty-ninth Annual Session Held in the City of Detroit, May 28–June 3, 1902*, ed. Isabel C. Barrows (Boston: Geo. H. Ellis, 1902), 270–71.

27. Trattner, *From Poor Law to Welfare State*, 200.

28. Abraham Flexner, "Is Social Work a Profession?" in *Proceedings of the National Conference of Charities and Correction at the Forty-second Annual Session Held in Baltimore, Maryland, May 12–19, 1915* (Chicago: Hildmann Printing, 1915), 581.

29. Ibid., 587.

30. William Healy, M.D. "The Bearings of Psychology on Social Case Work," in *Proceedings of the National Conference of Social Work at the Forty-fourth Annual Session Held in Pittsburgh, Pennsylvania, June 6–13, 1917* (Chicago: 1917), 105.

31. Crocker, *Mrs. Russell Sage*; Glenn et al., *Russell Sage Foundation*, 1:31–32, 59; Hammack and Wheeler, *Social Science in the Making*, 19; Stanley Wenocur and Michael Reisch, *From Charity to Enterprise: The Development of American Social Work in a Market Economy* (Chicago: University of Chicago Press, 1989), 47–77.

32. Agnew, *From Charity to Social Work*, 10.

33. Mary Richmond, *Friendly Visiting among the Poor: A Handbook for Charity Workers*, rev. ed. (New York: Macmillan, 1916), 8.

34. Ibid., 11. See also Gordon, "Social Insurance and Public Assistance."

35. Mary Richmond, *Social Diagnosis* (New York: Russell Sage Foundation, 1917), 29.

36. Mary Richmond, "The Social Case Worker's Task," in *Proceedings of the National Conference of Social Work at the Forty-fourth Annual Session Held in Pittsburgh, Pennsylvania, June 6–13, 1917* (Chicago, 1917), 112.

37. Richmond, *Social Diagnosis*, 26.

38. Ibid., 7–8.

39. Hilts, *Statist and Statistician*, 1.

40. Porter R. Lee, "The Administrative Basis of Public Outdoor Relief," in *Proceedings of the National Conference of Social Work at the Forty-fourth Annual Session Held in Pittsburgh, Pennsylvania, June 6–13, 1917* (Chicago, 1917), 149–50.

41. Angie L. Kellogg, "What Educational Psychology Can Contribute to Case Work with the Normal Family," in *Proceedings of the National Conference of Social Work at the Forty-fifth Annual Session Held in Kansas City, Missouri, May 15–22, 1918* (Chicago: Rogers & Hall, 1918), 330.

42. Ibid., 333–34.

43. Kusmer, *Down & Out*, 91.

44. Mary C. Jarrett, "The Psychiatric Thread Running through All Social Case Work," in *Proceedings of the National Conference of Social Work at the Forty-sixth Annual Session Held in Atlantic City, New Jersey, June 1–8, 1919* (Chicago: Rogers and Hall, 1919), 592.

45. See, e.g., John Carson, *The Measure of Merit: Talents, Intelligence, and Inequality in the French and American Republics, 1750–1940* (Princeton: Princeton University Press, 2007).

46. Dr. E. E. Southard, "Social Research in Public Institutions," in *Proceedings of the National Conference of Charities and Correction at the Forty-third Annual Session Held in Indianapolis, Indiana, May 10–17, 1916* (Chicago: Hildmann Printing, 1916), 383.

47. Maurice Parmelee, "A Scientific Basis for the Treatment of Problems of Criminology and Penology," in *Proceedings of the National Conference of Charities and Correction at the Thirty-seventh Annual Session Held in the City of St. Louis, Mo., May 19th to 26th*, ed. Alexander Johnson (Fort Wayne: Archer Printing, 1910), 81.

48. Charles Davenport, "Eugenics and Charity," in *Proceedings of the National Conference of Charities and Correction at the Thirty-ninth Annual Session Held in Cleveland, Ohio, June 12–19, 1912*, ed. Alexander Johnson (Fort Wayne: Fort Wayne Printing, 1912), 281.

49. Francis Gavisk, "The Scope of the Conference," in *Proceedings of the National Conference of Charities and Correction at the Forty-third Annual Session Held in Indianapolis, Indiana, May 10–17, 1916* (Chicago: Hildmann Printing, 1916), 3.

50. Viola Paradise, "Industry and the Home: Behind the Statistic," in *Proceedings of the National Conference of Social Work at the Fiftieth Anniversary Session Held in Washington, D.C., May 16–23, 1923* (Chicago: University of Chicago Press, 1923), 314.

51. Ibid., 319.

SELECTED BIBLIOGRAPHY

ARCHIVAL SOURCES

Family Service Association of Indianapolis Records, 1879–1971. Collection M0102. Indiana Historical Society (FAS).
Oscar C. McCulloch Collection. Indiana State Library, Indianapolis.
Richard Ely Papers. Wisconsin State Historical Society, Madison.

PRIMARY SOURCES

American Social Science Association. *Constitution, Address, and List of Members of the American Association for the Promotion of Social Science.* Boston: Wright & Potter, 1866.
Annual Reports of the Indianapolis Benevolent Society and Charity Organization Society. Indianapolis, 1883–84, 1903–1904, 1908–1909.
Bercovici, Konrad. *Crimes of Charity.* New York: Alfred A. Knopf, 1917.
Boies, Henry M. *Prisoners and Paupers: A Study of the Abnormal Increase of Criminals and the Public Burden of Pauperism in the United States; The Causes and Remedies.* New York: Putnam, 1893.
Burch, Henry Reed, and S. Howard Patterson. *American Social Problems: An Introduction to the Study of Society.* New York: Macmillan, 1919.
Butler, Amos W. *Indiana, a Century of Progress: A Study of the Development of Public Charities and Correction, 1790–1915.* Indianapolis: Indiana Reformatory Printing Trade School, 1916.
Campbell, Helen. *Prisoners of Poverty: Women Wage-Workers, Their Trades, and Their Lives.* Boston: Little, Brown, 1900.
Charities: A Weekly Review of Local and General Philanthropy. 1902–1906.
Charities Review. 1899–1900.
Charity Organization Society of the City of New York. *Hand-Book for Friendly Visitors among the Poor.* New York: G. P. Putnam's Sons, 1883.
Devine, Edward T. *The Family and Social Work.* New York: Association Press, 1912.
———. *The Practice of Charity: Individual, Associated, and Organized.* New York: Lentilhon, 1901.
———. *The Principles of Relief.* New York: Macmillan, 1904.
Donnelly, Ignatius. *Caesar's Column: A Story of the Twentieth Century.* Chicago: F.J. Schulte, 1890.

Dugdale, Richard. *The Jukes: A Study in Crime, Pauperism, Disease, and Heredity.* 3rd ed. New York: G. P. Putnam, 1877.

Estabrook, Arthur. "The Tribe of Ishmael." *Second International Eugenics Congress* (1921): 398–404.

Gurteen, Stephen Humphreys. "Beginning of Charity Organization in America." *Lend a Hand* 15, no 5 (November 1894): 353–67.

———. *A Handbook of Charity Organization.* Buffalo: Author, 1882.

———. *What Is Charity Organization?* Buffalo: Charity Organization Society of the City of Buffalo, 1881.

A Handbook on the Prevention of Tuberculosis, Being the First Annual Report of the Committee on the Prevention of Tuberculosis of the Charity Organization Society of the City of New York. New York City: Charity Organization Society, 1903.

Henderson, Charles. *An Introduction to the Study of the Dependent, Defective, and Delinquent Classes.* Boston: D. C. Heath, 1893.

Hill, Octavia. *Homes of the London Poor.* London, 1874.

———. "The Importance of Aiding the Poor without Almsgiving." In *Transactions of the National Association for the Promotion of Social Science: Bristol Meeting, 1869,* ed. Edwin Pears, 589–94. London, 1870.

———. *Life of Octavia Hill as Told in Her Letters.* Edited by Chares E. Maurice. London: Macmillan, 1913.

House, Edward M. *Philip Dru: Administrator.* New York: B. W. Huebsch, 1912.

Hubbard, Charles M. "Relation of Charity-Organization Societies to Relief Societies and Relief-Giving." *American Journal of Sociology* 6, no. 6 (May 1901): 783–89.

Hunter, Robert. *Poverty.* New York: Macmillan, 1904.

Indianapolis Journal. 1879–82, 1885–86.

Indianapolis News. 1879–82, 1885–86.

Indianapolis Recorder. 1899–1900.

Indianapolis Sentinel. 1879–82, 1885–86.

Indianapolis Year Book of Charities, 1889–90, 1890–91, 1891–92; *Year Book of Charities,* 1886, 1886–87, 1888–89; *Year Book of Charities Indianapolis,* 1892–93.

Johnson, Alexander. *Adventures in Social Welfare: Being Reminiscences of Things, Thoughts, and Folks during Forty Years of Social Work.* Fort Wayne, 1923.

———. *The Almshouse: Construction and Management.* New York: Charities Publication Committee, 1911.

Jordan, David Starr. *The Blood of a Nation: A Study of the Decay of Races through the Survival of the Unfit.* Boston: American Unitarian Association, 1902.

———. *The Days of a Man: Being Memories of a Naturalist, Teacher, and Minor Prophet of Democracy.* 2 vols. New York: World Book, 1922.

Kellogg, Charles D. "Charity Organization in the United States—Report of the Committee on History of Charity Organization." In *Proceedings of the National Conference of Charities and Correction at the Twentieth Annual Session Held in Chicago, Ill., June 8–11, 1893,* ed. Isabel C. Barrows, 552–89. Boston: Press of Geo. H. Ellis, 1893.

McCulloch, Oscar C. "Associated Charities." In *Proceedings of the Seventh Annual Conference of Charities, Held at Cleveland, June and July, 1880,* ed. F. B. Sanborn, 122–35. Boston: A. Williams, 1880. Also published as *Organized Charity in Cities: A Paper Read before the National Conference of Charities, Held at Cleveland, Ohio.* Indianapolis, 1880.

———. *The Open Door: Sermons and Prayers.* Indianapolis: Wm. B. Burford, 1892.

———. *The Tribe of Ishmael: A Study in Social Degradation.* Indianapolis, 1889.

Mothers Aid and Convalescent Work: An Investigation of Fifty-five Mothers Who Support Families by Their Own Labor. Indianapolis: Charity Organization Society, 1907.

Noble, Harriet. *The Indianapolis Friendly Visitor: Friendly Visiting.* Indianapolis: Society of Friendly Visitors Committee, 1903.

A Partial Report of Four Months' Work of the Unemployed by the Charity Organization Society of Indianapolis. Indianapolis: Hollenbeck Press, 1908.

Proceedings of the Conference of Boards of Public Charities. 1875–79.

Proceedings of the Conference of Charities. 1880–81.

Proceedings of the National Conference of Charities and Correction. 1882–1916.

Proceedings of the National Conference of Social Work. 1917–25.

Richmond, Mary. *Friendly Visiting among the Poor: A Handbook for Charity Workers.* Rev. ed. New York: Macmillan, 1916.

———. *Social Diagnosis.* New York: Russell Sage Foundation, 1917.

"Study Class in Social Science in the Dept. of Charity." In *Indianapolis Yearbook of Charities: 1889–1890,* 34–35. Indianapolis, 1891.

Thanet, Octave [Alice French]. "The Indoor Pauper: A Study," *Atlantic Monthly* 47 (June 1881): 749–61.

Tuckerman, Joseph. *On the Elevation of the Poor.* Boston, 1874.

Warner, Amos. *American Charities: A Study in Philanthropy and Economics.* New York: Thomas Y. Crowell, 1894; rev. ed., 1908.

Warner, Amos, Stuart Queen, and Ernest Harper. *American Charities and Social Work.* 4th ed. New York: Thomas Y. Crowell, 1930.

Watson, Frank Dekker. *The Charity Organization Movement in the United States: A Study in American Philanthropy.* New York: Macmillan, 1922.

SECONDARY SOURCES

Abel, Emily K. "Medicine and Morality: The Health Care Program of the New York Charity Organization Society." *Social Service Review* 71, no. 4 (December 1997): 634–51.

———. "Valuing Care: Turn-of-the-Century Conflicts between Charity Workers and Women Clients." *Journal of Women's History* 10 (Autumn 1998): 32–52.

Abzug, Robert H. *Cosmos Crumbling: American Reform and the Religious Imagination.* Oxford: Oxford University Press, 1994.

Agnew, Elizabeth N. *From Charity to Social Work: Mary E. Richmond and the Creation of an American Profession.* Urbana: University of Illinois Press, 2004.

Amenta, Edwin. *Bold Relief: Institutional Politics and the Origins of Modern American Social Policy.* Princeton: Princeton University Press, 1998.

Axin, June, and Mark Stern. *Social Welfare: A History of the American Response to Need.* 7th ed. Boston: Allyn & Bacon, 2007.

Bannister, Robert C. *Sociology and Scientism: The American Quest for Objectivity, 1880–1940.* Chapel Hill: University of North Carolina Press, 1987.

Bell, E. Moderly. *Octavia Hill: A Biography.* London: Constable, 1942.

Bergman, Jill, and Debra Bernardi, eds. *Our Sisters' Keepers: Nineteenth-Century Benevolence Literature by American Women.* Tuscaloosa: University of Alabama Press, 2005.

Bernard, L. L., and Jessie Bernard. *Origins of American Sociology: The Social Science Movement in the United States.* New York: Russell & Russell, 1965.

Bledstein, Burton J. *The Culture of Professionalism: The Middle Class and the Development of Higher Education in America.* New York: Norton, 1976.

Bodenhamer, David J., and Robert G. Barrows, eds. *The Encyclopedia of Indianapolis.* Bloomington: Indiana University Press, 1994.

Boyd, Nancy. *Three Victorian Women Who Changed Their World: Josephine Butler, Octavia Hill, Florence Nightingale.* Oxford: Oxford University Press, 1982.

Boyer, Paul. *Urban Masses and Moral Order in America, 1820–1920.* Cambridge: Harvard University Press, 1978.

Bradshaw, Jonathan, and Roy Sainsbury, eds. *Experiencing Poverty.* Aldershot: Ashgate, 2000.

———. *Researching Poverty.* Aldershot: Ashgate, 2000.

Bremner, Robert H. *From the Depths: The Discovery of Poverty in the United States.* New York: New York University Press, 1956.

———. *The Public Good: Philanthropy and Welfare in the Civil War Era.* New York: Alfred A. Knopf, 1980.

———. "'Scientific Philanthropy,' 1873–93." *Social Service Review* 30 (June 1956): 168–73.

Brenner, Johanna. "Feminist Political Discourses: Radical versus Liberal Approaches to the Feminization of Poverty and Comparable Worth." *Gender & Society* 1, no. 4 (December 1987): 447–65.

Broder, Sherri. *Tramps, Unfit Mothers, and Neglected Children: Negotiating the Family in Nineteenth-Century Philadelphia.* Philadelphia: University of Pennsylvania Press, 2002.

Brown, Dorothy M., and Elizabeth McKeown. *The Poor Belong to Us: Catholic Charities and American Welfare.* Cambridge: Harvard University Press, 1997.

Bruno, Frank. *Trends in Social Work, 1874–1956: A History Based on the Proceedings of the National Conference of Social Work.* New York: Columbia University Press, 1957.

Bulmer, Martin. *The Chicago School of Sociology: Institutionalization, Diversity, and the Rise of Sociological Research.* Chicago: University of Chicago Press, 1984.

Bulmer, Martin, Kevin Bales, and Kathryn Kish Sklar, eds. *The Social Survey in Historical Perspective, 1880–1940.* Cambridge: Cambridge University Press, 1991.

Burgess, Charles O. "The Newspaper as Charity Worker: Poor Relief in New York City, 1893–1894." *New York History* 43 (July 1962): 249–68.

Camic, Charles, and Yu Xie. "The Statistical Turn in American Social Science: Columbia University, 1890 to 1915." *American Sociological Review* 59, no. 5 (October 1994): 773–805.

Carlson, Elof Axel. *The Unfit: A History of a Bad Idea.* Cold Spring Harbor, N.Y.: Cold Spring Harbor Laboratory Press, 2001.

Carson, Mina. *Settlement Folk: Social Thought and the American Settlement Movement, 1885–1930.* Chicago: University of Chicago Press, 1990.

Carter, Paul A. *The Decline and Revival of the Social Gospel: Social and Political Liberalism in American Protestant Churches, 1920–1940.* Ithaca: Cornell University Press, 1954.

Cashman, Sean Dennis. *American in the Gilded Age: From the Death of Lincoln to the Rise of Theodore Roosevelt.* New York: New York University Press, 1984.

Cayton, Andrew R. L. *Frontier Indiana.* Bloomington: Indiana University Press, 1996.

Chamberlain, John. *Farewell to Reform: The Rise, Life, and Decay of the Progressive Mind in America.* New York: John Day, 1932.

Clemens, Elisabeth S. *The People's Lobby: Organizational Innovation and the Rise of Interest-Group Politics in the United States, 1890–1925.* Chicago: University of Chicago Press, 1997.

Cooper, John. *Pivotal Decades: The United States, 1900–1920.* New York: W. W. Norton, 1990.

Cotkin, George. *Reluctant Modernism: American Thought and Culture, 1880–1900.* New York: Twayne, 1992.

Cox Richardson, Heather. *West from Appomattox: The Reconstruction of America after the Civil War.* New Haven: Yale University Press, 2007.

Cravens, Hamilton. *The Triumph of Evolution: The Heredity-Environment Controversy, 1900–1941.* Baltimore: Johns Hopkins University Press, 1988.

Critchlow, Donald T., and Charles H. Parker, eds. *With Us Always: A History of Private Charity and Public Welfare.* Oxford: Rowman & Littlefield, 1998.

Crocker, Ruth. "'I Only Ask You Kindly to Divide Some of Your Fortune With Me': Begging Letters and the Transformation of Charity in Late Nineteenth-Century America." *Social Politics* 6, no. 2 (Summer 1999): 131–60.

———. "Making Charity Modern: Business and the Reform of Charities in Indianapolis, 1879–1930." *Business and Economic History,* 2nd ser., 12 (1984): 158–70.

———. *Mrs. Russell Sage, Women's Activism, and Philanthropy in Gilded Age and Progressive Era America.* Bloomington: Indiana University Press, 2006.

———. *Social Work and Social Order: The Settlement Movement in Two Industrial Cities, 1889–1930.* Urbana: University of Illinois Press, 1992.

Crunden, Robert. *Ministers of Reform: The Progressives' Achievement in American Civilization, 1880–1920.* New York: Basic Books, 1982.

Cuddy, Lois A., and Claire M. Roch, eds. *Evolution and Eugenics in American Literature and Culture, 1880–1940: Essays on Ideological Conflict and Complicity.* London: Associated University Presses, 2003.

Cumbler, John T. "The Politics of Charity: Gender and Class in Late Nineteenth-Century Charity Policy." *Journal of Social History* 14, no. 1 (Fall 1980): 99–112.

Davis, Allen F. "The Social Worker and the Progressive Party, 1912–1916." *American Historical Review* 60, no. 3 (April 1964): 671–88.

———. *Spearheads for Reform: The Social Settlements and the Progressive Movement, 1890–1914.* New York: Oxford University Press, 1967.

Dawley, Alan. *Struggles for Justice: Social Responsibility and the Liberal State.* Cambridge, Mass.: Belknap Press, 1991.

Deegan, Mary Jo. *Jane Addams and the Men of the Chicago School, 1892–1918.* New Brunswick: Transaction Books, 1988.

———. *Race, Hull-House, and the University of Chicago: A New Conscious against Ancient Evils.* Westport, Conn.: Praeger, 2002.

———. "The Second Sex and the Chicago School: Women's Accounts, Knowledge, and Work, 1945–1960." In *A Second Chicago School? The Development of a Postwar American Sociology,* ed. Gary Alan Fine, 322–64. Chicago: University of Chicago Press, 1995.

———, ed. *Women in Sociology: A Bio-bibliographical Sourcebook.* New York: Greenwood Press, 1991.

Denton, James A. *Rocky Mountain Radical: Myron W. Reed, Christian Socialist.* Albuquerque: University of New Mexico Press, 1997.

Depastino, Todd. *Citizen Hobo: How a Century of Homelessness Shaped America.* Chicago: University of Chicago Press, 2003.

Deutsch, Nathaniel. *Inventing America's "Worst" Family: Eugenics, Islam, and the Fall and Rise of the Tribe of Ishmael.* Berkeley: University of California Press, 2009.

Dowbiggin, Ian Robert. *Keeping America Sane: Psychiatry and Eugenics in the United States and Canada.* Ithaca: Cornell University Press, 1997.

Doyle, Don Harrison. *The Social Order of a Frontier Community: Jacksonville, Illinois, 1825–1870.* Urbana: University of Illinois Press, 1978.

Dunn, Jacob Piatt. *Greater Indianapolis: The History, the Industries, the Institutions, and the People of a City of Homes.* Chicago: Lewis, 1910.

Englander, David, and Rosemary O'Day, eds. *Retrieved Riches: Social Investigation in Britain, 1840–1914.* Aldershot: Ashgate, 1995.

Fitzpatrick, Ellen. *Endless Crusade: Women Social Scientists and Progressive Reform.* New York: Oxford University Press, 1990.

———. "Social Welfare." In *The Cambridge History of Science, Volume 7: The Modern Social Sciences,* ed. Theodore M. Porter and Dorothy Ross, 608–20. Cambridge: Cambridge University Press, 2002.

Fitzpatrick, Paul. "The Early Teaching of Statistics in American Colleges and Universities." *American Statistician* 9, no. 5 (December 1955): 12–18.

Fox Piven, Frances, and Richard A. Cloward. *Regulating the Poor: The Functions of Public Welfare.* New York: Pantheon Books, 1971.

Fredrickson, George. *The Inner Civil War: Northern Intellectuals and the Crisis of the Union.* New York: Harper & Row, 1965.

Freedman, Estelle B. *Their Sisters' Keepers: Women's Prison Reform in America, 1830–1930.* Ann Arbor: University of Michigan Press, 1981.

Furner, Mary. *Advocacy and Objectivity: A Crisis in the Professionalization of American Social Science, 1865–1905.* Lexington: University Press of Kentucky, 1975.

Gaither, Milton. "The Rise and Fall of a Pedagogical Empire: The Board of State Charities and the Indiana Philosophy of Giving." *Indiana Magazine of History* 96, no. 4 (December 2000): 336–46.

Gettleman, Marvin E. "Charity and Social Classes in the United States, 1874–1900, II." *American Journal of Economics and Sociology* 22, no. 3 (July 1963): 417–26.

———. "Philanthropy as Social Control in Late Nineteenth-Century America: Some Hypotheses and Data on the Rise of Social Work." *Societas* 5, no. 1 (1975): 49–59.

Gilens, Martin. *Why Americans Hate Welfare: Race, Media, and the Politics of Antipoverty Policy.* Chicago: University of Chicago Press, 1999.

Glenn, John M., Lilian Brandt, and F. Emerson Andrews. *Russell Sage Foundation, 1907–1946.* Vol. 1. New York: Russell Sage Foundation, 1947.

Goldberg, Chad Alan. *Citizens and Paupers: Relief, Rights, and Race, from the Freedmen's Bureau to Workfare.* Chicago: University of Chicago Press, 2007.

Gordon, Linda. "Black and White Visions of Welfare: Women's Welfare Activism, 1890–1945." *Journal of American History* 78, no. 2 (September 1991): 559–90.

———. *The Great Arizona Orphan Abduction.* Cambridge: Harvard University Press, 1999.

———. *Heroes of Their Own Lives: The Politics and History of Family Violence: Boston, 1880–1960.* Urbana: University of Illinois Press, 2002.

———. *Pitied but Not Entitled: Single Mothers and the History of Welfare, 1890–1935.* New York: Free Press, 1994.

———. "Social Insurance and Public Assistance: The Influence of Gender in Welfare Thought in the United States, 1890–1935." *American Historical Review* 97, no. 1 (February 1992): 19–54.

Greeley, Dawn. "Beyond Benevolence: Gender, Class, and the Development of Scientific Charity in NYC, 1882–1935." PhD diss., New York State University–Stony Brook, 1995.

Greenwald, Maurine W., and Margo Anderson, eds. *Pittsburgh Surveyed: Social Science and Social Reform in the Early Twentieth Century.* Pittsburgh: University of Pittsburgh Press, 1996.

Hacsi, Timothy A. *Second Home: Orphan Asylums and Poor Families in America.* Cambridge: Harvard University Press, 1997.

Hall, Stephen Ray. "Oscar McCulloch and Indiana Eugenics." PhD diss., Virginia Commonwealth University, 1993.

Haller, Mark. *Eugenics: Hereditarian Attitudes in American Thought.* New Brunswick, N.J.: Rutgers University Press, 1963.

Hammack, David C. *Power and Society: Greater New York at the Turn of the Century.* New York: Russell Sage Foundation, 1982.

Hammack, David C., and Stanton Wheeler. *Social Science in the Making: Essays on the Russell Sage Foundation, 1907–1972.* New York: Russell Sage Foundation, 1994.

Harrison, Robert. *Congress, Progressive Reform, and the New American State.* Cambridge: Cambridge University Press, 2004.

Haskell, Thomas. *The Emergence of Professional Social Science: The American Social Science Association and the Nineteenth-Century Crisis of Authority.* Urbana: University of Illinois Press, 1977.

Higbie, Frank Tobias. *Indispensable Outcasts: Hobo Workers and Community in the American Midwest, 1880–1930.* Urbana: University of Illinois Press, 2003.

Higham, John. *Strangers in the Land: Patterns of American Nativism, 1860–1925.* New Brunswick, N.J.: Rutgers University Press, 1955.

Hilts, Victor. "Obeying the Laws of Hereditary Descent: Phrenological Views on Inheritance and Eugenics." *Journal of the History of the Behavioral Sciences* 18 (January 1982): 62–77.

———. *Statist and Statistician.* New York: Arno Press, 1981.

———. "Towards the Social Organism: Herbert Spencer and William B. Carpenter on the Analogical Method." In *The Natural and the Social Sciences, Some Critical and Historical Perspectives,* ed. I. B. Cohen, 275–303. Boston: Kluwer Academic, 1994.

Hoffman, Charles. "The Depression of the Nineties." *Journal of Economic History* 16, no. 2 (June 1956): 137–64.

———. *The Depression of the Nineties.* Westport, Conn.: Greenwood, 1970.

Hofstadter, Richard. *The Age of Reform: From Bryan to F.D.R.* New York: Alfred A. Knopf, 1955.

———. *Social Darwinism in American Thought, 1860–1915.* Philadelphia: University of Pennsylvania Press, 1944.

Hopkins, Charles Howard. *The Rise of the Social Gospel in American Protestantism, 1865–1915.* New Haven: Yale University Press, 1940.

Huggins, Nathan Irvin. *Protestants against Poverty: Boston's Charities, 1870–1900.* Westport, Conn.: Greenwood, 1971.

Jacobson, Matthew Frye. *Barbarian Virtues: The United States Encounters Foreign Peoples at Home and Abroad, 1876–1917.* New York: Hill and Wang, 2000.

Jones, Gareth Stedman. *Outcast London: A Study in the Relationship between Classes in Victorian Society.* Oxford: Clarendon Press, 1971.

Jordan, John M. *Machine-Age Ideology: Social Engineering and American Liberalism, 1911–1939.* Chapel Hill: University of North Carolina Press, 1994.

Katz, Michael. *In the Shadow of the Poorhouse: A Social History of Welfare in America.* New York: Basic Books, 1986.

———. *Poverty and Policy in American History: Studies in Social Discontinuity.* New York: Academic Press, 1983.

———. *The Undeserving Poor: From the War on Poverty to the War on Welfare.* New York: Pantheon Books, 1989.

Katz, Michael, and Thomas Sugrue, eds. *W.E.B. Du Bois, Race, and the City: The Philadelphia Negro and Its Legacy.* Philadelphia: University of Pennsylvania Press, 1998.

Kershner, Frederick Doyle, Jr. "A Social and Cultural History of Indianapolis, 1860–1914." PhD diss., University of Wisconsin, 1950.

Kevles, Daniel. *In the Name of Eugenics: Genetics and the Uses of Human Heredity.* Cambridge: Harvard University Press, 1985.

Keyssar, Alexander. *Out of Work: The First Century of Unemployment in Massachusetts.* New York: Cambridge University Press, 1986.

Kidd, Alan. *State, Society, and the Poor in Nineteenth-Century England.* New York: St. Martin's Press, 1999.

Kimmelman, Barbara. "The American Breeders' Association: Genetics and Eugenics in an Agricultural Context, 1903–1913." *Social Studies of Science* 13 (1983): 163–204.

Kirschner, Don S. "The Ambiguous Legacy: Social Justice and Social Control in the Progressive Era." *Historical Reflections* 2 (Summer 1975): 69–88.

Kish Sklar, Kathryn. *Florence Kelley and the Nation's Work: The Rise of Women's Political Culture, 1830–1900.* New Haven: Yale University Press, 1995.

Kline, Wendy. *Building a Better Race: Gender, Sexuality, and Eugenics from the Turn of the Century to the Baby Boom.* Berkeley: University of California Press, 2001.

Knights, Peter R. *Yankee Destinies: The Lives of Ordinary Nineteenth-Century Bostonians.* Chapel Hill: University of North Carolina Press, 1991.

Kogut, Alvin B. "The Negro and the Charity Organization Society in the Progressive Era." *Social Service Review* 44, no. 1 (March 1970): 11–21.

Koven, Seth. *Culture and Poverty: The London Settlement House Movement, 1870–1914.* New York: Routledge, 2009.

———. *Slumming: Sexual and Social Politics in Victorian London.* Princeton: Princeton University Press, 2004.

Krainz, Thomas A. *Delivering Aid: Implementing Progressive Era Welfare in the American West.* Albuquerque: University of New Mexico Press, 2005.

Kramer, Elsa. "Recasting the Tribe of Ishmael: The Role of Indianapolis's Nineteenth-Century Poor in Twentieth-Century Eugenics." *Indiana Magazine of History* 104 (March 2008): 36–64.

Kusmer, Kenneth L. *Down & Out, on the Road: The Homeless in American History.* Oxford: Oxford University Press, 2002.

———. "The Functions of Organized Charity in the Progressive Era: Chicago as a Case Study." *Journal of American History* 60, no. 3 (December 1973): 657–78.

Lane, James B. "Jacob A. Riis and Scientific Philanthropy during the Progressive Era." *Social Service Review* 47, no. 1 (March 1973): 32–48.

Largent, Mark. *Breeding Contempt: The History of Coerced Sterilization in the United States*. New Brunswick: Rutgers University Press, 2008.

Larson, Edward. *Sex, Race, and Science: Eugenics in the Deep South*. Baltimore: Johns Hopkins University Press, 1995.

Leach, William. *True Love and Perfect Union: The Feminist Reform of Sex and Society*. New York: Basic Books, 1980.

Leaming, Hugo P. "The Ben Ishmael Tribe: A Fugitive 'Nation' of the Old Northwest." In *The Ethnic Frontier: Group Survival in Chicago and the Midwest*, ed. Melvin G. Holli and Peter d'A. Jones, 97–141. Grand Rapids: William B. Eerdmans, 1977.

Lears, T. J. Jackson. *No Place of Grace: Anti-modernism and the Transformation of American Culture, 1880–1920*. New York: Pantheon Books, 1981.

———. *Rebirth of a Nation: The Making of Modern America, 1877–1920*. New York: HarperCollins, 2009.

Lebsock, Suzanne. *The Free Women of Petersburg: Status and Culture in a Southern Town, 1784–1860*. New York: W. W. Norton, 1984.

Leiby, James. "Amos Warner's 'American Charities,' 1894–1930." *Social Science Review* 37, no. 4 (1967): 441–55.

———. "Charity Organization Reconsidered." *Social Service Review* 58, no. 4 (1984): 523–38.

———. *A History of Social Welfare and Social Work in the United States*. New York: Columbia University Press, 1978.

Lerner, Barron H. *Contagion and Confinement: Controlling Tuberculosis along the Skid Road*. Baltimore: Johns Hopkins University Press, 1998.

Lewis, Jane. *Women and Social Action in Victorian and Edwardian England*. Stanford: Stanford University Press, 1991.

Lewis, Verl S. "Stephen Humphreys Gurteen and the American Origins of Charity Organization." *Social Service Review* 40, no. 2 (June 1966): 190–201.

Link, Arthur S., and Richard L. McCormick. *Progressivism*. Arlington Heights, Ill.: Harlan Davidson, 1983.

Lubove, Roy. *The Professional Altruist: The Emergence of Social Work as a Career, 1880–1930*. Cambridge: Harvard University Press, 1965.

Ludmerer, Kenneth M. *Genetics and American Society: A Historical Appraisal*. Baltimore: Johns Hopkins University Press, 1972.

Madison, James H. *The Indiana Way: A State History*. Bloomington: Indiana University Press, 1986.

Mandler, Peter, ed. *The Uses of Charity: The Poor on Relief in the Nineteenth-Century Metropolis*. Philadelphia: University of Pennsylvania Press, 1990.

Marshall, Joan E. "Aid for Union Soldiers' Families: A Comfortable Entitlement or a Pauper's Pittance? Indiana, 1861–1865." *Social Service Review* 78, no. 2 (June 2004): 207–42.

———. "The Charity Organization Society and Poor Relief for the Able-Bodied Unemployed: Lafayette, Indiana, 1905–1910." *Indiana Magazine of History* 93, no. 3 (September 1997): 217–43.

May, Henry F. *Protestant Churches and Industrial America*. New York: Octagon Books, 1963.

McCarthy, Kathleen D. *Noblesse Oblige: Charity and Cultural Philanthropy in Chicago, 1849–1929*. Chicago: University of Chicago Press, 1982.

McGerr, Michael. *A Fierce Discontent: The Rise and Fall of the Progressive Movement in America, 1870–1920.* New York: Free Press, 2003.

McMath, Robert C. *American Populism: A Social History, 1877–1898.* New York: Hill and Wang, 1993.

Milkis, Sidney M., and Jerome M. Mileur, eds. *Progressivism and the New Democracy.* Amherst: University of Massachusetts Press, 1999.

Mowat, Charles Loch. *The Charity Organization Society, 1869–1913: Its Ideas and Work.* London: Methuen, 1961.

Muncy, Robyn. *Creating a Female Dominion in American Reform, 1890–1935.* New York: Oxford University Press, 1991.

Nugent, Walter. *Crossings: The Great Transatlantic Migrations, 1870–1914.* Bloomington: Indiana University Press, 1992.

Numbers, Ronald. *Almost Persuaded: American Physicians and Compulsory Health Insurance, 1912–1920.* Baltimore: Johns Hopkins University Press, 1978.

Oates, Mary J. *The Catholic Philanthropic Tradition in America.* Bloomington: Indiana University Press, 1995.

Oberschall, Anthony. "The Institutionalization of American Sociology." In *The Establishment of Empirical Sociology: Studies in Continuity, Discontinuity, and Institutionalization,* ed. Anthony Oberschall, 187–251. New York: Harper and Row, 1972.

———. "Paul F. Lazarsfeld and the History of Empirical Social Research." *Journal of the History of the Behavioral Sciences* 14, no. 3 (July 1978): 199–206.

O'Connor, Alice. *Poverty Knowledge: Social Science, Social Policy, and the Poor in Twentieth-Century U.S. History.* Princeton, N.J.: Princeton University Press, 2001.

Paul, Diane. *Controlling Human Heredity: 1865 to the Present.* Atlantic Highlands, N.J.: Humanities Press, 1995.

Phillips, Clifton J. *Indiana in Transition: The Emergence of an Industrial Commonwealth, 1880–1920.* Indianapolis: Indiana Historical Society, 1968.

Pickens, Donald K. *Eugenics and the Progressives.* Nashville: Vanderbilt University Press, 1968.

Pittenger, Mark, "A World of Difference: Constructing the 'Underclass' in Progressive America." *American Quarterly* 49, no. 1 (March 1997): 26–65.

Porter, Theodore. *The Rise of Statistical Thinking, 1820–1900.* Princeton: Princeton University Press, 1986.

Pratt, John Webb. *Religion, Politics, and Diversity: The Church-State Theme in New York History.* Ithaca: Cornell University Press, 1967.

Prochaska, F. K. *Women and Philanthropy in Nineteenth-Century England.* Oxford: Clarendon Press, 1980.

Rafter, Nicole Hahn. *Creating Born Criminals.* Urbana: University of Illinois Press, 1997.

———, ed. *White Trash: The Eugenic Family Studies, 1877–1919.* Boston: Northeastern University Press, 1988.

Recchiuti, John. *Civic Engagement: Social Science and Progressive-Era Reform in New York City.* Philadelphia: University of Pennsylvania Press, 2007.

Riis, Jacob. *How the Other Half Lives: Studies among the Tenements of New York.* New York: Scribner, 1890.

Ringenbach, Paul T. *Tramps and Reformers, 1873–1916: The Discovery of Unemployment in New York.* London: Greenwood Press, 1973.

Roberts, Michael J. D. "Charity Disestablished? The Origins of the Charity Organization Society Revisited, 1868–1871." *Journal of Ecclesiastical History* 54, no. 1 (January
2003): 40–61.

Rodgers, David. *Atlantic Crossings: Social Politics in a Progressive Age.* Cambridge:
Belknap Press, 1998.

Rose, Gregory S. "Hoosier Origins: The Nativity of Indiana's United States–Born Population in 1850." *Indiana Magazine of History* 86 (September 1985): 201–32.

————. "Upland Southerners: The County Origins of Southern Migrants to Indiana by
1850." *Indiana Magazine of History* 87 (September 1986): 242–63.

Rosen, Christine. *Preaching Eugenics: Religious Leaders and the American Eugenics Movement.* Oxford: Oxford University Press, 2004.

Rosenberg, Carroll Smith. *Religion and the Rise of the American City: The New York City
Mission Movement, 1812–1870.* Ithaca: Cornell University Press, 1971.

Rosenberg, Charles. *No Other Gods: On Science and American Social Thought.* Baltimore:
Johns Hopkins University Press, 1976.

Ross, Dorothy. *The Origins of American Social Science.* Cambridge: Cambridge University Press, 1991.

Rothman, David J. *The Discovery of the Asylum: Social Order and Disorder in the New Republic.* Boston: Little, Brown, 1971.

Rothman, Sheila M. *Living in the Shadow of Death: Tuberculosis and the Social Experience
of Illness in American History.* New York: Basic Books, 1994.

Ruswick, Brent. "Just Poor Enough: Gilded Age Charity Applicants Respond to Charity
Investigators." *Journal of the Gilded Age and Progressive Era* 10 (July 2011): 265–87.

————. "The Measure of Worthiness: The Rev. Oscar McCulloch and the Pauper
Problem, 1877–1891." *Indiana Magazine of History* 104 (March 2008): 3–35.

Rutman, Darrett B. *Winthrop's Boston: Portrait of a Puritan Town, 1630–1649.* Chapel
Hill: University of North Carolina Press, 1965.

Sanders, Elizabeth. *Roots of Reform: Farmers, Workers, and the American State, 1877–1917.*
Chicago: University of Chicago Press, 1999.

Schafer, Alice, Mary Wysor Keefer, and Sophonisba P. Breckinridge. *The Indiana Poor
Law: Its Development and Administration with Special Reference to the Provision of State
Care for the Sick Poor.* Chicago: University of Chicago Press, 1936.

Schäfer, Axel R. *American Progressives and German Social Reform, 1875–1920: Social Ethics, Moral Control, and the Regulatory State in a Transatlantic Context.* Stuttgart: Franz
Steiner Verlag, 2000.

Schneider, Dorothy, and Carl J. Schneider. *American Women in the Progressive Era, 1900–
1920.* New York: Anchor Books, 1993.

Schwartz, Joel. *Fighting Poverty with Virtue: Moral Reform and America's Urban Poor,
1825–2000.* Bloomington: Indiana University Press, 2000.

Silverberg, Helene, ed. *Gender and American Social Science: The Formative Years.* Princeton: Princeton University Press, 1998.

Sklansky, Jeff. "Pauperism and Poverty: Henry George, William Graham Sumner, and
the Ideological Origins of Modern American Social Science." *Journal of the History of
the Behavioral Sciences* 35, no. 2 (Spring 1999): 111–38.

Skocpol, Theda. *Protecting Soldiers and Mothers: The Political Origins of Social Policy in the
United States.* Cambridge: Belknap Press of Harvard University Press, 1992.

Skowronek, Stephen. *Building a New American State: The Expansion of National Adminis-trative Capacities, 1877–1920.* Cambridge: Cambridge University Press, 1982.

Slack, Paul. *English Poor Law, 1531–1782.* Basingstoke: Macmillan Education, 1990.

———. *From Reformation to Improvement: Public Welfare in Early Modern England.* Ox-ford: Clarendon Press, 1999.

Smith, Timothy L. *Revivalism and Social Reform in Mid-Nineteenth-Century America.* New York: Abingdon Press, 1957.

Stadum, Beverly. *Poor Women and Their Families: Hard Working Charity Cases, 1900–1930.* Albany: State University of New York Press, 1992.

Stanley, Amy Dru. "Beggars Can't Be Choosers: Compulsion and Contract in Post-bellum America." *Journal of American History* 78 (March 1992): 1265–93.

Stern, Alexandra Minna. *Eugenic Nation: Faults and Frontiers of Better Breeding in Modern America.* Berkeley: University of California Press, 2005.

———. "'We Cannot Make a Silk Purse Out of a Sow's Ear': Eugenics in the Hoosier Heartland." *Indiana Magazine of History* 103 (March 2007): 3–38.

Stocking Jr., George W. "Lamarckianism in American Social Science: 1890–1915." *Journal of the History of Ideas* 23, no. 2 (April–June 1962): 239–56.

Streightoff, Frances Doan, and Frank Hatch Streightoff. *Indiana: A Social and Economic Survey.* Indianapolis: W. K. Stewart, 1916.

Stromquist, Shelton. *Reinventing "The People": The Progressive Movement, the Class Problem, and the Origins of Modern Liberalism.* Urbana: University of Illinois Press, 2006.

Taylor, Bob Pepperman. *Citizenship and Democratic Doubt: The Legacy of Progressive Thought.* Lawrence: University Press of Kansas, 2004.

Thernstrom, Stephan. *The Other Bostonians: Poverty and Progress in the American Metrop-olis.* Cambridge: Harvard University Press, 1973.

———. *Poverty and Progress: Social Mobility in a Nineteenth-Century City.* Cambridge: Harvard University Press, 1964; New York: Atheneum, 1970.

Thornbrough, Emma Lou. *Indiana in the Civil War Era, 1850–1880.* Indianapolis: Indiana Historical Bureau, 1965.

Tice, Karen. *Tales of Wayward Girls and Immoral Women: Case Records and the Profes-sionalization of Social Work.* Urbana: University of Illinois Press, 1998.

Trattner, Walter. *From Poor Law to Welfare State: A History of Social Welfare in America.* New York: Free Press, 1974.

Trent, James. *Inventing the Feeble Mind: A History of Mental Retardation in the United States.* Berkeley: University of California Press, 1995.

Tropman, John E. *American Values and Social Welfare: Cultural Contradictions in the Wel-fare State.* New Jersey: Prentice Hall, 1989.

Vecoli, Rudolph J. "Sterilization: A Progressive Measure?" *Wisconsin Magazine of His-tory* 43, no. 3 (Spring 1960): 190–202.

Walkowitz, Daniel J. "The Making of a Feminine Professional Identity: Social Workers in the 1920s." *American Historical Review* 95, no. 4 (October 1990): 1051–75.

Ward, David. *Poverty, Ethnicity, and the American City, 1840–1925: Changing Conceptions of the Slum and the Ghetto.* Cambridge: Cambridge University Press, 1989.

Waugh, Joan. "'Give This Man Work!' Josephine Shaw Lowell, the Charity Organization Society of the City of New York, and the Depression of 1893." *Social Science History* 25, no. 2 (Summer 2000): 217–46.

———. *Unsentimental Reformer: The Life of Josephine Shaw Lowell.* Cambridge: Harvard University Press, 1997.

Weeks, Genevieve. "Oscar C. McCulloch: Leader in Organized Charity." *Social Service Review* 39 (June 1965): 209–21.

———. *Oscar Carleton McCulloch, 1843–1891: Preacher and Practitioner of Applied Christianity.* Indianapolis: Indiana Historical Society, 1976.

———. "Religion and Social Work as Exemplified in the Life of Oscar C. McCulloch." *Social Service Review* 39 (March 1965): 38–52.

Wenocur, Stanley, and Michael Reisch. *From Charity to Enterprise: The Development of American Social Work in a Market Economy.* Urbana: University of Illinois Press, 1989.

Wheatley, Steven C. *The Politics of Philanthropy: Abraham Flexner and Medical Education.* Madison: University of Wisconsin Press, 1988.

White, Leonard D. *The Republican Era, 1869–1901: A Study in Administrative History.* New York: Macmillan, 1958.

Wiebe, Robert. *Businessmen and Reform: A Study of the Progressive Movement.* Chicago: Quadrangle Books, 1962.

———. *The Search for Order, 1877–1920.* New York: Hill and Wang, 1967.

Wohl, A. S. "Octavia Hill and the Homes of the London Poor." *Journal of British Studies* 10, no. 2 (May 1971): 105–31.

Woodward, C. Vann. *The Strange Career of Jim Crow.* New York: Oxford University Press, 1955.

Zald, Mayer N., ed. *Social Welfare Institutions: A Sociological Reader.* New York: John Wiley, 1965.

Ziliak, Stephen Thomas. "Essays on Self-Reliance: The United States in the Era of 'Scientific Charity.'" PhD diss., University of Iowa, 1996.

———. "Self-Reliance before the Welfare State: Evidence from the Charity Organization Movement in the United States." *Journal of Economic History* 64, no. 2 (June 2004): 433–61.

INDEX

Note: italic page number indicates illustration; t. indicates table.

PHILANTHROPIC AND NONPROFIT STUDIES

Dwight F. Burlingame and David C. Hammack, editors

Thomas Adam. *Buying Respectability: Philanthropy and Urban Society in Transnational Perspective, 1840s to 1930s*

Thomas Adam, editor. *Philanthropy, Patronage, and Civil Society: Experiences from Germany, Great Britain, and North America*

Albert B. Anderson. *Ethics for Fundraisers*

Peter M. Ascoli. *Julius Rosenwald: The Man Who Built Sears, Roebuck and Advanced the Cause of Black Education in the American South*

Karen J. Blair. *The Torchbearers: Women and Their Amateur Arts Associations in America, 1890–1930*

Eleanor Brilliant. *Private Charity and Public Inquiry: A History of the Filer and Peterson Commissions*

Dwight F. Burlingame, editor. *The Responsibilities of Wealth*

Dwight F. Burlingame and Dennis Young, editors. *Corporate Philanthropy at the Crossroads*

Charles T. Clotfelter and Thomas Ehrlich, editors. *Philanthropy and the Nonprofit Sector in a Changing America*

Ruth Crocker. *Mrs. Russell Sage: Women's Activism and Philanthropy in Gilded Age and Progressive Era America*

Marcos Cueto, editor. *Missionaries of Science: The Rockefeller Foundation and Latin America*

William Damon and Susan Verducci, editors. *Taking Philanthropy Seriously: Beyond Noble Intentions to Responsible Giving*

Angela Eikenberry. *Giving Circles: Philanthropy, Voluntary Association, and Democracy*

Gregory Eiselein. *Literature and Humanitarian Reform in the Civil War Era*

Helen Gilbert and Chris Tiffin, editors. *Burden or Benefit?: Imperial Benevolence and Its Legacies*

Richard B. Gunderman. *We Make a Life by What We Give*

David C. Hammack, editor. *Making the Nonprofit Sector in the United States: A Reader*

David C. Hammack and Steven Heydemann, editors. *Globalization, Philanthropy, and Civil Society: Projecting Institutional Logics Abroad*

Jerome L. Himmelstein. *Looking Good and Doing Good: Corporate Philanthropy and Corporate Power*

Warren F. Ilchman, Stanley N. Katz, and Edward L. Queen II, editors. *Philanthropy in the World's Traditions*

Warren F. Ilchman, Alice Stone Ilchman, and Mary Hale Tolar, editors. *The Lucky Few and the Worthy Many: Scholarship Competitions and the World's Future Leaders*

BRENT RUSWICK has taught at the University of Central Arkansas and the University of Wisconsin, where he received his doctorate. He is currently researching a book on the "mutual aid" theory of evolution in American reform. *Almost Worthy* is his first book.